THE HISTORICAL NOVEL

The historical novel is an enduringly popular genre that raises crucial questions about key literary concepts, fact and fiction, identity, history, reading and writing. In this comprehensive, focused guide Jerome de Groot offers an accessible introduction to the genre and critical debates that surround it, including:

- the development of the historical novel from early eighteenth-century works to postmodern and contemporary historical fiction
- different genres, such as sensational or 'low' fiction, crime novels, literary works, counterfactual writing and related issues of audience, value and authenticity
- the many functions of historical fiction, particularly the challenges it poses to accepted histories and postmodern questioning of 'grand narratives'
- the relationship of the historical novel to the wider cultural sphere, with reference to historical theory, the internet, television and film
- key theoretical concepts such as the authentic fallacy, postcolonialism, Marxism, queer and feminist reading

Drawing on a wide range of examples from across the centuries and around the globe, *The Historical Novel* is essential reading for students exploring the interface of history and fiction.

Jerome de Groot is Lecturer in Renaissance Literature and Culture at the University of Manchester. His publications include *Consuming History* (2008) and *Royalist Identities* (2004).

THE NEW CRITICAL IDIOM

SERIES EDITOR: JOHN DRAKAKIS, UNIVERSITY OF STIRLING

The New Critical Idiom is an invaluable series of introductory guides to today's critical terminology. Each book: provides a handy, explanatory guide to the use (and abuse) of the term offers an original and distinctive overview by a leading literary and cultural critic relates the term to the larger field of cultural representation

With a strong emphasis on clarity, lively debate and the widest possible breadth of examples, *The New Critical Idiom* is an indispensable approach to key topics in literary studies. Also in the series:

THE HISTORICAL NOVEL

Jerome de Groot

LONDON AND NEW YORK

First published 2010 by Routledge
2 Park Square, Milton Park, Abingdon, Oxon OX14 4RN

Simultaneously published in the USA and Canada
by Routledge
270 Madison Avenue, New York, NY 10016

Routledge is an imprint of the Taylor & Francis Group, an informa business

Typeset in Garamond by Taylor & Francis Books
Printed and bound in Great Britain by
TJ International Ltd, Padstow Cornwall

British Library Cataloguing in Publication Data
A catalogue record for this book is available from the British Library

Library of Congress Cataloging in Publication Data
De Groot, Jerome, 1975-
The historical novel / Jerome de Groot. – 1st ed.
p. cm. – (The new critical idiom)
Includes bibliographical references and index.
1. Historical fiction – History and criticism. 2. Literature and history.
3. History in literature. 4. Fiction genres. I. Title.
PN3441.D4 2009
809.3'81 – dc22
2009014425

ISBN10: 0-415-42661-8 (hbk)
ISBN10: 0-415-42662-6 (pbk)
ISBN10: 0-203-86896-X (ebk)

ISBN13: 978-0-415-42661-9 (hbk)
ISBN13: 978-0-415-42662-6 (pbk)
ISBN13: 978-0-203-86896-6 (ebk)

CONTENTS

SERIES EDITOR'S PREFACE

The New Critical Idiom is a series of introductory books which seeks to extend the lexicon of literary terms, in order to address the radical changes which have taken place in the study of literature during the last decades of the twentieth century. The aim is to provide clear, well illustrated accounts of the full range of terminology currently in use, and to evolve histories of its changing usage.

The current state of the discipline of literary studies is one where there is considerable debate concerning basic questions of terminology. This involves, among other things, the boundaries which distinguish the literary from the non-literary; the position of literature within the larger sphere of culture; the relationship between literatures of different cultures; and questions concerning the relation of literary to other cultural forms within the context of interdisciplinary studies.

It is clear that the field of literary criticism and theory is a dynamic and heterogeneous one. The present need is for individual volumes on terms which combine clarity of exposition with an adventurousness of perspective and a breadth of application. Each volume will contain as part of its apparatus some indication of the direction in which the definition of particular terms is likely to move, as well as expanding the disciplinary boundaries within which some of these terms have been traditionally contained. This will involve some re-situating of terms within the larger field of cultural representation, and will introduce examples from the area of film and the modern media in addition to examples from a variety of literary texts.

J.D.

ACKNOWLEDGEMENTS

Many thanks to: staff at the British Library, Manchester John Rylands University Library and Manchester Central Library; the students on my Historical Novel special subject course at the University of Manchester; John Drakakis for incisive reading and thoughtful editing; Liz Thompson, Emma Nugent, and the team at Routledge; Andrew Biswell; Matthew Creasy and Ato Quayson for talk about misquotation so long ago, finally used; Sarah Waters; Kaye Mitchell for enormously helpful and generous comments, criticism and suggestions (I owe to Kaye many points in Chapter 1 particularly); Ann Hughes for books, references and enthusiasm; Anastasia Valassopoulos for elegantly nuancing my gauche thoughts on postcolonial writing and theory; colleagues who helped, discussed and supported my work, including in particular David Alderson, Hal Gladfelder and John McAuliffe; Mum for her help, books and discussion; Olivia for reading, talking through and being generally brilliant; Dad for long-distance delight and Chris for numerous interesting debates about history; Daniel and James for being rocks; all my friends for their excellent ways; and to Sharon, for ever and for everything. This book is for her.

J.d.G.

1

INTRODUCTION

The question has been asked by one or two critics of standing – What right has the Historical Novel to exist at all?

(Nield 1902)

Whatever the answer to this question, it is clear, surveying the field, that at present the Historical Novel is in robust health, critically, formally and economically. In particular, the last few decades have seen an explosion in the sales and popularity of novels set in the past. Visit a bookshop or book website and the Historical Fiction section, in itself a relatively new marketing innovation, will be groaning under the weight of new work published by authors from across the world, and in numerous styles. The shelves will be shared by writers as diverse as Philippa Gregory, Bernard Cornwell, Sarah Waters, Ken Follett, Robert Harris, Dan Brown and Amy Tan. Such bestsellers share space with perennial favourites Georgette Heyer, George MacDonald Fraser, Jean Plaidy and Margaret Mitchell; with genre-specific work from detective to horror to romance, such as that by Lee Jackson, Simon Scarrow, Candace Robb, Dan Simmons and C. J. Sansom; with translations of work by writers as diverse as Boris

Akunin, Naguib Mahfouz and Orhan Pamuk; and with literary fiction by Philip Roth, Gore Vidal, Margaret Atwood and Toni Morrison. The complexity of the bookshop's Historical Fiction section, then, its physical intermingling of genres, types of writer, and publishers, demonstrates the levelling ability of this mode of fiction, somehow linking Tracy Chevalier with George Eliot, Ellis Peters with Pat Barker.

The historical novel is a genre that is increasingly studied on university curricula and discussed at research level; it is also an immensely popular form, with global audience reach. This book attempts to trace the defining characteristics, key manifestations and cultural meanings of this particular type of fiction. Historical writing can take place within numerous fictional locales: romance, detective, thriller, counterfactual, horror, literary, gothic, postmodern, epic, fantasy, mystery, western, children's books. Indeed, the intergeneric hybridity and flexibility of historical fiction have long been one of its defining characteristics. A historical novel might consider the articulation of nationhood via the past, highlight the subjectivism of narratives of History, underline the importance of the realist mode of writing to notions of authenticity, question writing itself, and attack historiographical convention. The form manages to hold within itself conservatism, dissidence, complication and simplicity; it attracts multiple, complex, dynamic audiences; it is a particular and complex genre hiding in plain sight on the shelves of a bookshop. As the examples above demonstrate, historical fiction is written by a variety of authors, within an evolving set of sub-genres, for a multiplicity of audiences. One might suggest an alternative narrative of the rise of the novel focused through historical fiction, for instance, a form concerned with social movement, dissidence, complication and empathy rather than the more individualistic novel form we are familiar with, born of autobiographical, personal, revelatory narratives. Certainly figures that we might see as key exponents of the novel form, such as Gustave Flaubert, or Leo Tolstoy, considered their historical fictions not to be novels at all, but experiments and crucial interventions in important cultural debates.

This present study investigates the genre in a number of ways, considering popular novels (particularly those aimed at and marketed specifically to men or women), literary fiction and postmodern writing. A final section begins to consider the ways in which the challenge to orthodoxy and potential for dissent innate to historical fiction have been used to challenge mainstream and repressive narratives: by postcolonial authors to 'write back'; by lesbian and gay authors to reclaim marginalised identities; by politicians and public figures to posit or explore new ideological positions. This introduction outlines some of the key problems and oddities associated with the genre so we may begin to locate it as a type of writing, before turning in Chapter 2 to the chronological evolution and development of the form.

History is other, and the present familiar. The historian's job is often to explain the transition between these states. The historical novelist similarly explores the dissonance and displacement between then and now, making the past recognisable but simultaneously authentically unfamiliar. To use Alessandro Manzoni's metaphor, the historical novelist is required to give 'not just the bare bones of history, but something richer, more complete. In a way you want him to put the flesh back on the skeleton that is history' (Manzoni 1984: 67–68). The figures we meet in historical fiction are identifiable to us on the one hand due to the conceit of the novel form, in that they speak the same language, and their concerns are often similar to ours, but their situation and their surroundings are immensely different. How does this affect the writing and reading of fiction? Historical novelists concentrate on the gaps between known factual history and that which is lived to a variety of purposes:

> It's precisely the difference of the past that makes it exciting for me. I think we always need to be reminded that the moment that we live in is very temporary. Historical fiction at its best can remind us of that.
> (Waters, cited in Allardice 2006)

These thoughts of the novelist Sarah Waters attempt to define and understand the motives for reading and enjoying historical fiction. The genre is a knotty one to pin down, including within its boundaries a multiplicity of different types of fictional formats, but Waters' words give us a set of pointers towards articulating an understanding of the sort of writing that this present book calls the 'historical novel'. Here Waters asserts the virtue of historical fiction as something which enforces on the reader a sense of historicised 'difference' (and there is a *frisson* in the excitement which this otherness provokes in the author), and as a mode which has an effect on the normative experience of the everyday and the contemporary world. Of course, much historical fiction seeks to close down difference and works conservatively to promote universalising tendencies; however, the subversive potential of the form is innate within it at all points, as the various discussions that follow seek to demonstrate.

Historical fiction, for Waters, 'reminds' readers of their historical particularity and simultaneity. It follows, then, that the historical novel as a form is something which demands an unusual response from its audience: an active response, at the least, and a sense of otherness and difference when reading. The historical novel, then, is similar to other forms of novel-writing in that it shares a concern with realism, development of character, authenticity. Yet fundamentally it entails an engagement on the part of the reader (possibly unconsciously) with a set of tropes, settings and ideas that are particular, alien and strange. The experience of writing, reading and understanding historical fiction is markedly different from that of a novel set in the contemporary world. Knowingly or not, the three participants of the historical novel, writers, readers, students, bring a set of reading skills and premeditated ideas to the experience. An historical novel is always a slightly more inflected form than most other types of fiction, the reader of such a work slightly more self-aware of the artificiality of the writing and the strangeness of engaging with imaginary work which strives to explain something that is other than one's contemporary knowledge and experience: the past. In this a cognate genre is science fiction, which involves a conscious interaction with a clearly unfamiliar set of landscapes, technologies and circumstances. As Darko Suvin argues, SF is 'a literary genre whose necessary and sufficient conditions are the presence and interaction of estrangement and cognition' (cited and discussed in Roberts 2005: 7). This question of a fundamental 'estrangement' intertwined with a clear rational 'cognition' seems a clear analogue for the work that historical fiction undertakes, the compound between the two in the present case leading to something like 'faction', a conjunction of the fictional uncanny and the factually authentic.

Jonathan Nield's introduction to his *Guide to the Best Historical Novels and Tales* (1902) attempted to account for various concerns:

> More often than not, it is pointed out, the Romancist gives us gives us a mass of inaccuracies, which, while they mislead the ignorant (i.e., the majority?), are an unpardonable offence to the historically-minded reader. Moreover, the writer of such Fiction, though he be a Thackeray or a Scott, cannot surmount barriers which are not merely hard to scale, but absolutely impassable. The spirit of a period is like the selfhood of a human being – something that cannot be handed on; try as we may, it is impossible for us to breathe the atmosphere of a bygone time, since all those thousand-and-one details which went to the building up of both individual and general experience, can never be reproduced. We consider (say) the eighteenth century from the purely Historical standpoint, and, while we do so, are under no delusion as to our limitations; we know that a few of the leading personages and events have been brought before us in a more or less disjointed fashion, and are perfectly aware that there is room for much discrepancy between the pictures so presented to us (be it with immense skill) and the actual facts as they took place in such and such a year. But, goes on the objector, in the case of a Historical Romance we allow ourselves to be hoodwinked, for, under the influence of a pseudo-historic security, we seem to watch the real sequence of events in so far as these affect the characters in whom we are interested.
>
> (Nield 1902)

There is much food for thought here. Nield points out a set of problems associated with literary taste, concern for authenticity, anxiety that the form might mislead its readership. Writing about history involves approaching insurmountable barriers.

The 'spirit of a period' may not be reclaimed, and when approached through the lens of history the knowledge of this is uppermost; however, in reading fiction 'we allow ourselves to be hoodwinked'. Nield's formulations introduce key ideas about the concern for authenticity. Much criticism of the historical novel concerns its ability to change fact, and indeed those who attack the form are often concerned with its innate ability to encourage an audience into being knowingly misinformed, misled and duped. We will develop the idea of being consciously 'hoodwinked' throughout the following chapters, and indeed this fundamental strangeness is, it is argued, one of the most important attributes of the historical novel.

Nield also demonstrates neatly how throughout the nineteenth century what we might call the Historical Novel was often, problematically and pejoratively, referred to as 'Historical Romance'. This type of fiction was generically flexible and intransigent; its subject matter not worthy of the rationalist and civilising ideas associated with the high realist novel. The term 'Historical Romance' suggests the complexity and manipulability of the genre, its ability to meld high and low types of writing, its popular appeal. Such writing that was immensely important in the rise and development of the 'novel' due to the influence particularly of the work of Sir Walter Scott, but also stood to one side, was a mode apart from the concerns of the more straightforward type of literature as represented by the novel. This will be discussed in Chapter 2.

Nield's approach is influenced by critics who suggest the historical novel might be a force for educational good. He worries that some fictions are 'harmful', reminding the reader that 'History itself possesses interest for us more as the unfolding of certain moral and mental developments than as the mere enumeration of facts' (Nield 1902). He argues that critics were concerned that the type of scepticism common in approaches to the past was somehow something that the novel could not incorporate. The genre's 'pseudo-historic security' becalms the reader and makes them a passive recipient of all kinds of untruths. In contrast, it seems to me that the historical novel, whilst happily hoodwinking its audience, does so with their collusion, and that this complicity is more self-conscious and self-aware than Nield's critics might allow.

A good example of the dissonance innate to the form is the author's note. It might be a rule of thumb to define the historical novel as something which has an explanatory note from the writer describing their own engagement with the period in question, either through schooling or, more commonly, through their reading and research. This kind of external scholarly apparatus appears in the first commonly defined historical novel, Sir Walter Scott's *Waverley* (1814). The novel's extensive notes encompass ballads and poetry (sometimes made up), political occurrences, biography, culture and customs, classical learning, sword making, accounts of actual events. Much of this material is written by Scott but he also cites various authorities and sources to make his points sound. Furthermore in the General Preface to the 1829 edition Scott claims to have talked to many veterans about their experiences:

> I had been a good deal in the Highlands at a time when they were much less accessible and much less visited then they have been of late years, and was acquainted with many of the old warriors of 1745, who were, like most veterans, easily induced to fight their battles over again for the benefit of a willing listener like myself.
>
> (Scott 1985: 522)

These techniques demonstrate how from the very beginning the historical novel was keen to emphasise its authority. This is in order to defend the novel from accusations of frivolity and femininity (novels were associated with female readers in the eighteenth century). Scott is at pains to demonstrate that his work is educational, well versed in actual events and eye-witness accounts, a worthwhile exercise. It is also a collage of information and generic form, including ballad, historical information, heraldry, court intrigue, footnotes on culture and history, and quotation in a kind of ragbag of a novel which is itself interested in not being too authoritative. Edward Waverley has an interview with Colonel Gardiner in which his letters and his actions are reviewed, and this section demonstrates that there is another way of interpreting events, a self-reflexive moment in which Scott's narrative actively undermines itself. The extratextual information also has the effect of controlling the reader. On the one hand the reader is put in the position of the tourist (and indeed of the character of Edward

Waverley himself), unknowing and passive, prey to the worldly, clever, ironising narrator. At the same time the reader is presumed to have some historical knowledge and therefore gains a certain power over the narrative to the extent that the novel cannot shock or challenge events. The notes and extraneous meta-narratives of the novel point to the artificiality of the exercise, encouraging the audience of the work to acknowledge the multiplicity of history and the subjective version of it being presented by Scott. The collage effect of authority that Scott creates here is something that points to the generic mixture of the form as well as the indeterminacy of history, and it is something that infuses almost all historical novels. The form is obsessed with pointing out its own partiality, with introducing other voices and undermining its authority.

The habit of authorial paratextual commentary upon the process and development of work has continued to the present day, and most historical fiction will have introductions and disavowals such as the following:

> While this novel was based on a large number of factual sources (detailed below), the warning of the Author's Note preceding it should be repeated here: it is a work of fiction and the characters, even when recognizable from an external context, are behaving fictionally ... My general aim has been to avoid giving to any character dialogue or actions which the historical record indicates would have been impossible or unlikely. However, the dialogue, though trying to capture the cadence of their conversation as it is recorded in reality, is frequently invented.
>
> (Lawson 2006: 367)

> Certain things are always erased or distorted in a novel and this is no exception. It seems worth saying that this is not a representation of the politics or personalities of the Angry Brigade.
>
> (Kunzru 2007: 268)

> This novel is another fiction, based on another fact. That fact was found in the following sources.
>
> (Peace 2006: 349)

Apart from Jean's letter to Arthur, all letters quoted, whether signed or anonymous, are authentic.

(Barnes 2006: 505)

The self-consciousness of the authors here illustrates their awareness of the strange project in which they are involved. Each has a different approach to the way in which their practice as historical novelists intersects with 'reality' and with 'history'; but each is moved to articulate this to the readership of their novels. This articulation highlights the artificiality of the novel, introduces a fundamental **metafictional** element to the form, and demonstrates that as a genre the historical novel provokes a certain anxiety and disquiet on the part of the writer. Mark Lawson repeats the mantra that his work, though well versed in fact, is unreal; Hari Kunzru feels it 'worth saying' that his novelistic imagining of the 1970s is not a 'representation', as if any reader would assume it was anything other than a *fiction*; David Peace's nebulous formulation of 'fiction, based on another fact' reflects the uncertainty of his central character, Brian Clough, as to what is occurring to him at times, or his desire to tell a story according to his own version of events; Barnes's work is 'authentic'. This scrabbling of authors to cover themselves has various motivations, from those echoing Scott and attempting to ensure the reader is aware of their skill and authenticity, whilst also throwing the veracity of the entire narrative into doubt, to more practical legal issues; Peace was taken to court by the Leeds United footballer Johnny Giles, whom he represents in his novel, and forced to pay damages and apologise to him. Historical biography, a form distinct from but related to historical fiction, somehow manages to bridge this gap but towards the more extreme end, as in the case of Peter Ackroyd, the distinctions between genres working with 'fact' and those working with 'fiction' begin to blur (de Groot 2008: 35–9).

This latter incident points us to another of the problematic glitches thrown up by the historical novel as a genre, the concerns raised when a writer approaches a figure who is still alive and fictionalises their story. Is this something which is acceptable? Historical novelists take the bare bones of 'history', some facts, some atmosphere, some vocabulary, some evidence, and weave a story within the gaps. In the case of persons still living, though, there are issues of good taste and libel, as well as authenticity. Yet, to extrapolate, this is always the case when writing about real people, whether they are Tudor or contemporary, and so the historical novelist has to negotiate their own position as regards their 'duty' to history, veracity, and the various figures involved. This is one of the reasons, surely, why historical novels often tend to eschew dramatising the lives of well known 'real' figures. Again, Sarah Waters has interesting thoughts on the duty of the writer to their subject matter:

> I don't think novels should misrepresent history, unless it's for some obvious serious or playful purpose (though this suggests that we can represent history accurately – something I'm not sure we can do; in fact, I've always been fascinated by the ways in which historical fiction continually reinvents the past). I think we have a duty to take history seriously – not simply to use it as a backdrop or for the purposes of nostalgia.
>
> (Waters 2006)

Once more the complexity of the enterprise is foregrounded: Waters brings in issues of authenticity, misrepresentation, re-invention and seriousness, all concepts that would not arise as compellingly in relation to novels set in contemporary society. The historical novel has a quality of revelation in that it can change the past; it also encourages a particular set of responses and approaches.

The historical novel, then, provokes a series of genre-specific questions that this book explores in order to illustrate how complex, dissonant, multiple and dynamic this seemingly clear-cut and innocuous form is. Through a consideration of various types of historical novel, through a chronological account of the form's development, and by looking with a number of theoretical perspectives, we can start to account for the genre and think about how and why it works.

2

ORIGINS
EARLY MANIFESTATIONS AND SOME DEFINITIONS

This chapter demonstrates that a concern with history has been present since the beginning of the novel form in the early eighteenth century. This is a necessarily swift review of the evolution of the form which will provide the literary historical basis for discussion as well as demonstrating the exciting multiple valency of the genre. We look at the work of a key theorist, Georg Lukács, in particular considering his ideas of immersion and historio-psychological realism. We will also look at European novels which use the historical form to reflect on contemporary issues. How do different nations conceive of the historical novel? Is it a form of commentary or a way to build the imagined community of nation? What happens when history itself starts to fray during the modernist era?

Whilst the historical novel as a form is generally considered to have originated during the early nineteenth century, and particularly with the writings of Sir Walter Scott, this mode of writing clearly has many antecedents before that period. Scott himself was merely developing the novel's fascination with history, as many critics have pointed out. Similarly, he was concretising in novel form something that had been a mainstay of other types of literary production for centuries. The use of creative forms to conceptualise, question and simply present history is a fundamental cultural practice, as can be seen in early examples like Homer, Virgil or Wu Cheng'en. The rebirth of interest in the classical period in Europe during what has been termed the Renaissance led to a tranche of texts taking historical events as their subject, an early version being Chaucer's *Troilus and Criseyde* (*c.* 1380–87). History as a subject for dramatic consideration, for instance, found its initial flowering in the 1590s with the plays of William Shakespeare, Christopher Marlowe, Ben Jonson and others. Subsequently plays that took history as their subject became commonplace. Poetic considerations of historical events were similarly common, as can be seen in John Milton's account of human history in *Paradise Lost* (1667). Historical poetry and prose romances were commonplace during the medieval and early modern period (Hughes 1993; Fuchs 2004). The first historical fiction that might be considered a 'novel' is Marie-Madeleine de Lafayette's *The Princess of Clevès* (1678, trans. 1679), set during the reign of Henri II (Maxwell 2008: 65).

The most important publication for our current consideration, however, was the 1605 printing in Madrid of *Don Quixote de la Mancha* by Miguel de Cervantes. *Don Quixote* follows the increasingly delusional exploits of a landowner whose head has been filled with historical romances and who thinks of himself as a knight errant, part of a noble quest to save a damsel in distress. The **picaresque** prose romance warns of the folly of believing in fiction, as the first English translation of 1620 makes clear:

> His fantasie was filled with those things that he read, of enchantments, quarrels, battels, challenges, wounds, wooings, loues, tempests, and other impossible follies. And these toyes did so firmly possesse his imagination with an infallible opinion, that all Machina of dreamed inuentions which he read was true, as he accounted no History in the world to be so certaine and sincere as they were.

> (Cervantes 1620: 4)

The work is historical, in so far as it takes place 'not long since' (Cervantes 1620: 1), but the main importance of this work throughout Europe was to popularise the prose account which eventually developed into the novel form (Cruz 2005). *Don Quixote* dramatises the ways in which fictions of the past might infect the present and lead to romanticised madness, how accounts of history can have an effect on the contemporary mind. It demonstrates the ludicrousness of thinking history relevant now, as part of Quixote's insanity is to use archaic language, customs and practices in the 'modern' world. His overactive historical-fictional imagination turns windmills into vengeful knights and a donkey into a noble steed. *Don Quixote* was immensely influential in its form and its troubling of literariness; it also suggested various ways that history might be treated in prose fiction.

Before moving on to consider the novel as a form through the eighteenth century, it is crucial to recognise that this narrative of development is problematic in so far as we are tracing with hindsight a path that is logical to us only because we know the 'answer', that is, the final outcome. We also should be aware that critical stories of the 'rise' of the novel have long been considered by literary scholars with some suspicion; the novel is a hybrid genre which came to some form of accretion during the late 1700s, but it is not part of a progress towards anything or an expression of rational **Enlightenment** (McKeon 2000). Accounts of the rise of the novel also tend to ignore marginalised writing, such as that of women, for instance, and to see the development of the novel as moving towards the masterpieces of the Victorian period. The conservative tendency is obvious, for instance, in the case of Scott, who has been abstracted from his context due to the fact that he is considered the 'first' historical novelist, ignoring other writers and practitioners. This originary definition estab-lishes an authority for his writing that is in some way false. We also, finally, need to be aware that the story of the development of the historical novel is particularly **Eurocentric** (see Moretti 2007). Scott's example and influence were so wide-ranging throughout the nineteenth century that they have obscured other historical fictive writing, particularly that of non-Western cultures. Luo Guanzhong's *Three Kingdoms*, for instance, is a prose historical fiction first published in China in 1522. Recounting the downfall of the Han dynasty (168–280), the text concludes with a verse considering the purpose of fiction and the effect that historical distance has on our understanding of events: 'The kingdoms three are now the stuff of dream,/For men to ponder, past all praise or blame' (Guanzhong 2004: 936). The text is hugely influential in Chinese culture but has been little considered in the West.

With this caveat, it can be argued that the novel increasingly emerged as a definable form during the latter part of the eighteenth century. Historical fictions were written throughout the last decades of the century, drawing on earlier examples like the works of Daniel Defoe (?1660–1731), Lafayette's *Princess of Clevès* and Thomas Leland's *Longsword* (1762). Novel readers were generally thought of as less respectable than those of poetry. In the 1800 Preface to the *Lyrical Ballads* William Wordsworth famously derided novels as being sensational and demeaning. As a literary form, the novel developed out of other genres such as romance, epic, autobiography, and was consistently in dialogue with its origins, in particular with the prose romance. Romance traditionally dealt with chivalry, knights, feminine perfection and mythical elements. Some novels, particularly those by Samuel Richardson and Jane Austen, avoided this association, and were interested in newly detailed psychological realism. However, the form that we shall be looking at was clearly indebted to the romance, and in particular to the example of *Don Quixote*.

GOTHIC NOVELS AND THE FETISHISATION OF EUROPEAN HISTORY

A key type of historical fiction was that evinced by the Gothic novel, popular during the latter half of the eighteenth century. Gothic is a type of writing which is fascinated by the unknown and mysterious, with the terrifying and the haunting. Gothic novels fetishised European history. They were often set during the medieval period, and their interest in this past was a fascination with savagery and mystery. Horace Walpole's *The Castle of Otranto*, for instance, often taken to be the first Gothic novel, is fascinated by the horrific possibilities of the past. Walpole mixed 'ancient and modern romance in which contemporary characters are placed in feudal settings', and his example, the use of the past to scare these recognisably 'modern' characters, was influential to all subsequent Gothic novelists (Botting and Townshend 2004: 2). *Otranto* concerns the sins of the past (those of the fathers) being visited upon the present (their sons). The novel purports to be a translation of a sixteenth-century transcript of an eleventh-century Italian manuscript found in a library, and was published under the pseudonym William Marshal, the alleged translator. From the beginning, then, the novel troubles its own legitimacy and plays games with authority in ways that become commonplace. (See also the practice of Manzoni, Hogg and Eco, discussed below.) The text of *The Castle of Otranto* presents itself as a piece of evidence, an historical document itself, with all the mystery and partiality associated with the archive. The uncertainty of the translator in his preface leads him to tentatively date it to between 1095 and 1243: 'The principal incidents are such as were believed in the darkest ages of Christianity, but the language and conduct have nothing that savours of barbarism' (Walpole 1765: iii). Furthermore, he apologises for the credulity of the narrative:

> Miracles, visions, necromancy, dreams, and other preternatural events are exploded now even from romances. That was not the case when our author wrote; much less when the story itself is supposed to have happened. Belief in every kind of prodigy was so established in those dark ages, that an author would not be faithful to the *manners* of the times, who should omit all mention of them. He is not bound to believe them himself, but he must represent his actors as believing them.
>
> (Walpole 1765: v)

Walpole here articulates a sense of historical characterisation and authenticity that would be developed by Scott (see below). The writer must be 'faithful to the *manners* of the times'. This allows Walpole much latitude in writing a fantastical story of horror and ghostliness. It suggests that the European past is the site of Gothic terror, a place of possibility and credulity. Gothic novels, following Walpole, were fascinated by Europe and by this medieval past. In order to terrify the present, which is the purpose of the Gothic novel, it is necessary to ignore our contemporary rationality and present the chaotic, scary, Catholic past. The historical novel is here a vehicle for expressing terror and fear, a repository of horror. Fictional considerations of the past are interested in their ability to be other than now and, through that, to demonstrate that the present's nightmare is actually the past. Walpole establishes the novel as a form that might investigate, trouble and complicate the past; certainly as a way of communicating that past in innovative and complex ways (Maxwell 2008: 69–70).

Gothic novels were noted for their 'shameless interweaving of fiction and history ... the inaccuracy or even glaring anachronism of the genre's historiography' (Botting and Townshend 2004: 2). In this they see history not as a source of information or something to understand but as a place of horror and savagery. The historical place, in Gothic, be it the castle, grave or forest, is not a repository of pastness but a site where history might attack the visitor, a charnelhouse of remains that still have the power to harm. Contemporary critics were horrified by Gothic's disrespectful approach to the past, associating it with chaos and social upheaval. For our purposes, it is instructive that the short-lived Gothic novel's interest in history should be in disrupting that past to provoke horror and terror; the form's obsession with the artefacts and evidence of the past (manuscripts, graves, long-hidden passageways and rituals) demonstrates a nightmarish type of historical novel. Furthermore, as the example of Catherine Morland in *Northanger Abbey* (1818) demonstrates, the historical Gothic fictions of Ann Radcliffe use the setting 'as a fantasy space in which she [Radcliffe] can centralise a female consciousness and explore female fears and desires' (Wallace 2005: 2). That this type of writing was increasingly subsumed by the more ordered, decidedly less subversive fiction exemplified by Sir Walter Scott speaks volumes for the ways in which dissident and subversive works can be marginalised by society. The incipient historical novel, after the example of Scott, became a rational, realist form, shifting away from the excesses of the Gothic to emphasise process, progress and transcendent human values.

SIR WALTER SCOTT: THE *WAVERLEY* NOVELS AND THEIR INFLUENCE

Novels were a mass medium, widely available and popular. Generally people read novels from circulating libraries rather than buying them. Indeed, Sir Walter Scott himself describes doing this in his Introduction to *Waverley*. William Godwin, in an essay defending the historical romance or novel, noted that:

> The critic and the moralist, in their estimate of romances, have borrowed the principle that regulates the speculations of trade. They have weighed novels by the great and taken into their view the whole scum and surcharge of the press.
>
> (Godwin 1797)

Godwin here notices the problematic association of the novel with economics. The form was mass-produced, and critical distaste was due to this mercenary, 'trade' element. Technological innovations relating to printing meant that novels became the first mass-market literary medium, and the first novel to be published widely and also to be marketed to this new public was Scott's *Waverley* (1814). Scott's novel was massively, globally successful and influential; it introduced a new form, the 'historical' novel; and it demonstrated the range, reach and breadth of audience that the new type of writing might reach. *Waverley* and the ensuing series of anonymously published 'fictitious narratives, intended to illustrate the manners of Scotland' (Scott 1816: v), including *Guy Mannering* (1815), *The Antiquarian* (1816), *Rob Roy* (1817), *Heart of Midlothian* (1818) and *Ivanhoe* (1819), are generally taken to be the point at which the 'historical novel' is thought to have originated as a form. Therefore we must consider *Waverley* in some depth, as well as analyse the ways that the text conceives of itself. We should also be careful of using *Waverley* as a generic guide, as it is itself consciously a hybrid of styles. Ascribing it any kind of coherence is due to critical hindsight in the main, rather than any programmatic purpose on the part of the novelist.

That said, Scott himself had his antecedents, and we should be careful before ascribing him an originary role that we are not simply imposing a literary history or falsely suggesting that he departed from his forebears significantly. He is a 'great synthesiser' of 'what everyone before him had done' (Maxwell 2008: 75). Godwin, who himself wrote novels of history, defended the form and argued that:

> Romance, then, strictly considered, may be pronounced to be one of the species of history. The difference between romance and what ordinarily bears the denomination history, is this. The historian is confined to individual incident and individual man, and must hang upon that his invention or conjecture as he can. The writer collects his materials from all sources, experience, report, and the records of human affairs; then generalises them; and finally selects, from their elements and the various combinations they afford, those instances which he is best qualified to portray, and which he judges most calculated to impress the hearer and improve the faculties of his reader. In this point of view we should be apt to pronounce that romance was a bolder species of composition than history.
>
> (Godwin 1797)

Godwin is iconoclastic in approach here, arguing that romance is 'bolder' than history and at least as worthy of being considered as a similar type of writing. He has already pointed to the subjectivity of history, suggesting that the 'reader will be miserably deluded if, while he reads history, he suffers himself to imagine that he is reading facts' (Godwin 1797). It seems that what Godwin is pointing to here is what was suggested in Chapter 1, namely that fictionalising about history is a more honest way of creating a narrative about something which is essentially unknowable. In some ways the novelist's ability to generalise, for Godwin, allows them to communicate something more profound than the historian, 'confined to individual incident'. This poet–historian binary suggesting that the artist has creative latitude, in contrast to the more constrained ability of the chronicler to render reality, had been a commonplace of literary discussion from Sir Philip Sidney's *A Defence of Poesie* (1592) onward; indeed, the distinguishing between modes of the universal and the particular, and the allegation that the poet should be able to communicate something more vital and truthful than the historian, can be found in the philosophy of Plato and Aristotle.

Godwin brilliantly and characteristically argues that the historian can never know the character of those they write about:

> But we never know any man's character. My most intimate and sagacious friend continually misapprehends my motives. He is in most cases a little worse judge of them than myself and I am perpetually mistaken. The materials are abundant for the history of Alexander, Caesar, Cicero and Queen Elizabeth. Yet how widely do the best informed persons differ respecting them? Perhaps by all their character is misrepresented. The conjectures therefore respecting their motives in each particular transaction must be eternally fallacious. The writer of romance stands in this respect upon higher ground. He must be permitted, we should naturally suppose, to understand the character which is the creature of his own fancy. The writer of romance is to be considered as the writer of real history; while he who was formerly called the historian, must be contented to step down into the place of his rival, with this disadvantage, that he is a romance writer, without the arduous, the enthusiastic and the sublime licence of imagination, that belong to that species of composition. True history consists in a delineation of consistent, human character, in a display of the manner in which such a character acts under successive circumstances, in showing how character increases and assimilates new substances to its own, and how it decays, together with the catastrophe into which by its own gravity it naturally declines.
>
> (Godwin 1797)

Godwin's argument here is that history is clearly othered from us, as completely as our fellow human beings are, and we would be foolish to think otherwise. Instead, the historical romance writer can create 'authentic' characters within a factual-led framework, and write stories about them which will communicate as much as is necessary of the past. The final formulation might be taken as a good working definition of the historical novel. It certainly is what many theorists have argued Scott was doing, in so far as his analysis of recognisable human character within a specific set of circumstances is what supposedly makes him innovative:

> What matters therefore in the historical novel is not the retelling of great historical events, but the poetic awakening of the people who figured in those events. What matters is that we should re-experience the social and human motives which led men to think, feel and act just as they did in historical reality.
>
> (Lukács 1962: 42)

Godwin is essentially arguing this before Scott has put pen to paper, and in doing so he suggests to us a few key things. First, the writing of historical fiction, since its origins in romance, has been something which has effectively communicated narrative and character. Second, the very mode of imaginative writing about history demonstrates the innate falsity of History and the subjective ways in which we know, engage with, and understand the past.

What Scott demonstrates is the integration of a newly successful type of historical fiction. As he suggests in the opening of *The Antiquary*, 'I have been more solicitous to describe manners minutely, than to arrange in any case an artificial and combined narration' (Scott 1816: vii). Scott was interested in the ways that people act, rather than the effects and purposes of their actions. That said, he also (confusingly) argues in *Waverley* that 'From this my choice of an era the understanding critic may further presage, that the object of my tale is more a description of men than manners' (Scott 1985: 35). Again, this suggests an interest in psychology rather than in custom. It is clear that Scott thought of his novels as somehow both romance and novel, demonstrating its slippery definition.

Waverley follows the fortunes of Edward Waverley, a foolish English gentleman who visits the Highlands of Scotland and becomes embroiled in the nascent rebellion of the Jacobite Bonnie Prince Charlie. He is particularly drawn to the impudent and charming clan leader Fergus Mac-Ivor and his sister Flora. Waverley is a dreamy romantic who is seduced by the Scottish way of life and allows himself to get caught up in events; it is not until the conclusion of the novel that he attains self-consciousness and understands the force and consequence of his actions. Scott is generally credited with 'making respectable the denigrated, feminized genre of romance by infusing it with the masculine, empirical essence of real history' (Russell 2005: 385). The fusion of the two modes is the key, creating a narrative which combines strong characterisation with historical background.

The character of Edward Waverley is presented to us as a foolish dreamer, fired by romantic fiction to seek adventure but discovering the relatively grim realities behind the flourish: 'It was up the course of this last stream that Waverley, like a knight of romance, was conducted by the fair Highland damsel, his silent guide' (Scott 1985: 175). This idealised version of things is seen to be a fiction. For instance, even during the clan celebrations Fergus Mac-Ivor admits he does not really like the Highland celebrations but he partakes for the sake of his men. The romanticism of the novel is generally problematic, and Scott himself calls his protagonist a 'sneaking piece of imbecility' (Scott 1985: 20). When we are introduced to Waverley the name of Quixote is mentioned and it is clear that he is something akin to the eccentric knight, but he is also a young man learning about himself through a journey which is a key trope of the novel. The novel draws on the traditions of the Gothic novel particularly in the presentation of its hero: 'Waverley spends much of the novel in a state of polite ignorance' (Russell 2005: 386). This lack of agency associates him with passive female characters in Gothic novels, although the rejection of romance in the novel has been read as Scott 'explicitly distancing himself from these female forerunners' (Wallace 2005: 9).

Don Quixote is a clear motif for *Waverley*. Cervantes is referred to as a model and Scott argues:

> My intention is not to follow the steps of that inimitable author, in describing such total perversion of intellect as misconstrues the objects actually presented to the senses, but that more common aberration from sound judgement, which apprehends occurrences indeed in their reality, but communicates to them a tincture of its own romantic tone and colouring.
>
> (Scott 1985: 55)

As this demonstrates Scott is interested in the ways in which 'reality' can be misinterpreted by the imagination. The novel also meditates on the nature of reading fiction and the experience of the reader. Scott's rationalist perspective leads him to suspect the romanticising tendency of those who read fiction. Again, this model suggests that in writing his historical novel Scott was concerned to clearly delimit his practice. Scott wanted to write of 'men not manners'. Customs and behaviour are mere external fripperies, whereas Scott's purpose was to reveal the actuality of the past. *Waverley* has its roots in romance, and there is a clear dialogue between the rational realism of England and the romantic, sublime, passionate romance of the Highlands. This kind of dialogue is seen in a debate by Flora and Edward over Scottish ballads and verse. However, Scott firmly comes down on the side of rationality, and the book presents to us 'a series of apparently heroic situations being collapsed by realistic punctures' (Harvey Wood 2006: 40). Flora, for instance, becomes exiled from society after the fall of her hero, Prince Charles, and her bitterness is shocking; her brother moves from charming clan leader to condemned prisoner, executed for treason. As Waverley travels through Scotland he sees the devastation wrought upon the land by war (Scott 1985: 432), and this experience upsets his simple view of things.

Waverley as a character is quintessential Scott, an exemplar for all his protagonists as well as many of those in subsequent historical novels, 'poised accidentally on the cusp of historical events, influenced in different directions by reason and upbringing' (Harvey Wood 2006: 38). He sees historical events but experiences them personally and from a variety of perspectives, very few of them a clear, insightful understanding. His witnessing of key battles, for instance, is generally from the sidelines. Furthermore, as someone who takes a long time coming to an understanding of the significance of events, Waverley stands metonymically for the audience's engagement with the historical past: as something consciously understood only with the benefit of hindsight. The novel shows Waverley's 'gradual disillusionment' with the rebellion and his 'growing maturity' (Harvey Wood 2006: 41) as a person. He learns from his experience, understanding finally, through a kind of hindsight, the consequences and meanings of his actions. This reconciliatory compromise leads him to happiness, finally, and demonstrates 'the theme of the opposition of romance and realism that was to recur in so many of his [Scott's] later novels' (Harvey Wood 2006: 42). As various critics have argued, Scott was concerned about the political instability that the presence of the past might have in contemporary society, and his writing sought to answer this: 'his consistent goal, across a number of literary genres, was to anatomize and neutralize such sinister energies of this past while at the same time commercially exploiting the appeal of that past to the reader' (MacAlman 1999: 692). The novel, for all its celebration of the traditions and lives of the Highlanders, consistently undermines them. As Richard Humphrey argues, his attitude to Jacobitism is mixed: '*Waverley* is the novel in which he is able vicariously to live out both sides of this divided political self' (Humphrey 1993: 34).

Scott's contemporary readers were delighted and excited by his works, but some critical minds were not so certain. As Wordsworth's comments, already noted, suggested, the novel was considered dangerous because of its ability to reach a broad section of society and take hold of their imagination. The critical *Letter to the Author of Waverley* by Timothy Touchstone worries about his influence: 'You possess, Sir, a most powerful influence over the imagination of your readers, the engine by which the passions are oftenest excited' (Touchstone 1820: 11). Scott's lack of moral seriousness, his ambivalence and political havering, his celebration of low characters and criminals, as well as his representations of the vice of religion and the fact that his novels have no tone of ethical guidance, led to various critiques and attacks on his works. Responses to his work, and, particularly, to his success, highlighted the duty of the writer of popular fiction to attend to the morals of the audience: 'I cannot divest myself of the opinion that popular works of amusement *ought* to have their MORAL tendency *clearly* defined; and that the precepts they inculcate should be of that high tone which have the word of God for their foundation' (Touchstone 1820: 13). Popular fiction has always been feared, and Touchstone's concern here for the lack of moral direction in Scott's work demonstrates the worry of critics and conservatives alike that the novel has a dissident, problematic quality that should be controlled.

THEORETICAL PARADIGMS: GEORG LUKÁCS AND THE BIRTH OF THE HISTORICAL NOVEL

What, then, if anything, did Scott do that was new, and what are the generic rules that he laid down? In order to analyse this it is instructive to turn to the most influential and thoughtful critic of the historical novel, Georg Lukács. This section will outline his work as a way of investigating the significance of Scott and of setting up key thematic models that we will be concerned with throughout the remainder of this book. Marxist literary theorist Lukács's essay *The Historical Novel*, published in 1955, was part of his wider contribution to analysis of the novel form and particularly his influential move to see literary works as products of social forces. *The Historical Novel* takes Scott as its subject, and seeks to understand the 'social and ideological basis from which the historical novel was able to emerge' (Lukács 1962: 20). Lukács also analyses why his historical novels work and what their significance is. He suggests that historical work before Scott is 'mere costumery'; what he brings is 'the specifically historical, that is, derivation of the individuality of characters from the historical peculiarity of their age' (Lukács 1962: 19). There were novels with 'historical themes' before Scott, argues Lukács, yet in contrast to them Scott does not use history simply as background but seeks to understand individuals historically.

Lukács posits that Scott's novels emerged at a unique historical moment. The revolutionary and Napoleonic wars of the late eighteenth and early nineteenth centuries, and the emergence of capitalism as an economic structure after the Enlightenment, had a direct cultural consequence which was the realist novel. The economic grounds for realism, the appearance of capitalism, meant that the novel evolved into something which reflected a new sense of 'the concrete (i.e. historical) significance of time and place, to social conditions, and so on, it created this spatio-temporal (i.e. historical) character of people and places' (Lukács 1962: 21). Before the end of the Enlightenment 'history' as such did not really exist. Incipient capitalism and the emerging separation of the workers (in this instance in agriculture) from the means of production and capital led to a sense of history as specific, although this sense was instinctive because Marx had not been born to theorise it yet: 'this, as in the economics of Steuart, was a product of realistic instinct and did not amount to a clear understanding of history as a process, of history as the concrete precondition of the present' (Lukács 1962: 21). After the French revolution a sense of historical perspective and progress was imported, leading to 'a new humanism, a new concept of progress' (Lukács 1962: 29); before this, history had been the story of unalterable Man, unchanging and **reified**. Lukács posits the 'invention' of a sense of historicalness, a sense post-revolution of the continuation and development of history as something non-static.

Essentially, what Lukács is interested in here is to prove that economic and social tumult created a dynamic sense of progress and, most of all, of history as *process*. Before the **Enlightenment**, for Lukács, 'history' did not exist in a way that normal people might understand. There was no sense of progress and change, for **Marxists** the fundamentals of history. It took the French revolution and the following wars to create a subject who had a sense of history: '[they] for the first time made history a *mass experience* and moreover on a European scale' (Lukács 1962: 23). Lukács discusses the German philosopher Hegel, and in particular his theories of history:

> Hegel, however, sees a process in history, a process propelled, on the one hand, by the inner motive forces of history and which, on the other hand, extends its influence to all the phenomena of human life, including thought. He sees the total life of humanity as a great historical process.
>
> (Lukács 1962: 29)

So the point about history is that it is in a state of flux, and entirely prevalent throughout society. All of life is historical, or steeped in the process of history. The geographical breadth of the Napoleonic wars was also key:

> if experiences such as this are linked with the knowledge that similar upheavals are taking place all over the world, this must enormously strengthen the feeling first that there is such a thing as history, that it

is an uninterrupted process of changes and finally that it has a direct effect upon the life of every individual.

(Lukács 1962: 23)

The wars introduced Europe to the first 'mass' experience of a series of events, and provoked what you might call historical anxiety:

Hence the concrete possibilities for men to comprehend their own existence as something historically conditioned, for them to see in history something which deeply affects their daily lives and immediately concerns them.

(Lukács 1962: 24)

This experience was linked to the emergence of nationalism at the same time, a clear development of which was a need to communicate a sense of national history: 'The appeal to national independence and national character is necessarily connected with a reawakening of national history' (Lukács 1962: 25). Essentially, then, the uproar of the times led to a new sense of historicity, manifest in the notion of historical progress, the possibility of change, and the individuated importance of these concepts. Specifically, these changes were expressed through the emergent realist novel, and, particularly, through the historical form of that genre: 'These events, this transformation of men's existence and consciousness throughout Europe form the economic and ideological basis for Scott's historical novel' (Lukács 1962: 31).

What, then, of the novels themselves? Their context is the moment Europe awoke into historicity, but how do they work and why are they important? At base the form is something which communicates and educates through fiction: 'the historical novel therefore has to *demonstrate* by *artistic* means that historical circumstances and characters existed in precisely such-and-such a way' (Lukács 1962: 43). They have the ability to create a sense of human connection which is key: we do not 'regard the particular psychology and ethics which arise from them as an historical curiosity, but should re-experience them as a phase of mankind's development which concerns and moves us' (Lukács 1962: 42).

This clear sense of connection with the past, and an awareness that the events of history have an impact upon the contemporary, is something which has profound consequences for the way we live our lives and conceive of ourselves. The historical novel gives us this connection and insight, and therefore is of keen importance.

For Lukács the importance of Scott's novels is that he was able to express history through character:

> Scott's greatness lies in his capacity to give living human embodiment to historical-social types. The typically human terms in which great historical trends become tangible had never been so superbly, straightforwardly and pregnantly portrayed. And above all, never before had this kind of portrayal been consciously set at the centre of the representation of reality.
>
> (Lukács 1962: 35)

Scott's authentic character portrayal avoids romanticising figures. This key interest in historicised character, in giving the reader insight into the mind of a member of a past society, is for Lukács the political importance of the historical novel, as it induces historical empathy and a sense of process: 'This historical faithfulness of Scott is the authenticity of the historical psychology of his characters, the genuine *hic et nunc* [here and now] of their inner motives and behaviour' (Lukács 1962: 60). Yet it goes further than simply good characterisation; to some degree Lukács demands that the historical novel creates a living empathy, a live connection between then and now:

> What matters therefore in the historical novel is not the retelling of great historical events, but the poetic awakening of the people who figured in those events. What matters is that we should re-experience the social and human motives which led men to think, feel and act just as they did in historical reality. And it is a law of literary portrayal which first appears paradoxical, but then quite obvious, that in order to bring out these social and human motives of behaviour, the outwardly insignificant events, the smaller (from without) relationships are better suited than the great monumental dramas of world history.
>
> (Lukács 1962: 42)

The key element here is to communicate through character a sense of empathy and thence of historical process. The 'retelling of great historical events' is not important, as the **historiography** of the historical novel, for Lukács, is that it enables a sense of connection which is deeply politicised. In this, the novel is best when it concentrates on the minor details and the marginalised characters in order to communicate the 'social and human motives of behaviour'. The realism of Scott's novels, his 'disclosing the actual conditions of life' and his interest in low characters means that he can demonstrate the real cause and consequence of events:

> Scott discovers the only possible means whereby the historical novel can reflect historical reality adequately, without either romantically monumentalizing the important figures or dragging them down to the level of private, psychological trivia ... Scott represents simultaneously the historical necessity of this particular individual personality and the individual role which he plays in history.
>
> (Lukács 1962: 47)

This dynamic sense of the individual within history is what Lukács calls 'historical faithfulness' (Lukács 1962: 44). The individual in his novels is both historical and of history, both individual and emblematic.

One final aspect of Scott's writing is the concept of the 'necessary anachronism': the knitting of a fictional narrative out of 'reality':

> Scott's 'necessary anachronism' consists, therefore, simply in allowing his characters to express feelings and thoughts about real, historical relationships in a much clearer way than the actual men and women of the time could have done. But the content of these feelings and thoughts, their relation to their real object is always historically and socially correct.
>
> (Lukács 1962: 63)

This is how Lukács squares the fiction–fact circle, something that, as we shall see, Manzoni amongst others will have problems with. In order to attend to his wider project, communicating historical events through character, Scott and all historical novelists will have to sculpt reality somewhat and, effectively, make things up.

The form of *Waverley* reflects Lukács's idea of history as the form of a **Bildungsroman** or journal towards personal redemption in some ways demands the sense of a 'life' as something which can encompass progress. In the same way that Lukács talks of the masses achieving historical consciousness the hero of the *Bildungsroman* achieves a sense of 'then' and 'now' in relation to his personal identity. Yet Waverley himself is, as Lukács points out, entirely middling as a character. This is key for Lukács in that it allows Scott to explore the 'reality' of history through a figure who is without prejudice. The ordinariness of the central character is the point, as there is a sense that the figures in Scott stand for more (metonymically) than just characters: 'Scott's unequalled historical genius shows itself in the individual characteristics which he gives his leading figures so they really concentrate in themselves the salient positive and negative sides of the movement concerned' (Lukács 1962: 40).

For Lukács, then, the historical novel is keenly important for various reasons. It represents historical process, and in doing so gestures towards actual historical progress. The realism of the novel allows the reader to engage with and empathise with historical individuals and thence gain a sense of their own historical specificity. It is able to communicate to people a sense of their own historicity, and the ways that they might be able to construct historically inflected identities for themselves. The historical novel has a humanist impulse to teach and educate, and this pedagogical element is crucial for Lukács; it is the movement to historicised revelation and understanding which is the point of the exercise.

THEORETICAL PARADIGMS: MANZONI, THE 'NAKED HISTORIAN'

What, though, did contemporaries of Scott make of historical fiction? Lukács sees Scott with theoretical and historical hindsight, claiming his example for his own ideology. How did those who responded immediately to Scott's work conceptualise his importance? There was constant debate through the nineteenth century about the relationship of the novel to history, and how the historical novel worked aesthetically. Alfred de Vigny argued in the preface to his historical novel *Cinq mars* that 'history is a romance of which the people are the authors', claiming that art could infuse the past with life and see into the hidden areas of the human heart (de Vigny 1829). Alessandro Manzoni's *c.* 1828 (published 1850) essay on the historical novel begins by articulating the two key criticisms of the form. In his view these are that 'fact is not clearly distinguished from invention', preventing such works from giving 'a faithful representation of history' (Manzoni 1984: 63); and conversely, that in some novels 'the author does plainly distinguish factual truth from invention', destroying the 'unity that is the vital condition of this or any other work of art' (Manzoni 1984: 65). Disarmingly, Manzoni simply concludes, 'How to answer these critics? To tell the truth, they are probably right' (Manzoni 1984: 67). By beginning his essay in this fashion Manzoni demonstrates several things: that critics of the historical novel have always existed and have generally been pretty rigidly dogmatic in their approach to the form; that the genre might be maddeningly inconsistent, and indeed that this might be innate to this mode of writing; that the weaving of fact and fiction which is the central characteristic of the historical novel is crucial to its manifestation; and that this provokes disquiet. He points out that both criticisms are inconsistent with actual novelistic practice, and suggests that the reader *knows* before they pick up the book that they will find 'things that occurred and things that have been invented, two different objects of two different, fully contrary, sorts of belief' (Manzoni 1984: 70). He asserts, therefore, an active engagement on the part of the reader that the critic disavows. Manzoni distinguishes between the reader's 'historical' belief in fact and 'that other unique, exclusive, and ineffable belief that we lend to things known to be merely verisimilar, and that I call poetic' (Manzoni 1984: 69). This need to hold two very different types of system in mind when reading historical fiction argues an impossible complexity to the activity:

> I had hoped to show, and I think I have shown, that the historical novel is a work in which the necessary turns out to be impossible,

and in which two essential conditions cannot be reconciled, or even one fulfilled. It inevitably calls for a combination that is contrary to its subject matter and a division contrary to its form ... In short it is a work impossible to achieve satisfactorily, because its premises are inherently contradictory ... here precisely is its critical flaw.

(Manzoni 1984: 72)

The genre is fundamentally fractured, contradictory and flawed. It holds two things in tension that cannot come together, and the effect of this is 'disquieting'; the ethical problems associated with it are huge (Manzoni 1984: 74). However, 'Try as you may to prove that these [Scott's] novels ought not to succeed, the fact is they do' (Manzoni 1984: 78). The historical novel 'is hardly unique in the inherent contradiction of its premises and its resulting inability to take on a convincing and stable form' (Manzoni 1984: 81). In the instability of form and constant flux of the genre lies its protean complexity; in order to square the illogical circle inherent within it, the historical novel must keep on evolving, shifting and changing. Manzoni in many ways is critical of the historical novel, mainly due to its blurring of history and concomitant ethical problems, but he has sympathy with the attempt and places the form with epic and tragedy as forms in which writers have tried to combine history and story. His criticisms of the historical novel, in particular its innate falsehood, are still commonly deployed today, and might be said to be inextricably bound up in the form. Similarly, his insight that the historical novel is inherently contradictory might to a modern reader suggest something interesting rather than be grounds for disapproval.

The essay was begun just after the publication of Manzoni's own historical novel *The Betrothed* (1827), in which he demonstrates some of his key arguments. *The Betrothed* divorces the writing of history from the narrative; certain chapters might stand on their own as historical disquisitions. Chapters 31 and 32, for instance, consist of a lengthy narrative history, with footnotes, of the coming of plague to Italy: 'Our aim in this account is to tell the truth, not only to represent the conditions in which our characters will find themselves, but to make known at the same time, as far as our restricted space and limited abilities allow, a page or our country's history which is more celebrated than it is known' (Manzoni 1997: 429). Similarly at an earlier point the narrator breaks away 'in order to make clear the remaining private events which we have to relate, we simply must preface them by some account of these public ones' (Manzoni 1997: 387). As Goethe said of him, at this point Manzoni 'divests himself of the poet's garb and stands revealed for some considerable time as a naked historian' (Manzoni 1997: 675). Where many historical fiction writers are content to add footnotes or suggest history, even, as in Dickens's *Barnaby Rudge*, having long sections describing events such as the storming of Newgate that are not strictly related to the central story, Manzoni takes it as his purpose to present the reader with the scholarly historical framework. Fundamentally, this is given in order that the private stories of those in the novel might be further understood. Rather than gaining a greater insight into history through the experience of individuals, here the reader is allowed to understand the story of those individuals through their historical context. As his most recent editors have pointed out, this makes him 'unique among the historical novelists of the nineteenth century' (Manzoni 1997: xxiv) in so far as he clearly conceived of a mode of writing history as being apart from fictionalising the past, but also allowed that the two types of writing might sit easily as part of the same work. *The Betrothed* seems to consciously demonstrate Manzoni's idea of the 'poetic' and the 'historical' belief by showing how history might work in various ways with fiction (Gladfelder 1993). Manzoni's essay concludes by worrying that the historical novel is a flimsy, corrupt genre that tends towards obfuscation and falsehood; he prophesies its immediate demise. He finds in Scott the only example of someone who might hold all the contradictions together and make something flawed but beautiful. Yet in his own practice he wrote a romance which clearly articulated a way in which history and fiction might coexist, and inform one another; in his words, to effectively 'represent the human condition in a historical era through invented actions' (Manzoni 1984: 76).

NINETEENTH-CENTURY HISTORIES

The example of Scott's work was profoundly influential, not just over the writers of fiction but the writers of history, too. It is difficult to overstate how important his example was to writers, historians and readers during the nineteenth century, throughout the world (see Chapter 4). Historian Thomas Macaulay argued in 1854 that 'those parts of the duty which properly belong to the historian have been appropriated by the historical novelist' (cited in Sanders 1978: 5). Macaulay thought that the historian should be making the past familiar and understandable, but that this was what Scott had done instead. Mark Twain even argued that the new nationhood suggested by the works of Scott was responsible for the American Civil War (Hayden 1970: 537–9). Of course, the centrality of Scott to the discussion of the historical novel is not simply due to the fact that he was an important exponent of that particular form. His example as an historical writer spread throughout Europe and the world, and he was mimicked and echoed repeatedly. He also had a crucial impact upon the development of the 'pure' realist novel form, as his importance to Dickens, Balzac, Manzoni, Pushkin and Tolstoy among others demonstrates (Shaw 1983: 23; Sanders 1978: 11). The remainder of this chapter will trace further manifestations of the historical novel throughout the nineteenth century and conclude by looking at ways that history itself was troubled by Modernist writers.

The profession of History had been increasingly codified and organised during the nineteenth century (Levine 1986; Slee 1986), particularly due to the influential writings of Leopold von Ranke (Iggers and Powell 1990). Ranke's *History of the Latin and Teutonic Nations* (1824) inaugurated a powerful style of narrative history allied to the study of primary sources and famously claimed:

> History has had assigned to it the office of judging the past and of instructing the present for the benefit of the future ages. To such high offices the present work does not presume: it seeks only to show what actually happened.
>
> (Ranke 1824)

This increasing sense of history as a pseudo-scientific, self-governing discipline began to divorce it from an amateur pursuit. As a consequence, the historical novel became intertwined with a newly emerging discipline rather than developing as an offshoot of the literary novel.

The British historical novel during the nineteenth century took the example of Scott and analysed the processes of history: 'The past could be seen to reflect the present, and, as a consequence, modern problems could be judged more detachedly for being considered within an historical perspective' (Sanders 1978: 11). The historical novel had the potential to develop moral and social issues, and in tandem with realist tropes was thought to have significant importance (Sanders 1978: 13–14). The British historical novel is concerned with society in a way that European manifestations are not; they tend to be more interested in the grand sweep of history than in reflecting upon the contemporary (see below). In Britain there was also a popular trend for medievalism (Ganim 2005), a cultural trend influenced in part by Henry Kenelm Digby's work on chivalry, *The Broad-stone of Honour* (1822), and best seen in Edward Bulwer Lytton's *The Last of the Barons* (1843) and Arthur Conan Doyle's *The White Company* (1891). However, writers such as George Eliot, Charles Dickens, William Makepeace Thackeray, Edward Bulwer-Lytton and Elizabeth Gaskell used the historical novel to contemplate social change. Charles Reade's *The Cloister and the Hearth* (1861) was the most popular and influential of this tranche of writings, and adhered to a naturalist realism in order to communicate something that cold history could not:

> The general reader cannot feel them, they are presented so curtly and coldly: they are not like breathing stories appealing to his heart, but little historic hailstones striking him but to glance off his bosom: nor can he understand them; for epitomes are not narratives, as skeletons are not human figures.
>
> Thus records of prime truths remain a dead letter to plain folk: the writers have left so much to the imagination, and imagination is so rare a gift. Here, then, the writer of fiction may be of use to the public – as an interpreter.
>
> (Reade 1861)

This is a model of historical fiction which allows the reader to understand history through 'breathing stories appealing to his heart', the flesh on the bones of the past.

As Sanders argues, to Charles Dickens history 'is as much of a nightmare as the present can be, even though the present has succeeded in alleviating some of the abuses and prejudices which once made for disorder' (Sanders 1978: 71). Dickens's first historical novel includes sharp observation of mob violence and the consequences of extremist anti-religious sentiment. *Barnaby Rudge* (1841) is set during the anti-Catholic Gordon riots of 1780, the most destructive in Britain, which involved the storming of Newgate prison. The action is set sixty-six years before the present, within living memory (and invoking the sixty years hence of *Waverley*). Dickens intertwines the public story of the violence with the personal narratives of his characters, often caught up in the horror and at times leading it. The attack on Newgate and the various waves of mob violence against persons and property are narrated with a precise, journalistic excitement. The spectre of such violence on the streets of London is terrible, but Dickens is keen to suggest that it is mainly undertaken by criminals and lunatics. The violence of the crowd is explicitly non-English, as is demonstrated when they destroy the Maypole Inn. The mindless wrecking of this venerable institution in Chigwell that has stood placidly for centuries illustrates the threat posed to the nation by such inexcusable destruction. *Barnaby Rudge* warns of the consequences for society of following mobs, attacking minorities, and intolerance. In contrast, the noble middle classes, in particular the locksmith Varden, stolidly resist such mayhem. The novel therefore celebrates a kind of ordinary Englishness and derides the violence of revolution, asserting a historiography of abiding and stability rather than process and progress. The Maypole is rebuilt, the mob subsides, and all is good in the country. *Barnaby Rudge* was written at the same time as the Chartist uprisings in England, and many critics have taken it to be a warning against revolution (Fleishman 1971: 102). It is, though, an extremely complex and bleak work which understands how mobs work and sees a viciousness at the heart of the country which the virtuous need to guard against.

Similarly, *A Tale of Two Cities* (1859) berates the Parisians for destroying nobility and virtue during the French revolution and its aftermath. In his preface to the novel Dickens claims the evidentiary support of 'the most trustworthy witnesses', continuing that it 'has been one of my hopes to add something to the popular and picturesque means of understanding that terrible time, though no one can hope to add anything to the philosophy of Mr Carlyle's wonderful book' (Dickens 1860: preface). Dickens sees his purpose as contributing to the myriad ways that audiences might understand the revolution. He also cites a greater authority, Thomas Carlyle's famous *French Revolution: A History* (1837), and suggests through association that his novel, whilst inferior, is similar in its ability to communicate the events of the past. Dickens's well known opening to the novel suggests differences of historical interpretation before reflecting on the relative unchanging nature of things:

> It was the best of times, it was the worst of times, it was the age of wisdom, it was the age of foolishness, it was the epoch of belief, it was the epoch of incredulity, it was the season of Light, it was the season of Darkness, it was the spring of hope, it was the winter of despair, we had everything before us, we had nothing before us, we were all going direct to Heaven, we were all going direct the other way – in short, the period was so far like the present period, that some of its noisiest authorities insisted on its being received, for good or for evil, in the superlative degree of comparison only.
>
> (Dickens 1860: 1)

George Eliot's historical fiction is less interested in the traumatic events of history. Her masterpiece, *Middlemarch*, is subtitled *A Study of Provincial Life*, and she looks for meaning and significance in the margins, away from the central occurrences. Eliot's Prelude to the novel invokes the story of St Theresa, whose:

> passionate, ideal nature demanded an epic life: what were many-volumed romances of chivalry and the social conquests of a brilliant girl to her? Her flame quickly burned up that light fuel, and, fed from within, soared after some illimitable satisfaction, some object which

would never justify weariness, which would reconcile self-despair with the rapturous consciousness of life beyond self.

(Eliot 1871 I: vi)

Theresa rejects idealised history and contemporary society alike in her desire to become self-aware and self-defining. Theresa is a recurring female type through history: 'Many Theresas have been born who found for themselves no epic life wherein there was a constant unfolding of far-resonant action' (Eliot 1871 I: vi). Lacking opportunity and social satisfaction, these women who desire something more than their lot find only disappointment. They have no historical agency and cannot impact upon and change society. They have no 'epic' life, no narrative other than that imposed upon them. The heroine of *Middlemarch*, Dorothea, is a woman who strives and is often punished for her attempts to break free from the social, historical and cultural identities that she is offered. She wishes to be part of the 'far-resonant action' but cannot, due to forces out of her control. Eliot's reflection on historical circumstance therefore suggests that it allows us to see the ways in which people are caught and to reflect on the reasons for this; a kind of politicised hindsight which then allows the individual to reflect upon their contemporary circumstance. Yet the most important elements of the historical process, for Eliot, were those things that are not seen or understood:

the effect of her [Dorothea's] being on those around her was incalculably diffusive: for the growing good of the world is partly dependent on unhistoric acts; and that things are not so ill with you and me as they might have been, is half owing to the number who lived faithfully a hidden life, and rest in unvisited tombs.

(Eliot 1871 IV: 371)

This argues an interest in the particular and the unseen of history; rather than the progress outlined by historians, a desire to understand that the lives of forgotten individuals are as significant as anything else. The movement from then to now is not simply one of 'historical' development but the accretion of 'unhistoric acts' by forgotten people which make life better than it might be.

These small everyday kindnesses and virtuous actions are worthy of remembering, and celebration. *Middlemarch* sees the importance of minutiae in clear contrast with the epic sweep of other historical novels, such as *War and Peace*, which seek to use the historical novel to explain great public historical processes. Eliot defined the 'Historic Imagination' in her notebook: 'the working out in detail of the various steps by which a political or social change was reached, using all extant evidence and supplying deficiencies by careful analogical creation' (cited in Fleishman 1971: 158). She presents her evidence and traces the minor shifts of the personal past in order to understand the personal present, as expressed in *Felix Holt, the Radical* (1866):

> These social changes in Treby parish are comparatively public matters, and this history is chiefly concerned with the private lot of a few men and women; but there is no private life which has not been determined by a wider public life ... the lives we are about to look back upon do not belong to those conservatory species; they are rooted in the common earth, having to ensure all the ordinary chances of past and present weather.
>
> (Eliot 1977: 129)

The interrelationship of private and public demonstrates that history is the preserve of all of society, be they male, female, poor, or rich. Eliot's historical fictions *Middlemarch*, *Romola* (1853) and *Felix Holt*, all explore historical periods in forensic philosophical, cultural and social detail with a view to understanding political process and change through the experience of a range of ordinary people.

EUROPEAN VERSIONS: HUGO, PUSHKIN, FLAUBERT AND TOLSTOY

The historical novel was developed in Europe as a form not distinct from the novel itself but clearly part of the genre and something worth our investigation. The practice of the key novelists in France, Germany and Russia demonstrates this, as innovative writers from Honoré de Balzac, Stendhal, Gustave Flaubert and

Alexander Pushkin to mainstream practitioners like Alexandre Dumas and Victor Hugo all wrote successful and interesting work. The European historical novel also produced some of the most famous and impressive works of the century, in particular Leo Tolstoy's *War and Peace* (1865).

Pushkin imitated Scott, and his work was an attempt to circumvent censorship and create nationalist sentiment through literary engagement with Russian history. He wrote of Scott, 'we get to know past times ... as though we were living a day-to-day life in them ourselves' (Pushkin 1962: 13), arguing that the imaginative re-creation of this kind of historical empathy was the key to the form. In contrast, Tolstoy had a much more mechanical and developed sense of historiography, and *War and Peace* is an attempt at both writing narrative and seriously communicating something historical. Tolstoy wrote to his publisher, 'the work is not a novel and is not a story, and cannot have the sort of plot whose interest ends with the denouement'; he asked for the work not to be called a novel at all (Tolstoy 2007: viii). He was attempting to create something which eluded both history and fiction; an epic of pastness which somehow maintained the integrity of history and truth whilst creating a compelling narrative. As Shaw argues, 'Of all historical novelists, Tolstoy comes closest to capturing the total spectrum of human existence in history' (Shaw 1983: 119). The book opens with a contemporariness of tone, with little by way of historical explanation: 'These were the words with which, in July 1805, the renowned Anna Pavlovna Scherer, lady-in-waiting and confidante of the empress Maria Fedorovna, greeted the influential and high-ranking Prince Vasily' (Tolstoy 2007: 5). The narrative develops in this state of simultaneity, moving from the initial comments by Pavlovna from place to place via characters, with little descriptive detail. It is not until later that a metahistorical voice is introduced. This distinguishing of tone is intentional, as Tolstoy wished to introduce historical conflict and to be both historian and novelist. Wachtel reminds us that Tolstoy includes a map of the battlefield of Borodino and therefore presents the fictional and the factually historic 'in dialogical contrast' (Wachtel 2002: 181). By avoiding simplicity and order, sidestepping Lukács's 'necessary anachronism' of coherence and connecting plot, for instance, Tolstoy achieves an epic scope that seeks to communicate the vastness of history and its courses. He interleaves and adds various philosophical arguments about the nature of history, which contribute to the 'novel's overall attempt to achieve a general vision of historical process without falsifying its particularities' (Shaw 1983: 124).

French novelist Gustave Flaubert's fascination with history led him to be the most stylistic innovator of the century in the genre. Historical novelists strove for accuracy whilst acknowledging their inability to achieve it, and Flaubert took this further than most: 'willing to see beyond the need for historical accuracy, he recognised that creative "misunderstandings" of the past could open up new literary possibilities' (Green 2004: 88). The work he produced as a consequence was fiercely interested in challenging conventional ways of writing 'history' and in undermining the authority of the past. His *La Tentation de Saint Antoine* (1849) is a strange, night-marish re-creation of the life of the saint; hardly even a novel, it is a series of 'historically authentic' hallucinations. Flaubert realised that the novelist's misunderstanding, or misappropriating, of history was extremely important to the ways that they might write. In stepping outside of conventional historicity by having characters out of time appear to Antoine, Flaubert begins the process of fiction's unravel-ling of history which was taken up tentatively by modernist writers and with gusto by the **postmodernists**.

Salammbô (1862), his 'Realistic Romance of Ancient Carthage', demonstrates further 'the continuing tension between his passionate, visceral engagement with the past and his scholarly, analytical approach' (Flaubert 1886: frontispiece; Green 2004: 92). The very notion of a 'Realistic Romance' suggests an inquisitive, rational and particularly 'contemporary' approach to the genre. As he argued in a letter to a critical Sainte-Beuve, 'I have sought to fix a mirage by applying the methods of the modern world to anti-quity, and have tried to be simple' (Flaubert 1886: 340–1). Flaubert particularly uses strange language to convey distance and oddness (Sainte-Beuve complained he needed a lexicon to under-stand the novel; Flaubert 1886: 342). The text is full of odd ellipses and mysterious aspects. Flaubert attempted to convey impressionistic atmosphere rather than detail, which he considered 'of very secondary importance' (Green 2004: 95). He had a conception that the historical background was in thrall to his literary creations: 'There is not an isolated, gratuitous description in my book; they are all *subservient* to my characters, and have an influence immediate or remote upon the action'; 'I make no pretence ... to archaeology' (Flaubert 1886: 343, 351).

The novel is complex, non-linear, and the strangeness of his composition meant that on publication critics were divided by what it actually was (Green 2004: 95). It attempted to be an historical novel but clearly was not one in the conventional sense of the term. Again, then, Flaubert's striving to create a clear sense of historical otherness led to his troubling of generic boundaries and the evolution of a new set of ways of approaching the past fictively. Flaubert thought long about how to write an historical novel, how to be true to a past whilst also representing it in print, and the consequence was these two strange, unearthly books which between them challenge and undermine conventional narrative and form. In refusing to communicate educationally, but trying to convey something more ineffable, he undermined the rationality of the historical novel form and pointed towards something more experimental and potential.

By the end of the century Scott's historical novel practice had been examined and expanded upon in multiple contexts and for various reasons. The historical novel fed nascent nationalism, developed fiction as a form, allowed for actual historical investigation; it had been theorised and discussed, critiqued and defended. As a genre it had some working definitions, but these were in a state of flux. The form had been used to attack contemporary conditions or to defend political stability; it was used to further particular arguments or as a way of reflecting on society. The historical novel had flourished in America, Europe, Latin America and Australia; it had been commented upon and developed in varying ways (Leisy 1950: 9–20).

MODERNISM AND THE END-OF-HISTORY NOVEL

Virginia Woolf argued for a new way of writing novels. In her famous 1925 essay 'Modern Fiction' she claimed that innovation was central to the development of the genre:

> if we can imagine the art of fiction come alive and standing in our
> midst, she would undoubtedly bid us break her and bully her, as well as
> honour and love her, for so her youth is renewed and her sovereignty
> assured.
>
> (Woolf 2000: 744)

This troubling image personifies fiction assailed by lovers, continually reshaped according to their desires and her masochistic
demands. Strange motif aside, what Woolf argues for is the constant re-creation of the genre. Current fiction, she argues, 'spend[s]
immense skill and immense industry making the trivial and the
transitory appear the true and the enduring' (Woolf 2000: 740).
Instead, writers should attend to the massive complexity of the
world:

> Life is not a series of gig lamps symmetrically arranged; but a luminous
> halo, a semi-transparent envelope surrounding us from the beginning
> of consciousness to the end. Is it not the task of the novelist to
> convey this varying, this unknown and uncircumscribed spirit, what-
> ever aberration or complexity it may display, with as little mixture of
> the alien and external as possible?
>
> (Woolf 2000: 741)

Woolf argues for an interest in interiority, rather than the 'alien
and external', a return to the individuation of experience. She
criticises convention and urges novelists to remember that
'everything is the proper stuff of fiction, every feeling, every
thought; every quality of brain and spirit is drawn upon; no perception comes amiss' (Woolf 2000: 744). This desire to adumbrate
the detailed complications of life, allied to a clear interest in representing the psychological and in breaking formal conventions, forms
the outline of what is often defined as literary **modernism**.

Woolf brought this investigative, fracturing approach to bear
on history in her next novel, *Orlando* (1928). Subtitled *A Biography*, the book follows Orlando through history from the Tudor
period to the 'present time'; he never dies, and at a certain point
changes gender: 'Let biologists and psychologists determine. It is
enough for us to state the simple fact; Orlando was a man till the

age of thirty; when he became a woman and has remained so ever since' (Woolf 1928: 139). The novel quite consciously fractures historicity, attacking patriarchal modes of knowing and being in order to suggest alternative, fluid knowledges and identities. *Orlando* challenges hierarchies and gendered norms, subverting ordering narratives to present a space of flux and possibility: 'she had a great variety of selves to call upon, far more than we have been able to find room for, since a biography is considered complete if it merely accounts for six or seven selves, whereas a person may well have as many as a thousand' (Woolf 1928: 309). In particular, *Orlando* undermines the historical novel, **queering** it in order to upset the rational realism of the form and to bend it as far out of shape as possible. This was, as she argued, in order to avoid the dullness of convention and to try to describe the world in better detail. Woolf clearly desired a kind of authenticity, and in the preface to the novel she praises 'my husband for the patience with which he has invariably helped my researches and for the profound historical knowledge to which these pages owe whatever degree of accuracy they attain' (Woolf 1928: ix). Yet the equivocation of 'whatever degree of accuracy' betrays the fact that she was not wedded to it; accuracy was not her central purpose. Woolf therefore points out the (male) convention of realism in writing about history, in deploying a certain set of rational, ordering tropes. Historical fiction has become something which can be formally undermined by someone seeking to reorder the novel form itself. *Orlando* breaks the historical novel apart by demonstrating that its cleaving to realistic narrative, to the 'truth' of explication, might be somehow flawed and aesthetically problematic. The novelist should, instead, be exploring possibilities and potentialities:

> They attempt to come closer to life, and to preserve more sincerely and exactly what interests and moves them, even if to do so they must discard most of the conventions which are commonly observed by the novelist. Let us record the atoms as they fall upon the mind in the order in which they fall, let us trace the pattern, however disconnected and incoherent in appearance, which each sight or incident scores upon the consciousness.

> (Woolf 2000: 740)

Her practice in *Orlando* was part of a wider movement interested in formal innovation and complication. Fleishman sees Woolf's practice in *Orlando* and *Between the Acts* (1941) as bringing 'the tradition of the English historical novel to a self-conscious close' (Fleishman 1971: 232), demonstrating how critics tend to privilege the literary mode of the form but also illustrating the way in which these novels consciously tried to forcibly reconfigure a particular form of writing.

Whilst she had little time for him, H. G. Wells had done something similar to Woolf in his *Time Machine* (1895). This novel undermines history by presenting it as a linear development that might be destabilized, and introduces to the imagination the sense of the past as something which is traversable, rather than inescapable. *The Time Machine* points to a future time when 'now' is forgotten, locating the reader at a strange point and forced to anticipate their incipient historicalness as they, too, will become 'the past'. The novel demonstrates how science has defeated history, bypassing the specificity of the historical moment with ease:

> There are really four dimensions, three which we call the three planes of Space, and a fourth, Time. There is, however, a tendency to draw an unreal distinction between the former three dimensions and the latter, because it happens that our consciousness moves inter-mittently in one direction along the latter from the beginning to the end of our lives.
>
> (Wells 1895: 3)

The Time Traveller has the ability to move in the fourth dimen-sion, and hence undermines the linear, progressive direction of the past towards the present. By creating a sense of history as something navigable and fluid both Wells and Woolf signalled new cultural modes of thinking about the past and contributed to the literary move away from 'then' to a predilection with 'now'. The historical novel became a popular form, rather than a literary one, and was increasingly allied to history itself, whereas the novel became increasingly baroque in its attempts to explore and explain contemporary experience.

'NOT TIME OR INCLINATION TO STUDY THE MORE SERIOUS HISTORIANS': HERBERT BUTTERFIELD AND THEORIES OF THE HISTORICAL NOVEL DURING THE TWENTIETH CENTURY

During the twentieth century the historical novel became a more prevalent sub-genre but also one which was increasingly marginal in discussion of the novel proper. It has been argued that literary fiction became divorced from the historical: 'it is only after the second world war and the rise of post-modernism that the historical novel again attracts the attention of major writers' (Danytė 2007: 35). There were various sophisticated manifestations, including Sigrid Undset's Nobel Prize winning trilogy *Kristin Lavransdatter* (1920–22), Robert Graves's *I, Claudius* (1934) and Sylvia Townsend Warner's *The Corner that Held Them* (1948). Georg Lukács's *The Historical Novel*, discussed above, was published in 1937, demonstrating particularly the left-wing and Marxist interest in the form during the early twentieth century (Hopkins 2006: 95–101).

Alfred Sheppard in his *The Art and Practice of Historical Fiction* (1930) suggested that the First World War had given historical novelists pause, and certainly the effects of the war on literary culture were the fragmenting and fracturing of legitimacies described by Woolf. By 1951 B. J. Whiting could mourn the exhausted form and argue that 'Something has clearly given the historical novel a shot in the arm but just as clearly the stimulus has affected quantity rather than quality' (Whiting 1951: 337). The historical novel became dissociated from the development of the novel form itself, and developed as a sub-genre at a tangent from the mainstream. However, it is still the case that most serious novelists approached the genre at least once, from Vita Sackville-West's *The Edwardians* (1930) to Evelyn Waugh's *Helena* (1950). Waugh considered *Helena* his best work, suggesting that the historical novel still had literary merit and valency despite becoming somewhat becalmed. The historical novel increasingly becomes a form written and read by women, suggesting that the decline in interest is due to a patriarchal literary history rather than a shift in practice and quality (Montefiore 1996: 2–3; Wallace 2005). This issue, and women's historical fiction, is discussed in Chapter 3.

Throughout the early twentieth century introductory guides were published to audit the wide variety of historical novels, demonstrating that the form was becoming a clear sub-genre of its own and that the breadth of its scope ensured a demand for an accurate typology. These guides are suggestive in the ways they define the genre, as well as their situating of the historical novel as something distinct from the mainstream novel. Jonathan Nield's 1902 *Guide to the Best Historical Novels and Tales* defended the form from its critics (see Chapter 1). Nield argued that the historical novel existed:

> primarily as Fiction, and, even though in our waking moments we may be persuaded of the unreality of that 'dream' which a Scott or a Dumas has produced for us, we shall still be able to place ourselves again and again under the spell of their delightful influence.
>
> (Nield 1902)

This attempt to remind the critic of the aesthetic purpose of the novel signalled how historical fiction's creativity was increasingly subsumed into the educational element. As Nield himself argued, within the boundaries of such fiction 'we are to some extent educated historically' (Nield 1902). Ernest Baker published his two-volume *History in Fiction* soon after, in 1908, a bibliography that began as an appendix in 1903 to his *Guide to the Best Fiction*. This demonstrates the burgeoning scope and variety of the historical novel, but also the division between the realist contemporary novel and its historical counterpart. Defining the historical novel as 'stories that in any way whatsoever portray the life of the past, even though actual persons and actual public events have no place in them' (Baker 1968: vii), Baker lists 1,899 entries from around the world, an attempt to articulate the historical novel as a global form, where before it had been generally considered as an **Anglophone** or European genre. He described the distinction between his book on fiction and his text on the historical novel:

although many books appear in both, the two works do not really overlap, their aims being widely different. The whole arrangement of this, the descriptive notes, and the indexing are designed for the particular benefit of the teacher and student of history, and for the reader interested in history who has not time or inclination to study the more serious historians.

(Baker 1968: vii)

This clearly suggests that the historical novel has a purpose which is distinct and different to that of the more mainstream novel; or, perhaps, that it might be at least used in a different way by its readership. Despite the fact that he thinks the historical novel distinct from the actual novel, it has an important intervention to make, particularly in historical thought.

Historical fiction is not history, but it is often better than history ... may easily teach more and carry a deeper impression than whole chapters of description and analysis ... will probably succeed in making a period live in the imagination when textbooks merely give us dry bones.

(Baker 1968: viii)

He continued to argue that the historical novel 'may have a positive value as a contribution to knowledge ... [it] gives us something beyond the scope of the historian, but none the less true for that' (Baker 1968: viii). Indeed, he concluded, the historical novel might be something that would surmount history:

[It] is as sincere and valid reconstruction as the best efforts of the serious historian, and much the same methods are employed. Neither can possibly be more than an approximation to the reality; neither can help us to anything but a partial realization of the past which is no more.

(Baker 1968: viii)

Therefore from the beginning of the twentieth century the historical novel began to be theorised as something educational, a mode or genre distinct from the mainstream novel, and as a form which in some ways was in dialogue with history rather than with the aesthetic strategies of fiction. The guides written to service this new way of thinking about the novel give us an interesting insight into the ways in which the historical novel was conceived to be thought about: how it was imagined as a useful genre, particularly pedagogically. Teachers J. A. Buckley and W. T. Williams prefaced their *Guide to British Historical Fiction* confident that historical novels should be used by History teachers: 'No attempt need be made to demonstrate the value of historical fiction as a handmaiden to history proper' (Buckley and Williams 1912: v). The historical novel here has become something that might be used by teachers to supplement their classes and introduce students to the period. Buckley and Williams's guide is a massive chronological account which in many ways demonstrates the various effects and pedagogic uses of the historical novel: 'efforts have been made to include books which treat of the events from different, and often conflicting, points of view' (Buckley and Williams 1912: v). They list 700 or so items covering the period from the Eolithic Age to 1900.

The historian Herbert Butterfield wrote a treatise on historical novels in 1924, and his work demonstrates the ways in which the form was increasingly thought of in tandem with historical writing, rather than with other literary forms (Sewell 2005). Butterfield has a keen sense of the historical novel as a hybrid form, or 'fusion', to use his word (Butterfield 1924: 6). His essay was 'an attempt to find some relation between historical novels on the one hand and history treated as study on the other' (Butterfield 1924: preface), demonstrating the ways in which history and the historical novel were perceived as overlapping and somehow symbiotic:

> Whatever connection the historical novel may have with the history that men write and build up out of their conscious studies, or with History, the past as it really happened, the thing that is the object of study and research, it certainly has something to do with that world, that mental picture which each of us makes of the past ... the historical novel is a 'form' of history. It is a way of treating the past.
>
> (Butterfield 1924: 2–3)

This impressionistic sense of historical fiction as having a profound effect upon the historical imagination is key to a particular way of thinking about this type of novel. Indeed, we might suggest that the cultural forms of history and memory such as film, television or literature are extremely influential in creating and sustaining a particular type of historical imaginary, and one which is probably at odds with or at least a simplified version of the historical 'reality' (de Groot 2008).

Butterfield has a nostalgic turn of phrase which betrays his romanticised version of history and fiction: 'history is full of tales half told, and of tunes that break off in the middle; she gives us snatches from the lives of men, a peep at some corner of a battlefield, just enough to make us long for a fuller vision' (Butterfield 1924: 15–16) and his account of the historical novel is interested in the ways it can communicate the unknowability of the past to the contemporary reader. He has an idea of historical empathy: 'When history tells us that Napoleon did a certain thing, it is the work of each of us, in trying to bring history home to ourselves, to amplify in our imagination what the history-book gives us, and to *see* Napoleon doing the action' (Butterfield 1924: 22). The historical novel enables this imaginative understanding. Like Manzoni and Lukács (Lukács 1962: 25), Butterfield understands the value of the historical novel as a means of furthering nationalism: 'It is often born of a kind of patriotism; it can scarcely avoid always being the inspiration of it … the historical novel itself becomes a maker of history' (Butterfield 1924: 42). Globally from Scott through to the late nineteenth-century novels of Polish writers Joseph Kraszowski and Henryk Sienkiewicz, from Chinua Achebe's *Things Fall Apart* (1959), from John Cowper Powys's *Owen Glendower* (1940) to Yukio Mishima's *Sea of Fertility* tetralogy (1966–71), one of the major elements of the historical novel has been as an expression of national character and self-definition.

Daniel McGarry and Sarah Harriman White's *World Historical Fiction Guide* (1973) saw their audience as the educational community: 'This work is designed especially for use by adults and by students in senior high schools, colleges and universities; but books suitable for junior high school students as well as adult readers are also included' (McGarry and Harriman White 1973: iii). They list 6,455 novels from Antiquity onwards across the world, and define the genre as something both interested in the past but also incorporating an element of literary quality: 'fiction is historical if it includes reference to customs, conditions, identifiable persons, or events in the past ... among factors considered are literary excellence, readability, and historical value' (McGarry and Harriman White, 1973: iv). Other bibliographies included those by Hannah Logasa (for children and young adults, 1927), James R. Kaye (1920), Ernest F. Leisy (American novels, 1950) and A. T. Dickinson (American novels, 1971). The most recent of these guides, Sarah Johnson's *Historical Fiction: A Guide to the Genre* (2005), which covers 1995–2004, runs for 830 pages and 3,800 entries. This demonstrates the huge breadth of the novel, and also the desire to categorise and list it in order that the 'user' might be able to discern a pathway through the cacophony. Johnson's definition of the historical novel is more proscriptive than others: 'set before the middle of the last century ... in which the author is writing from research rather than personal experience' (Johnson 2005: 1). Almost a century after Baker, she describes the continuing problems of genre definition which mean that the historical novel still lives in the shadows: 'The problem is not that historical fiction is too narrow to deserve its own section in libraries and bookstores, but that it's too broad, and that it overlaps with other genres' (Johnson 2005: 11). This diffusion of genre will be discussed in the following chapters.

3

GENRE FICTION

This chapter concentrates on novels that are not generally judged literary and therefore are often unconsidered by critics. The sections look at novels aimed at women, those marketed for men and those written for children. How monolithic is the history being presented here? How authentic is it, and how authentic does it want to be? The key ideas we will consider are those of genre, reception, gender dynamics and authenticity. We will look at the notion of the historical novel as an educative medium and as an uncomplicated leisure choice. We also wonder about the phenomenon of serialisation. Men tend to read novels about one fictional character in a range of situations, where women tend to concentrate on one historical period or figure. 'Genre' historical fiction often tends to be extremely rigid in its underwriting of dominant cultural ideologies, and the exploration of the key issues involved in writing and consuming such fiction can show us how and why these practices are sustained.

NOVELS FOR WOMEN: ROMANCE AND HISTORY

Historical romance

This section considers historical fiction written by women for a predominantly female audience, in particular the form that is known as historical romance. Romance fiction prioritises loving and sexual relationships. Much serious historical fiction from the nineteenth century considered itself 'romance', and the morphing of the genre into something culturally marginal demonstrates the way in which historical writing became devalued through the twentieth century (Hughes 1993). Romance is a sub-genre in which sexual or romantic desire figures high, and has often been characterised as empty and conservative, in so far as it seems to sustain the dominant models of social ordering: family, hetero-normative relationships and strictly defined gender roles. As a genre it is closely associated with popular culture and with escapism: 'Romance is the original form of popular fiction. Its primary function of wish-fulfilment is the characteristic element of narratives that propel the reader into a fantasy world where a full and complete identity can be imagined' (McCracken 1998: 75).

One of the most important theorists for the study of women's genre fiction is Janice Radway. Her book *Reading the Romance* (1984) provided a set of feminist approaches to romance fictions which had been traditionally ignored or marginalised by literary critics. Radway's study concentrated on the experiences of a group of women in the American town of Smithton, and recorded their reading experiences, preferences and desires through interview, questionnaire and conversation. Her study is ethnographic, in so far as it attempts to analyse through a small study the character-istics of a certain set of ritual approaches to a cultural or social entity, in this case the romance text. She is interested in the ways that romances are read and used by their audiences, rather than in what they might mean to the critic. In the ways, particularly, that women might use the texts as sites of dissidence, revelation, community, escapism, subversion and personal agency (Radway 1987: 91–118). Radway's argument is that to simply dismiss romance novels, or writing specifically for women, as perpetuating the hegemonic structures of a patriarchal dominant culture is to miss the subtle ways that these texts are used and read. We might, therefore, posit historical romance fiction as something that is similarly part of this continuum and that could be used in a set of competing, possibly contradictory, and subversive ways. As Lisa Fletcher argues, 'historical romance fiction is constituted by an awareness of the instability of its narratological and ideological foundations' (Fletcher 2008: 14). Of course, it also might be used to serve a set of conservative, traditional discourses.

The association of women's historical writing with the romance is one of the reasons why it has been generally critically ignored (Wallace 2005: 150). Allied to this is the further issue that most of the fiction discussed in this chapter is popular, in genre and in market. Yet it seems clear that the historical version of the romance is an extremely important and a very particular type of genre. The notion of 'distance' is key to the romance (Wallace 2005: 153), and similarly 'The setting of historical romance provides just that necessary mingling of "distance" and "reality" which allows the combining of "surrogate experience" and "wish-fulfilling motifs" that are crucial to the genre' (Hughes 1993: 1). This has led to the historical romance being one of the most popular, long-running and widely read types of writing in the world. There are also sub-genres of the historical romance, in particular the 'erotic historical', which developed in the 1970s (Thurston 1987). The development of mainstream, relatively formulaic, historical romance fiction is outlined by Helen Hughes (Hughes 1993: 2–3, 132–4). Having been normally what most historical fiction was called (from Scott to Flaubert), the increasing association of historical 'romance' with a particular type of sub-generic writing led to its marginalisation. Hughes argues that after 1930 the form became increasingly associated with women, particularly in the practice of Georgette Heyer (who was first published by Mills & Boon) and subsequent practitioners such as Barbara Cartland and Catherine Cookson. Their novels reject the more rational model of historical fiction that Scott had inaugurated, with the clear sense of historical process being central, in favour of creating 'a self-sufficient past world whose attractions are seductive, drawing the reader into an uncritical experience of history as real life' (Hughes 1993: 8). Historical romances cleave to realism as a way of communicating ideology, and are relatively conservative in their outlook (Hughes 1993: 27).

Sophie Cole's *Arrows in the Dark* was Mills & Boon's first novel in 1909. The company quickly began to specialise in light romantic fiction and became immensely successful at publishing magazine serials and novels. Mills & Boon developed a formula for romance throughout the period 1930–60, concentrating on love and passion, although the books had their fair share of heartache and unpleasantness for the women in them (McAleer 1999: 158). However, they were intended to 'provide escape and entertainment', as one of their novelists, Violet Winspear, wrote in 1973 (cited in McAleer 1999: 264). Mills & Boon are now part of Harlequin, the world's largest publisher of romances, with sales of hundreds of millions around the world. Massively successful, ideologically conservative, these types of global, mass-market novels have rarely been considered by critics. These books are a set length, published monthly and reach millions of women through direct subscription, library circulation and online marketing. This is a readership constituency which is hardly ever addressed by literary critics. They are clearly an important context for our consideration, however, as the Mills & Boon 'Historical Romance' series has been one of the company's key strands since 1972 and it has been publishing historical romances throughout its history (McAleer 1999: 287; Wallace 2005: 151–2). The ways in which the books articulate historical events, identity and particularly personal relationships mean that they are an important adjunct to the generic definition of the historical novel form.

The Mills & Boon formula of light romantic fiction is relatively simple, being the story of a relationship between a woman and man from the female point of view. The marketing sells them as being particularly caricatured in their approach to history:

> Dramatic in scope, enjoy tales from chivalrous knights, roguish rakes and rugged cattlemen to impetuous heiresses, unconventional ladies and defiant bluestockings. These rich and vivid romances will capture your imagination.

> (Mills and Boon 2008)

The historical romances produced by Mills & Boon are repetitive and present history as a simplistic backdrop for the straightforward plot. The writing is straightforward and uncomplicated: heroes are 'preposterously handsome'; heroines are 'gently bred' (Brendan 2008: 7, 12). Mary Brennan's Regency-set *The Virtuous Courtesan* exemplifies many of the standard qualities of these novels. The conditions of a dead man's will are that his brother will inherit his house on the condition that he keeps his brother's former mistress living there 'in the manner to which she has become accustomed' (Brennan 2008: 16). In order to claim the fortune the brother must maintain the woman. She has little agency in the matter, and is effectively the prize superadded to economic fortune. The situation is clearly similar to that of Georgette Heyer's *Regency Buck*, discussed below, with the conflict between the protagonists the mainspring of the narrative. In many ways this is the point, as the historical period of the novel dictates the narrative structure or formulaic story, rather than anything more complex. This is why the fifteenth-century setting of June Francis's *Rebel Lady, Convenient Wife* includes accusations of witchcraft and questing pilgrimages. Yet, for all their apparent conservatism, Mills & Boon novels have been considered by several feminist critics as shifting the focus of society from masculine to feminine (Wallace 2005: 153; Dixon 1999).

Mainstream historical romances have a more complex manifestation. Catherine Cookson's first novel, *Kate Hannigan* (1950), concerns a cross-class romance between a child of the slums and a doctor. Set during the Edwardian period, the novel presents the past as a place of privation that might be escaped, where women are particularly downtrodden. It is a place of poverty, fear, drunkenness, neglect, illegitimacy and dirt. Even when the desired declaration of love in the relationship happens it is preceded by violence:

> As she dropped off to sleep again, he thought of the strangeness of the past twelve hours; most of all, that she had to be beaten almost to death for her prayer to be answered, and that through her suffering he had been saved from himself.
>
> (Cookson 1969: 150)

Kate sacrifices herself for her lover's happiness here, confessing her love after being injured and attaining a strange, almost uncanny understanding. Romance fiction is often interested in the relationship between professional male and 'subject', particularly in the doctor–nurse novels that Mills & Boon have been producing since their inception. They dramatise a particular power relationship and an escapist fantasy. That Cookson's first book also does this is interesting in so far as she sees the same relationship developing, but within a historically constrained moment. She also queries the relationship by having Kate be Doctor Rodney Prince's patient, both when injured and when giving birth. The final resolution seems almost painful, and is clearly difficult and problematic despite its initial wonder:

> she was choked by a rush of feeling, so poignant that no words could express it ... Love and tenderness seemed small parts of its ingredients; there was a protective and maternal urge mixed with her passion for him, all so intertwined that they were inseparable. And, as his lips gropingly sought hers, her own being was transported, even while her heart was rent by his tears which were wetting her face.
>
> (Cookson 1969: 222)

This variety of feelings, revelatory but complex, in the context of an embrace which is accompanied by weeping, means that the conclusion of the novel has a hubristic release as well as a melancholic sadness.

Cookson's novels refuse to compromise their message about the privations suffered by women in the past, and in doing so they present a type of historical romance which is idealistic about relationships but clear-sighted about history. These novels are not nostalgic, but articulate a clear understanding of the horrors of what women in particular went through. Furthermore, they celebrate relationships between women such as motherhood, friendship, and sisterhood as being the only thing that sustains identity and happiness through the grimness. Kate escapes her past through her beauty, her friendships and her education (Cookson 1969: 77–80). *Kate Hannigan* articulates a challenge to the ideologies of class rigidity: 'It was, as she had once read, that people like

Father O'Malley were only put there to stop people like her from thinking; for, if she once started thinking, she and her like wouldn't put up with things as they were' (Cookson 1969: 15). In pointing out the workings of hegemonic structures such as capitalism, religion and patriarchy such romances work to suggest that dominant cultural orderings might be challenged, subverted or questioned. In particular, the novel suggests that predatory, violent, selfish men are the problem, with their domineering, aggressive ways, and that whilst true love might be found it is more unusual than anything else. Having had her head turned by this new philosophy (education being important to self-realisation in Cookson's novels), Kate decides that she can break the constraints of class and that 'she was beautiful, that she was fit to marry anybody' (Cookson 1969: 16). Despite the fact that 'the path is all mapped out' (Cookson 1969: 126) for her, she strives through learning and virtue to better herself. This desire for class mobility is, therefore, presented as the romantic ideal: to escape into the arms of the better sort. Similarly, the working classes are celebrated as the posh Doctor learns to love them. So where in standard romance the aspirations of the romantic heroine work to sustain dominant cultural modes such as family, heteronormative relationships, economic, social and class structures, the manifestation of the romance in historical fiction might ask more questions than it answers, and cause the reader to question these discourses. These are the things that keep women in bondage, the novel suggests, and implicit in that suggestion is the sense that the reader might recognise that they themselves are ordered and constrained by similar forces. This self-reflexivity is common to the historical novel, in so far as it invites distance in that the past is the past; but also, in highlighting through hindsight the ways in which society works, it suggests similarity. As Wallace argues, this potentiality is key to the historical romance: 'By foregrounding historical change, women's historical novels offer the reader a retrospective view of how things *were* (particularly in relation to the restrictions imposed upon women) and thus point the way to possible change in the future' (Wallace 2005: 154).

Of course, much historical romance is clearly not interested in challenging such structures, and the work of Georgette Heyer and

Barbara Cartland is much more conservative in its representation of an idealised, nostalgic past of beauty and harmony: 'The historical setting allowed a return in imagination to a time when sexual morality was strict and gender roles clearly defined' (Hughes 1993: 116). Heyer's immensely influential historical romances of the 1930s set the pattern for most subsequent fiction in this genre (Hughes 1993: 124; Mills & Boon's historical series has a dedicated Regency strand). Heyer's historical works conceive of spirited women who gradually come to accept a patriarchal system because it offers them the opportunity of love. *Regency Buck* (1935) established the Austenesque romance, complete with a hero in the Darcy of *Pride and Prejudice* mould. The novel concerns a strong-willed heroine being slowly tamed by the society she finds herself in and the man whom she initially hates but comes to love. Judith Taverner is forced to accept the judgement of the patriarchal state as her freedom is constrained by a new legal guardian, Julian St John Audley, the man she eventually falls in love with: 'I had offended beyond forgiveness ... Shall I ever forget my dismay at what you must have been thinking?' (Heyer 1991: 330). This acceptance of the inevitability of formal relationships, although leavened by romantic love, is an important structure for such novels. In Cartland the love is even more important, and more enthusiastically expressed. Her novel *The Little Pretender*, also published in 1950, contrasts strongly with the type of bleak social realism found in Cookson. Cartland claims that she 'contented myself with making use of only two historical facts ... The rest of this book and its characters are entirely a product of my imagination' (Cartland 1971: 6). Cartland's novel is set in 1750 and concerns the Stuart Jacobites of whom Scott wrote. The sole function of this backdrop is to allow her to write of love across the classes, an extremely common theme in historical romance. The novel concludes with the wished-for embrace and the subsuming of the female, Iona, into the male, the Duke of Akrae:

> The deep passion in his voice made her tremble, and the colour rose in her cheeks.
> 'Are you afraid of me, my Dearest Heart?' he asked.

'No ... no,' she stammered, 'it ... is ... just ... that ... I love ... you so much ... I am ... afraid it is only ... a dream.'

He swept her close to his breast.

'It is true, my wife, my darling, my precious little love, you are mine now and for ever.'

(Cartland 1971: 256)

The formulaic ending here gives the male (aristocrat) precedence over the frightened female (commoner). The duke, who is never named, makes her promise repeatedly 'that you belong to me. I want to hear you say it,' and the final words, expressed while Iona 'quivered not with fear but with a strange new excitement she could not name' are 'I am ... yours' (Cartland 1971: 256). Cartland's historical romances do not seek to present social conditions but sustain conservative modes of cultural and social behaviour. In this her work is less conservatively problematic than Heyer's, which at least dramatises a certain complexity and dissonance before the harmonious conclusion.

Materiality, marketing and the text

Janice Radway is particularly interested in the materiality of romances within popular culture, and in particular how 'Literary texts are the result of a complicated and lengthy process of production that is itself controlled by a host of material and social factors' (Radway 1987: 19). As such she is a writer who exemplifies a Cultural Studies and Marxist way of thinking about texts. One central idea is that texts have physical and social aspects, and that the physical production and marketing of a book are key:

Book buying, then, cannot be reduced to a simple interaction between a book and a reader. It is an event that is affected and at least partially controlled by the material nature of book publishing as a socially organized technology of production and distribution.

(Radway 1987: 20)

The reason for this interest in materiality is that Radway argues that the book industry generated a need for romance: 'the astonishing success of the romance may constitute evidence for the effectiveness of commodity packaging and advertising and not for actual changes in readers' beliefs or in the surrounding culture' (Radway 1987: 20). In her opening section Radway considers the development of popular fiction publishing throughout the nineteenth century. She traces the gradual change from an initial period in which authorial control over the publication of books was uppermost to the changing attitude of publishers towards thinking about the book as a saleable commodity. Also important are physical and technological shifts (printing, glue, cheaper paper) that have expanded the potential market for books and the extension of literacy. She outlines the gradual growth of genre fiction in order to create a constant demand for books, and the increasing use of subscription and serialisation in the move towards publishing becoming a 'consumer-orientated industry' (Radway 1987: 26). The popular novel is cheap to produce, consumed as a product and marketed as part of an industry: 'contemporary romance publishing is guided by this entrepreneurial vision of the book as an endlessly replicable commodity' (Radway 1987: 23). This has led to massive sales figures and reach, and increasing strategies deployed by publishers to predict sales, particularly using subscription publishing and the branding of publishing houses. Female readers constitute half of the public and are catered for in particular ways; romance novels provide an enjoyable reading experience for women who wish then to repeat it regularly. Radway argues that this type of reading is particular to women, but we might also suggest that (as is argued below) male readerships are assumed to read in a particular, regularised fashion too.

A good example of the complexities of book circulation is the Book of the Month Club, founded in 1923. This is a mail-order system for selling and circulating novels. The system works on a negative response model, as subscribers are offered a novel and if they do not refuse it is mailed to them. Members are often offered the books at a substantial discount on the publisher's price which is offset by the terms of their commitment to the club in that they have to accept a minimum number of books in a time period. Using the postal system as a way of circulating cheap and popular fiction had been common practice since 1839, when Park Benjamin and Rufus Wilmost Griswold started up the 'story newspaper' *Brother Jonathan*. The Book of the Month system is useful for publishers and marketing departments as it generally guarantees a particular size of readership for a work but similarly it skews the reading audience towards particular genres and types of writing. Coinciding with the development of more efficient presses, this new type of distribution network radically changed the way that books were read, circulated and marketed in the United States and the world; it paved the way for subsequent developments such as Pocket Books, American Mercury Books and the UK's Penguin imprint. Whilst primarily and originally aimed at a popular market, literary fiction published by quality presses is increasingly sold in this fashion (McAleer 1999: 113–44).

Shortly after this change in publishing practice, Allen Lane (director of the publisher Bodley Head) was browsing the station bookshop in Exeter, having spent a weekend with Agatha Christie. He found nothing but reprinted classics and pulp novels and realised that there was a gap in the market for contemporary writing aimed at a wide audience; furthermore, he recognised that this market wanted books to be convenient and both easily accessible and readable. He founded Penguin Books to cater for this need, mass-producing contemporary crime, biography and fiction. The Penguin paperbacks had distinctive covers and were colour-coded by subject: dark blue for biography, green for crime, orange for fiction. The public appetite was much as Lane thought, and the company sold a million books within ten months. In 1937 the Pelican imprint began to develop the list, printing 'educational' books of history, politics or economics; in 1945 they began the Penguin Classics list. The paperbacks were light and small, making them easy to read, and printed very cheaply but with relatively high production values. The introduction of these volumes revolutionised literary production and the book market in the United Kingdom. The books invited buyers to read them in unfamiliar spaces. They were sold in Woolworth's, in corner shops and on station bookstalls as well as in traditional book-shops. In doing so they attempted to change reading habits and enfranchise readerships. They marketed 'quality' writing of all kinds in the way that most cheap print genre fiction had been presented, in effect making literary writing a mass-market commodity. In 1955 Penguin was selling 11 million copies a year, and other imprints like Corgi and Pan were selling in their millions (McAleer 1999: 116).

These two key events in the early twentieth century created and catered for a massive popular market. The innovations provide a set of contexts for considering the various different types of marketing, publication and circulation of fiction. They also provoke us to think a little about the ways in which texts are physically published and marketed. The material elements of production and circulation can tell us much about the meanings of a text:

> Traditional textual criticism, with its concentration on the linguistic text, is thus happily married to traditional hermeneutics, which elucidates meaning – which *locates* meaning – entirely in linguistic symbologies. Bibliographical signifiers, on the other hand, immediately call our attention to other styles and scales of symbolic exchange that every language event involves. Meaning is transmitted through bibliographical as well as linguistic codes.
>
> (McGann 1991: 57)

The ways in which we interpret a text are too much vested in the linguistic, McGann argues, and instead we should consider the bibliographical codings that mean one can judge a book by its cover. Furthermore, we need to be aware of the extraneous aspects of a physical text which strive to change our interpretation of it:

> The paratext is what enables a text to become a book and be offered as such to its readers, and, more generally, to the public ... It is an 'undefined zone' between the inside and the outside, a zone without any hard and fast boundary on either the inward side (turned toward the text) or the outward side (turned toward the world's discourse about the text), an edge, as Philippe Lejeune put it, 'a fringe of the printed text which in reality controls one's whole reading of the text'. Indeed, this fringe, always the conveyor of a commentary that is authorial or more or less legitimated by the author, constitutes a zone

between text and off-text, a zone not only of transition but also of *transaction*: a privileged place of a pragmatics and a strategy, of an influence on the public, an influence that – whether well or poorly understood and achieved – is at the service of a better reception for the text and a more pertinent reading of it (more pertinent, of course, in the eyes of the author and his allies).

(Genette 1997: 2)

Historical novels are obsessed with paratexts: footnotes, additions, acknowledgements, bibliographies, author information, maps. From these materials we can garner a huge amount of information about the text itself, how it is being presented and represented. A brief example comes in Philippa Gregory's *The Other Boleyn Girl*, as the note on the author, reached before the text itself, informs the reader that Gregory has a PhD and advises the BBC's television series *Time Team*. This information legitimises Gregory as an author, and ensures that the reader feels a sense of authority and authenticity. The novel itself has already been placed into a recognisable set of familiar historical romance tropes by the branded cover. These various bibliographical pointers and paratextual elements influence our interpretation of the text and change its meaning (Squires 2007). As we have seen, paratexts are an important element of the historical novel's purpose, and they are similarly important for the women's historical fiction considered in this chapter.

Historical fiction is presented and sold in particular ways, from the authorial branding of books by best-selling writers to the use of particular types of cover image. Pulp fiction, popular fiction and romance fiction are identifiable by external tropes that work to pigeonhole them as modes of cultural production. In order to understand this process we have to consider what the French theorist Pierre Bourdieu called the 'sociology of art':

The sociology of art and literature has to take as its object not only the material production but also the symbolic production of the work, i.e. the production of the value of the work, or, which amounts to the same thing, of belief in the value of the work. It therefore has to consider as contributing to production not only the direct producers of the work in its materiality (artist, writer, etc.) but also the producers of the meaning and value of the work – critics, publishers, gallery directors and the whole set of agents whose combined efforts produce consumers capable of knowing and recognizing the work of art as such, in particular teachers (but also families, etc.).

(Bourdieu 1993: 37)

The meaning of a text is produced not simply by those directly involved in authoring it but in the ways that it works within society. The book has both a meaning and a cultural value, it works both as a text with content and as something that has an effect within society. It is created by critics, marketing executives, by book clubs and agents. If we attempt to analyse this mode of consumption we can audit and study the various 'producers' of the text. Increasingly blogs, reading groups, review sites, user-generated critical content and online forums impact upon the ways in which a text is situated and engaged with (Hartley and Turvey 2001; de Groot 2008). This non-author-centric model might change the way we approach or understand a book. From the point of view of historical fiction, then, it is key that we conceptualise each novel as a work that has multiple valencies and is 'produced' in numerous ways. We need to think about the ways it might be produced, consumed, read and used in order to understand the complex entity that is the historical novel (Hughes 1993: 29–33).

Continuations: *Mr Darcy Takes a Wife* and the rewriting of Austen

The production of texts, then, depends upon their material and cultural contexts. We have to be attentive to various external elements that might influence or complicate the status of a text. This section considers one minor aspect of this approach. One of the ways in which romance fiction has created a 'historical' imagination for itself is the recycling and reuse of particular classic narratives, as can be seen in the continuing rewriting and response to the work of Jane Austen. The 1996 adaptation of *Pride and Prejudice* created a massive surge in public interest in

Jane Austen's fiction (de Groot 2008: 189–90). Not 'historical' romance, *per se*, nonetheless the increase in interest in reading Austen demonstrated a desire for historical novels and settings from the Regency period. They are books that only work in the cultural matrix that Bourdieu outlines, as part of a set of textual transactions given value by external forces.

The importance of reading Austen to women's self-definition and notions of agency was demonstrated by the film *The Jane Austen Book Club* (Robin Swicord, 2007) and ITV's *Lost in Austen* (2008). *Pride and Prejudice* has taken on a further life of its own: in continuation romances, including Jane Dawkins, *Letters from Pemberley* (2002), Linda Berdoll, *Mr Darcy Takes a Wife* (2004) and *Darcy and Elizabeth* (2006), Emma Tennant, *Pemberley Revisited* (2005), Helen Halstead, *A Private Performance* (2005) and *Mr Darcy Presents his Bride* (2007), Regina Jeffers, *Darcy's Passions* (2007), Elizabeth Aston, *The True Darcy Spirit* (2007) and *The Darcy Connection* (2008), Maya Slater, *Mr Darcy's Diary* (2008), Amanda Grange, *Mr Darcy's Diary* (2008), Isobel Scott Moffat, *The Mistress of Pemberley* (2008); in a series of romance 'variations' published by Abigail Reynolds, including *The Last Man in the World* (2007), *Impulse and Initiative* (2007), *Without Reserve* (2007) and *From Lambton to Longbourn* (2008); and in the 'Mr and Mrs Darcy Mystery' series by Carrie Bebris, including *Pride and Prescience* (2004), *North by Northanger* (2005), *Suspense and Sensibility* (2005) and *The Matters at Mansfield* (2008). Whilst there have been adaptations and continuations of Austen throughout the twentieth century, including Dorothy Alice Bonavia-Hunt's *Pemberley Shades* (1949) and Sybil Brinton's *Old Friends and New Fancies* (1913), the sheer number of responses over the past decade demonstrates the cultural valency and significance of Austen and Austenesque romance fiction. This cultural industry of fiction inspired by and continuing Austen's most famous novel has been less considered than the film and television adaptations of her work (see MacDonald and MacDonald 2003; Wagner 2002). These books show that the interest in Regency romance associated with the work of Georgette Heyer is still current; they also demonstrate how particular cultural entities, in this case film and television adaptations of Austen, can create a demand for novels.

The continuations of Austen attempt tonal pastiche, in so far as they mimic her style and her character palette. This adaptation/continuation creates a modern version of a historic novel, but the contemporary version is itself a historical romance, in so far as it is created around a set of events, characters and discourses from the past, although a past which is authenticated not by history but by the world of Austen's fiction (see Sanders 2005). This is not solely a phenomenon associated with Austen, although she is clearly the most responded to, as there have been continuations of Daphne du Maurier's *Rebecca* (Susan Hill, *Mrs de Winter*, 1993) and the James Bond franchise (Sebastian Faulks, *Devil May Care*, 2008). In all these instances the cultural capital of the original is somehow alchemised into a new text.

Linda Berdoll's *Mr Darcy Takes a Wife* (subtitled *Pride and Prejudice Continues*) makes the case for continuation:

> As befitting a maiden's sensibilities, her novels all end with the wedding ceremony. What throbs fast and full, what the blood rushes through, is denied her unforgettable characters and, therefore, us. Dash it all!
> We endeavour to right this wrong by compleating at least one of her stories, beginning whence hers leaves off. Our lovers have wed.
>
> (Berdoll 2004: preface)

Berdoll's disingenuousness here is revealing. Tonally she mimics Austen's archaic spellings and syntax ('compleating', 'whence'). She suggests that modern romance is interested in what comes after the wedding (a physical relationship which is denied by the virginal Austen) but also illustrates how romance in general is a genre in which readers desire a particular outcome and are not happy if it is denied. The book displays no quotes from critics, just comments from other readers, demonstrating the way that it is marketed at a particular constituency of (mainly female) buyers. In these novel continuations the textual world of Austen's fiction becomes the 'historical' backdrop to romance, and therefore these are historical novels, or 'historicesque' might perhaps be a better term. They perform the same trick as the historical novel, using a set of 'facts' to hang a set of conjectures and thoughts upon. The continuations inhabit a shady, liminal world of pastiche and imitation: validated or authorised by Austen's name, addressing a desire on the part of her readers for more fulfilling, or simply more, narratives.

Historical novels for women

Historical novels by women for women, then, whether romance or more literary, have often been dismissed by literary critics and marginalised by standard accounts, but there is a weight of argument which suggests this is an error: 'historical fiction has been one of the major forms of women's reading and writing in the second half of the twentieth century' (Light 1989: 60). This is reiterated by Wallace: 'the historical novel has been one of the most important forms of women's reading and writing during the twentieth century' (Wallace 2005: ix). Wallace, particularly, reads the historical novel as a form which has 'offered women readers the imaginative space to create different, more inclusive versions of "history", which are accessible or appealing to them in various ways' (Wallace 2005: 3). She considers the critique of women's historical novels as standard gendered criticism, and argues that the lack of attention to this important form is due to mis-apprehension and misunderstanding of the possibilities and poten-tialities of the genre. Wallace posits a different genealogy for the women's historical novel, arguing that it develops from the hybrid potentialities of the Gothic novel rather than the rationality of Scott. She argues that the form has allowed women writers a freedom and licence not granted them in other genres. As we saw in the case of Virginia Woolf (Chapter 2) and will see in the cases of Angela Carter and Jeanette Winterson (Chapter 5), women writers have used the historical novel to express multiple, complex identities and used them as sites of possibility and potential. Wallace suggests that this is something that is true of women's historical novels throughout the twentieth century. Similarly critics such as Sarah Waters, Laura Doan and Julie Abrahams have seen in the lesbian historical novel the opportunity for novelists to explore and conceptualise identities and otherness throughout the century (see Chapter 6).

The feminist historian Alison Light is an eloquent proponent of the ways that historical fiction for women might be thought of in progressive ways. Light suggests that many of the historical novels which inspired her as a child to study history are not particularly attractive on first view to feminists, as they are part of the romance genre. However, she argues that this misses the point and the subversive potentiality of the novels. Taking as their subjects female subjectivity, domestic private/public politics or the marginalisation of weaker subjects means these texts create a dissonant space in which various issues of legitimacy, authority and identity might be considered. The novels have a historiographical radicalism, 'giving femininity, which usually has a walk-on part in the official history of our times, the lead role in the national drama' (Light 1989: 60). In particular, 'For those who are normally left out of history altogether such an emphasis is very welcome' (Light 1989: 59). The romance novelist is attracted to Anne Boleyn, for instance, for her story and her significance, but cannot pin her down into a conventional narrative as her story eschews generic boundaries. This is in many ways down to the peculiarity of the historical novel form, its refusal, because of the particularity of subject, to sit easily with other genres. The historical novel is one of the most hybrid of forms, but, strangely, it possesses the ability to skew and compromise whatever it is being merged with because of its very particular oddness. In the context of our discussion, below, of Anne Boleyn, this becomes even stranger, as discussions of her life must necessarily present unidealised anti-romance elements such as death and miscarriage. In narratives of Henry VIII, Elizabeth, Anne Boleyn and other Tudor women, marriage, motherhood and family life are presented as things to avoid or be wary of. It is not just Tudor women who suffer, of course, as the question of privation pervades historical fiction from Sandra Gulland's *The Many Lives and Secret Sorrows of Joséphine B.* (1999) to Emma Donoghue's tale of the horror of eighteenth-century prostitution, *Slammerkin* (2001).

Light argues that in the women's historical novel of the midcentury is found a fantasy of female power and agency not found in other cultural production; that the books opened a volatile site of possibility that was crucial to her formation as a radical historian. She suggests that 'At best popular historical novels may have helped open up a space within which different groups of women have started to perceive how marginal their needs and concerns have usually been taken to be. They offer a number of new perspectives on the past, which sit less easily alongside textbook history' (Light 1989: 70). This suggestive thesis, then, can tell us much about one particular way in which gendered historical fiction might be read against the grain as creating potentiality. Indeed, this echoes Radway's thinking about the ways in which the romance as a genre might be read and appropriated. Robin Maxwell's acknowledgement in *The Secret Diary of Anne Boleyn* (1997) demonstrates the matrilineal genealogy of women's historical romance:

> This book is the result of twenty-five years of passionate interest in the brilliant world of Tudor England. My indoctrination began with a pair of novels by Norah Lofts that introduced me to the two female titans of the early sixteenth century, Anne Boleyn and Katherine of Aragon.
>
> (Maxwell 1997: acknowledgements)

Historian Alison Weir has similarly written of the importance of historical romance to her burgeoning sense of herself, and, particularly, of the resonance of Anne Boleyn: 'She is a romantic heroine in the truest sense' (Weir 2003: 94). Weir found history at school 'dull and uninspiring, a dreary succession of dates, acts and battles' (Weir 2003: 94), whereas historical romance novels brought the past alive. They are places of feminine solidarity (both Weir and Light shared the reading of these novels with their mothers and grandmothers), of female becoming independent of masculinised institutions (schools, **Whig history**), and sites of the creation and inspiration of an historical imagination.

Case study: Anne Boleyn

The story of Anne Boleyn, Henry VIII's second queen, has been returned to constantly by female novelists. An examination of books about her can illustrate many of the key issues relating to this type of historical novel. Irene Goodman argues that 'her story pushes all the right buttons. It has sex, adultery, pregnancy, scandal, divorce, royalty, glitterati, religious quarrels, and larger-than-life personalities' (Goodman 2005: 15). Henry VIII took control of the Church from Rome in order that he might divorce his wife, Katherine of Aragon, and marry Boleyn; she failed to provide an heir and he tired of her, after which circumstances and conspiracy led to her trial and execution as a witch. Boleyn's life is sensational and also historically important. She was a key player in the **Reformation**, arguably the first woman to demand to be considered equal to a man, the first female commoner to be made a peer by direct creation and to hold a title in her own right (*suo jure*) rather than through marriage, the mother of Elizabeth I, lover of a famous king, and wife executed by her husband after he falsely accused her of adultery, incest and witchcraft (a refutation of most of the charges is provided by Ives 2004: 344–52). She is represented as ambitious, a sexual predator, erudite, vengeful, independent, able, beautiful, fearless and intelligent; she was also destroyed by a political system that needed to be rid of her. Goodman has other, more simplistic, arguments to account for the success of novels about Boleyn:

> Another factor in success with historical fiction is that the majority of the readers are women, and they like to read about other women. Much of history is dominated by men, which means you have to look for subjects that include women. The most common device is to take a woman who really lived and to let her tell her own story, free from the alleged 'misrepresentation' of history.
>
> (Goodman 2005: 15)

This sense of the rewriting of history is common to revisionist feminist histories of the last three decades, and situates female historical fiction writers as 'writing back', bringing their subjects from darkness to light. In the particular case of Boleyn the main sources of contention concern her guilt (most writers refute it) and the importance of her political and amorous engagements. There is a lack of historical information about Anne, and the absence of verifiable sources has allowed novelists great latitude with certain elements of her biography (as well as often repeating the same apocryphal myths; Warnicke 1989: 242). The novels regarding her change very little about the story, or the canonical contexts, ideas and characters. Anne is a figure who is attractive to novelists for her agency, her poise, her beauty and the spectacle of her fall. As Miriam Burstein points out, the standard narrative of Boleyn's life in fiction is rarely deviated from (Burstein 2007). The figure of Anne Boleyn, therefore, is at an interesting historical nexus point which allows novelists to explore all manner of issues: female agency; the dynamic between personal relationship and how this is manifest in the public sphere; martyrdom; women's cruelty to women in her hatred of Katherine of Aragon; religious fanaticism; the struggles of women in the early modern period. It is these last which particularly have been brought out in novels about Boleyn and her daughter, Elizabeth I.

Jean Plaidy's *Murder Most Royal* (1949) is prefaced with a poem Boleyn wrote in the Tower of London whilst awaiting her execution:

> Defiled is my name, full sore
> Through cruel spite and false report ...
> For wrongfully ye judge of me; [giving]
> Unto my fame a mortal wound.
>
> (Plaidy 2006: preface)

These lines, and the title of the book, make it clear what the novelist thought about the execution of Anne Boleyn. Indeed, she explicitly calls her treatment at Henry's hands murder, and likens him to a common criminal preying upon innocent women:

> She was sure that he intended to murder her; in cold blood he planned this, as any commoner might plan to put away a wife of whom he had tired, by beating her to death or stabbing her with a knife or throwing her body into the dark river. She was terrified, experiencing all the alarm of a woman who knows herself to be followed in the dark by a footpad with murder in his heart.
>
> (Plaidy 2006: 483)

This is powerful, and plaintive, as well as being quite clear about the vulgarity of the actions of the King. The novel makes the process of history a personal, hypocritical, violent action. She quotes at length from Boleyn's letters to Henry from the Tower, allowing her own words to defend her (these documents are also used in Philippa Gregory's *The Other Boleyn Girl* as illustrations to the front and end papers of the book). This use of primary sources as part of the narrative is common, although often less explicit. The various contemporary narratives, particularly the recollections of Thomas Kingston, Constable of the Tower during Anne's time there before her death, are recycled by these novels. There are certain moments that are reused in nearly every narrative about Boleyn: her claim that the apartments in the Tower are too good for her now she is no longer Queen, her comments at her trial and execution, an overheard joke about her being a headless lady, poems and several letters to Henry. These stories, themselves based on dubious provenance, just like the evidence against her, create a canon of events which leaves the narrative of her fall unchanged from novel to novel (Ives 2004: 319–44).

The paratextual elements of the romances about Boleyn are themselves of great interest. Norah Lofts' *The Concubine* (1963) has on the title page the note 'A novel based upon the life of Anne Boleyn, Henry VIII's second wife, to whom the Spanish Ambassador often referred in his dispatches as "the Concubine"' (Lofts 1963: title page); this does not appear in the most recent edition of the book, demonstrating how paratextual elements lost in new editions might shift the interpretation of the novel. Lofts prefaces her chapters with evidence, from letters of Henry VIII to excerpts from historical biography such as Cavendish's *Life of Cardinal Wolsey* (1810) and Mattingly's *Life of Katherine of Aragon* (1942). This reliance on authority, and interleaving of fictional account with historical information and inference, gives the work a certain authenticity but also a self-consciousness about its artificiality.

Plaidy's novel makes a heroine of Anne Boleyn: 'She was reckless of herself, and though she may have been foolish and vain she clung to her magnificent courage' (Plaidy 2006: 483). Her reading of Boleyn's case is plainly sympathetic, suggesting that Thomas Cromwell manipulated the facts in order to gain control of a pliant and jealous King. Plaidy has a very long section outlining Cromwell's torture of Mark Smeaton for information about the

Queen (Plaidy 2006: 444–58), for instance, and makes clear the unsisterly actions of Jane Rochford, George Boleyn's wife, in repeating rumour, innuendo and gossip (Plaidy 2006: 470–3). Plaidy acknowledges the help of various sources, and asserts that where 'the authorities differ on various points I have used my own discretion, endeavouring to keep as near to the truth as possible' (Plaidy 2006: 647). Her desire for the 'truth' is as a means to refute the accusations made against Boleyn. Despite the generic romance form of the novel Plaidy's work is politicised; she gives Boleyn agency as a mover of history and as an individual woman literally brought down by jealous and unscrupulous men. Diana Wallace argues that Plaidy's novels in general offer 'the historical evidence of women's oppression across history' and that they 'demonstrate that it is a matter of historical fact that women have been locked up, mistreated, violently abused, raped, and even killed, often by their husbands' (Wallace 2005: 137). *Murder Most Royal* demonstrates how reading these texts as simply romances is problematic. Whilst they deal in sensation, love, intrigue and passion, by the end of the text everything is turned to ashes and death. The story of Boleyn and Henry fulfils the genre demands of a romance, with the heteronormative desire of Anne to be married, the wild love affair and seduction. However, their marriage destroys the state and another marriage, sex is problematic at best, family is also not a happy situation and the outcome of love is death and destruction, not happiness. In this we see the complexity of using Boleyn within this generic context (Burstein 2007). Her story is attractive and well known, but it is about dissenting from and challenging the dominant cultural norms; her example is that of the woman who created herself and, for a brief time, through her brilliance and her beauty and her will, maintained herself in a society in which quasi-independent female empowerment and political agency were relatively unknown. Boleyn's story is, in the main, shot through with tragedy rather than romance. This demonstrates how an historical subject might query generic form; the romance cannot make Boleyn's story fit.

In contrast to Plaidy's clear concern with presenting Boleyn as a victim, Jane Lane's *Sow the Tempest* (1960) presents a less querying narrative. Henry's obsession with Anne leads to a Reformation driven by sexual desire, and the consequences are personal – as shown by Katherine of Aragon's sadness, the weeping Princess Mary, the martyred Thomas More – and national, exemplified by the querulous population and the split with Rome. Lane is much more interested in the mechanics of the Reformation and the ways in which it was forwarded through torture, execution and confession. Thomas Cromwell, as usual, becomes the attack-dog zealot reduced to torturing and hoping 'that by rigorous and prolonged cross-examination he would induce these sick and lonely old men to slip from a refusal to acknowledge the King's supremacy to a denial of it' (Lane 2001: 242). Cromwell appears as Machiavellian villain in C. J. Sansom's *Dissolution* (2003) and *Dark Fire* (2004), plotting the downfall of the Church in order to pursue power, and it is interesting how this important figure has been reduced in popular culture to a plotting bureaucrat spymaster. It is particularly striking that Anne's and Cromwell's intellectual project, the cause of Protestant Reform, is reduced and traduced. Secular modern Britain is in many ways still a Protestant country yet these novels often simply understand and dismiss the Reformation as a consequence of the jealousies of the King and further see the motives of significant and important historical change as petty and vengeful. Significantly, in such narratives the martyrdom of Thomas More is often foregrounded and the role of Cardinal Wolsey, more significant in the divorce from Rome and the breaking of Aragon, is underplayed. Lane's book more than most mourns the end of a religious way of life, and ends with a bloated and lonely Henry wishing on his deathbed for the succour of the old Catholic life and wishing for the return of his first wife. The nation outside his window is crumbling and horrible, full of poverty and horror due to the dissolution of the monasteries. Lane reads the relationship between Henry and Boleyn as destructive to the fabric of the nation, as the personal impacts horrendously on the political. The binary between the two treatments here, either Anne as political and problematic or Anne as romantic, passionate and mistreated, is characteristic of the way in which Boleyn becomes defined through the second half of the twentieth century. For every work in which she is independent and articulate there is a book such as Gregory's *The*

Other Boleyn Girl which suggests that she was in fact guilty of incest and attempting witchcraft.

Novels about Boleyn, then, tell a similar narrative with slightly different inflections. Evelyn Anthony's *Anne Boleyn* (1957) is a relatively explicit account which celebrates her subject's beauty, political ability and vivacity. Margaret Campbell Barnes's *Brief Gaudy Hour* (1949) presents Boleyn's seduction of Henry as revenge for the brutal ending of her juvenile relationship with Henry Percy, Earl of Northumberland. Her French maid encourages her to keep Henry VIII in thrall to her 'to the exclusion of all decency and conscience' (Campbell Barnes 1949: 141). She suggests that she is the temptress Circe, as 'Have not all women who hold a man in thrall something of the sorceress in them?' (Campbell Barnes 1949: 141). Throughout, her ability to keep Henry sexually enthralled is compared to witchcraft. As she is being accused in court she remembers him saying to her, 'my witch, I should have you burned for enslaving my senses' (Campbell Barnes 1949: 320). The novel attempts to make Anne's historical association with magic both something that is created by men as an attractive quality and something intertwined with sexual obsession. Yet ultimately each of these novels is interested in the fall of a woman they present as being sharp, alert and important.

Other novels about Boleyn include Olive Lethbridge and John de Stourton, *The King's Master* (1912); Reginald Drew, *Anne Boleyn* (1912); Mary Hastings Bradley, *The Favour of Kings* (1912); E. Barrington, *Anne Boleyn* (1932); Francis Hackett, *Queen Anne Boleyn* (1939); Jean Plaidy, *The King's Secret Matter* (1962) and *The Lady in the Tower* (1986); Margaret Heys, *Ann Boleyn* (1972); Aileen Armitage, *The Tudor Sisters* (1975); Maureen Peters, *The Rose of Hever* (1976); Victoria Allen, *I, Anne Boleyn* (1978); Mollie Hardwick, *Blood Royal* (1988); Sylvia Lover, *Reap the Storm* (1998); Wendy J. Dunn, *Dear Heart, How Like You This?* (2002); Caroline Meyer, *Doomed Queen Anne* (2002); Susannah Dunn, *The Queen of Subtleties* (2004); Alison Prince, *Anne Boleyn and Me* (2004); Laurien Gardner, *A Lady Raised High* (2006); Robin Maxwell, *Mademoiselle Boleyn* (2007). Miriam Burstein's survey of fictional Boleyns takes in forty-five texts, most of them published after 1950 (Burstein 2007); and most of the more popular novels, in particular Evelyn Anthony's and Jean Plaidy's, have been regularly reprinted since their first publication. As this suggests, Boleyn has been a constant of historical romances by women. Furthermore, it is testament to the popularity of this figure that she is written about so often; certainly as much as nearly any other historical personage.

During the nineteenth century, novels about the Tudor period were more interested in the broader religious and political issues associated with the time, including William Harrison Ainsworth's *Windsor Castle* (1844), Emma Robinson's *Westminster Abbey* (1854), Frank Mathew's *Defender of the Faith* (1889) and M. Imlay Taylor's *House of the Wizard* (1900). Ainsworth's novel briefly dramatises the relationship between Boleyn and Thomas Wyatt, which is returned to repeatedly by authors, within a pastoral romance about Herne the Hunter (Ainsworth 1844). Robinson's novel, subtitled *The Days of the Reformation*, celebrates the coming of Protestantism in a book which is keenly interested in tracing the path of religious and political change rather than the fortunes of the Queen (Robinson 1854). What is clear, though, is that these novels are more interested in the broader elements than simply relating the narrative of Boleyn's rise and fall. The books of the early twentieth century that focus on Boleyn demonstrate the growing market for fiction aimed at and written by women, particularly that within the popular historical romance genre. By contrast, earlier versions are often merely dramatised versions of the historical events. Hackett's *Queen Anne Boleyn*, for example, is a dry and thorough account of Boleyn's rise and fall with a strangely passive narrative voice: 'Anne tossed her head. Her confidence in her own strength was based not only on Henry's tenderness but on Henry's dependence' (Hackett 1939: 394). There has been a clear upsurge of interest in Boleyn in the early twenty-first century, due in part to the success of Gregory's *The Other Boleyn Girl* but also because of the explosion of the women's historical novel and its interest in writing strong female characters. Furthermore, historiography has some influence. Agnes Strickland's 1844 popular biography of Boleyn influenced mid-nineteenth-century versions of her life; Paul Friedmann's 1884 biography similarly contributed to a sense of Boleyn as guilty somehow, if not of the crimes of which she was actually accused; the impetus of Eric Ives's work towards reading her life as part of a wider network of courtly factional intrigues from 1972 onwards has impacted on modern versions of Boleyn; and Retha Warnicke's controversial but challenging version of her as 'a victim of her society's mores and of human ignorance about conception and pregnancy' (Warnicke 1989: 242) has clear significance for recent Boleyns trapped by a patriarchal society.

Such is the multivalency of her life that the print industry around Boleyn even includes a supernatural novel about her mercenary executioner which meditates on her extreme courage in the face of death, C. C. Humphreys' *The French Executioner* (2002). This hybrid novel is an alternative history, a conspiracy thriller, a quest adventure narrative and a supernatural story. Boleyn's mythical six-fingered hand becomes a magical relic chased from London to Siena by ruthless churchmen hoping to use its power for their own ends; only the virtuous man who took her life can protect it. Humphreys' novel is interesting to us for a number of reasons. As a novelist associated with 'male' historical fiction (he is the author of the Jack Absolute series) his work demonstrates the intertwining of 'romance' subject with masculine treatment. His hero, Jean Rombaud, is a war veteran who uses his sword to cut a path through Europe. Even in the paratextual elements we find a kind of masculine performance; the idea for the book came, Humphreys tells us in his author's introductory note, whilst he was in the gym doing sets of weights in front of a mirror. The novel is a standard quest narrative of valour and adventure, something rarely associated with the Tudor court. Humphreys admits to writing something grounded in fact but that he was also happy to explore unknown likelihood: 'I was writing an adventure, not an historical document, but it all seemed possible. Who *really* knows what happened back then anyway?' (Humphreys 2002: vi). This makes a virtue of the lack of facts regarding Boleyn's life. He returns to the 'witchcraft' myth of Anne Boleyn, but undermines it (or makes it a virtue), in contradistinction to most female writers, who seek to give the lie to such accusations. In this novel the 'extraordinary' Anne is the graceful good witch, offering the sinner a vision of happiness in exchange for his service (Humphreys 2002: viii). Rombaud has a vision of her at the close of the novel, 'dressed in a simple shift of silk, and her brow was encircled with a wreath of meadow flowers' (Humphreys 2002: 365). She is a fantasy of pastoral magic, an icon to be addressed and worshipped. The importance of her hand as a religious relic echoes the fetishising of Catholic saints and, most important, of the Virgin Mary. Boleyn here becomes a saviour, proponent of good magic and the repository of grace. Humphreys therefore celebrates her agency and independence whilst at the same time returning her narrative to the clichés of witches and female caricature. The angelic actions associated with Boleyn here are the female clichés of male historical fiction, to which we now turn.

NOVELS FOR MEN: AUTHENTICITY, ADVENTURE AND HEROISM

This section analyses the key attributes of historical fiction marketed at men. In particular we consider the adventure genre, how heroism works in the novels, constructions of masculinity and the importance of detail. War and conflict are in general the situations explored by these novels, and the section looks at how the books construct various exemplars for male behaviour in these situations. We look at the much greater emphasis on authenticity and the popularity of secondary historical publications for these novels. The section traces briefly the evolution of historical fiction for men, from its roots in romance adventure to the extremely popular, heavily marketed and conservative novels like those written by Bernard Cornwell and Patrick O'Brian. Unlike popular fiction for women, there is little theoretical consideration of these types of writing, despite the fact that men appear to approach them in similar ways to those outlined above, and therefore might be using and reading them against the grain or to articulate a sense of community and personal identity.

What is immediately striking is that historical fiction for men tends to be more based in adventure and concerned in the main with warfare. The series of novels by Frederick Marryat, G. A. Henty, R. M. Ballantyne, C. S. Forester, Richard Woodman, Bernard Cornwell, Patrick O'Brian, Simon Scarrow and Dudley

Pope all consider the careers of soldiers and sailors and their particular contribution to history through their participation in combat. These novels present a set of possible masculinities within a relatively conservative nationalistic narrative. Their models of heroism are largely straightforward, dutiful, resourceful, violent and homosocial. They present a process of history in which the central character is repeatedly tested in some way before achieving some form of martial success. The books abound with detail, mainly military, martial and technical. What can be seen with early twentieth-century historical fiction is the bifurcation of historical romance into that for men and that for women; the one concerned with adventure and quest, the other with love and relationships (Hughes 1993: 10–11). Novels for girls and women, as demonstrated in the previous section of this chapter, are generally historical romances, with an element of adventure at times but more narratives of social, personal and cultural development and crisis rather than journeys, quests or achievements. This problematic gendering, seeing violent men interested in factual detail, dissident women concerned with relationships and love, is increasingly a feature of historical fiction throughout the twentieth century. It is also the case that women's historical fiction is more interested in challenging and problematising, particularly by the account of women's repression, whereas male historical novels articulate a masculinity that may be marginalised by class but is still very much articulate, with some agency and means of self-expression. Whilst a soldier may be constrained by the rules of the army, these novels do not consider the lot of men to be so bad, and, indeed, their enhanced physical and social mobility is in clear contrast to the women in female romance novels.

The key genres of which male historical fiction is a hybrid are adventure narratives, which have their grounding in nineteenth-century adventure romances, military history, fantasy and epic. Two key novelists provide some of the important paradigms for twentieth-century historical adventure fiction. Alexandre Dumas's novels of the Musketeers considered French seventeenth-century history as part of a narrative of excitement, valour and honour. *The Three Musketeers* (1844), *Twenty Years After* (1845) and *The*

Vicomte de Bragelonne (1847) all contain long, involved adventure quests. They introduce the key idea of the team of adventurers, probably soldiers, whose virtuous actions are the template for the reader's fantasy self-projection. This combination of bravery, political honour and excitement is itself a distillation of standard adventure-quest narratives from the medieval romance onward. Baroness Emmuska Orczy's *The Scarlet Pimpernel* (1905, with numerous sequels) abstracted the adventurous romance novel and added elements from the swashbuckling fictions of Dumas. Her version of the French revolution presents the participants as inhumanly unfeeling:

> A surging, seething, murmuring crowd, of beings that are human only in name, for to the eye and ear they seem naught but savage creatures, animated by vile passions and by the lust of vengeance and of hate.
>
> (Orczy 1905: 1)

The populace execute the aristocrats, but the Scarlet Pimpernel and his friends help to liberate them and set them safely in England. The elusive Pimpernel takes an active part in the historical event of the revolution, attacking the new French government and establishment through his subversive tactics: 'this band of young Englishmen had ... bearded the implacable and bloodthirsty tribunal of the Revolution, within the very walls of Paris, and had snatched away condemned victims, almost from the very foot of the guillotine' (Orczy 1905: 37). The examples of Orczy and Dumas were to create a genre of historical adventure fiction. These swashbucklers were combined with the narratives of piracy familiar from Robert Louis Stevenson's *Treasure Island* (1883) and in work such as that by Rafael Sabatini, whose *The Sea Hawk* (1915), *Scaramouche* (1921) and *Captain Blood* (1922) all conceptualise a history in which conflict and revolution are the background for acts of adventure and heroism. In *Captain Blood* Sabatini combined the actual biographies of two real people, Henry Pitman and Sir Henry Morgan (MacDonald Fraser 2004). These novels represent a masculinity that is martial, honourable and active.

C. S. Forester's Hornblower novels (1937–67) instigated a military historical romance which was read by both men and women, although following, to a certain extent, Frederick Marryat's series of naval novels. Massively successful, *Hornblower* is the archetypal historical adventurer military series. Named after the character in *Hamlet* and also Admiral Nelson, Horatio Hornblower is a complex, solitary figure. Plagued by anxieties and uncertain of his abilities, his ascent through the ranks is constantly prey to disappointment and accident. Hornblower has a series of fictional experiences on the edge of 'significant' events: he foils an attempt to rescue Napoleon from St Helena, meets Clausewitz, falls in love with Wellington's (fictional) sister. The series runs to eleven novels and various short-stories, and through the sequence Hornblower rises to become viscount and admiral of the fleet. The novels have been read as propagandist, particularly those published during the Second World War and afterwards, for the maintenance of sea power and a sense of British naval influence (Sternlicht 1999: 161). As a character Hornblower has proved uniquely attractive and well loved. This is as much down to his vulnerability as his heroism. In contrast to many of the subsequent heroes of historical fiction Hornblower's existential qualms of conscience present a masculinity that is perceptive, worried by violence, and self-aware. The *Hornblower* novels demonstrated that the minutiae of military life are an important part of how readers conceived of the past, and as such they have had a great impact on how historical fiction is written. The setting of the novels would influence subsequent novelists such as Bernard Cornwell and O'Brian. The *Hornblower* books also have a significant life in film and on television, and as such have dictated the way that Napoleonic history is imagined in the United States and the United Kingdom.

Subsequently historical adventure fiction has taken the *Hornblower* route and created serials around one central character. Bernard Cornwell has made his reputation on writing historical novels of fantasy and adventure, in the main associated with warfare or military events. He has written novel series about Arthurian Britain, the American Civil War, the quest for the holy grail in the fourteenth century, and Alfred the Great. A sense of serial and authorial brand coherence is key to 'male' historical fiction, a demographic that tends to stick with what they know and recognise. This can be seen in the covers of his books, with tele-vision tie-in images and the name of the series often given far greater importance than the novel's title. His sequence of Sharpe novels involves some twenty-three adventures of the rough-and-ready soldier on the fringes of official history. The books have an immense audience, selling some 12 million copies worldwide and making him one of the most popular novelists of the past decade. He has global reach, being a best-seller in Brazil and Japan, for instance; he is also hugely prolific, writing forty-three books in twenty-five years. His hero Richard Sharpe is the personification of uncivilised chaos and violence:

> 'I know what you think of the law, Richard, but it is the one barrier between man and bestiality.'
>
> 'Didn't do too much to stop the French.'
>
> 'War is above the law, which is why it is so bad. War lets loose all the things which the law restrains.'
>
> 'Like me,' Sharpe said.
>
> 'You are not such a bad man,' Vicente said with a smile.
>
> (Cornwell 2004: 130–1)

He is unapologetically violent, and this exchange suggests some-thing about why warfare is such a popular canvas for these novels. It allows the extremes of history to be presented, the transgressive and the uncivilised (de Groot 2008: 196–9). The model of mas-culinity being suggested here is unreconstructed: violent, selfish and awkward.

Cornwell's approach is to narrate stories in the margins of 'greater' historical events as a means to reflect and explain those occurrences. His notion of the past is interested in the experience of the common man within the wider sweep of events, the microcosmic relationships and occurrences that make a life within history. Sharpe is a fictional character who has extraordinary and improbable access to some of the most important moments in colonial and Napoleonic history. For instance, in *Sharpe's Triumph* (1998) Cornwell conjectures that someone must have replaced the Duke of Wellington's orderly when he was killed in action, but no one knows who, and Sharpe therefore becomes this forgotten figure. Sharpe is an observer of history as well as someone who makes decisive interventions. The novels have quite an odd **historiography**, continually suggesting that history is something which happens despite the actions of the individual but simultaneously celebrating the historically significant actions of that individual. Well drilled soldiers win through and luck plays a part. Modern warfare might be seen to be analogous with the processes of history, as it is chaotic, possibly but unusually changed by the actions of one man, and something which treats humans as a mass. In this context Sharpe's individual actions increasingly have a significant effect. He is not ancillary to the action and an observer but an actor with minor but important agency. His altruism and heroism lead in many cases to victory. In *Sharpe's Escape*, for instance:

> He knew the food had to be taken away if the French were to be beaten, yet for a moment he was tempted to let the whole thing slide. To hell with it. The army had treated him badly, so why the hell should he care? Yet he did care, and he would be damned before Ferragus helped the French win the war.
>
> (Cornwell 2004: 214)

Sharpe sets fire to a warehouse in the Portuguese city of Coimbra, the food store that had meant 'the [French] Army of Portugal was safe' (Cornwell 2004: 219). As a seemingly direct consequence Wellington's scorched-earth policy holds, and the French stumble to defeat. The British fall back to the lines of Torres Vedras to hold and defeat their starving enemy. In his historical note Cornwell admits that the significance of Sharpe's actions is amplified: 'though the hungry French discovered plenty of food in the city, they managed to destroy most of it' (Cornwell 2004: 349). At the same time Sharpe has a clear sense of historical irrelevance:

> 'You have a simple view of life.'
> 'You're born, you survive, you die,' Sharpe said. 'What's hard about that?'
> 'It's an animal's life,' Sarah said, 'and we are more than animals.'

'That's what they tell me,' Sharpe said, 'but when war comes
they're grateful for men like me.'

(Cornwell 2004: 249)

Cornwell is keen on detail: of regiment, of arms, of combat techniques and, particularly, of geographical detail. The central use of maps and a very clear sense of the importance of the geography of the battlefield or city under attack pervade the novels. This has two effects, first, situating the novels extremely specifically and, second, sharing the military historian's obsession with the importance of terrain in combat. They also allow us to suggest that there is a dynamic interaction between the 'reality' of the map and the 'fiction' of Sharpe's actions within it. They further suggest that the map is a **metonym** for History and Sharpe's actions for the historical novel. History imposes an inflexible form within which the historical novel can explore the gaps. The Sharpe novels have their roots in historical adventure romance but develop the serial genre. They are interested in the past as a backdrop to character, and create an experience for the audience which is acquisitive as well as inquisitive, about the gaining of knowledge of Sharpe as much as the understanding of the period. As Cornwell argues, 'Heroes live impossible lives' (Adkin 1998: xvii) and whilst he clearly understands that his audience is interested in the actuality of events, he is similarly aware of the demands of fiction.

One extremely interesting phenomenon associated with male historical fiction is that of the fan and the various extratextual elements created to service this community. The books of O'Brian and Cornwell, for instance, are marketed as part of a series, branded so that the readership can purchase familiar books and collect the entire set. There are numerous official fan clubs, and those who are interested in Cornwell's creation can read Mark Adkin's *Sharpe Companion* (1998) and his *Sharpe Cut* (2006), an introduction to the television series. Adkin's text is an historical guide to the military elements of each Sharpe novel, and 'guides, explains and helps to understand what Sharpe achieved' (Adkin 1998: xix) with images, maps, factual narratives and biographical accounts. This interleaving of the historical and fictional, whilst clearly aware that Sharpe himself is fictional, serves a need for authentification among the readership of the novels. It also introduces a key meta-fictional element to the series. They have a manifestation outside of their imaginative universe. Similarly Brian Lavery's *Jack Aubrey Commands* (2003) provides the reader of Patrick O'Brian's novels with historical information about the navy and its tactics during the period 1793–1815, although it is much more a work of maritime history than a specific companion. These secondary materials buttress the authenticity of the novels, ascribing them a gravitas and a meaningfulness. The interaction with scholarly history demonstrates the striving for realism that is crucial to the male historical novel. These texts illustrate how these types of novels have become abstracted from their generic background and turned into self-defining entities.

Certain other types of male-focused historical writing need to be briefly considered. Since Arthur Conan Doyle's *The White Company* (1891) and Lew Wallace's *Ben Hur* (1880), epic historical romances have been an adjunct to the adventure novel. *The White Company* has two maps at the beginning, and seemingly consists of a fictional intervention into historical debate on the part of Conan Doyle (Hughes 1993: 26–7). The novel is challenging to the reader, suggesting historicity rather than realistic fiction, and this element of authenticity is influential in the presentation of historical fiction. Bernard Cornwell is one of the key contributors to a fiction of historicised fantasy which develops this kind of writing, particularly his Grail Quest novels and *Stonehenge* (1999).

Historical novels and male-oriented crime fiction have many points of overlap, and the combination of historical novel and detective genre fiction more specifically has been particularly fruitful. In the same way that mainstream detective fiction tends to serialisation, creating a branded and connected series of novels in which the central figure is the key attraction, historical detective writing has created specific investigative characters. Historical detective-investigators include monks (Ellis Peters's Cadfael, Umberto Eco's William), policemen (Edward Marston's Colbeck, Lee Jackson's Inspector Webb, Anne Perry's William Monk and Thomas Pitt), railway police (Andrew Martin's Jim Stringer), lawyers (C. J. Sansom's Shardlake), journalists (David Peace's Red

Riding Quartet) and medical doctors. The historical crime genre tends to accrue around particular institutional sites, such as the monastery or religious community (Sansom's *Dissolution*, Maria McCann's *As Meat Loves Salt*, 2002). The scholar-historian-detective investigates the intrusion of chaos into a site of order: 'Prior Robert, very erect and austere on a bench beside the window, looked down his nose with a marked suggestion of disapproval and withdrawal. The complexities of law and murder and man-hunt had no business to enter into the monastic domain' (Peters 1988: 88). Sansom's *Dissolution* works neatly with generic tropes, particularly those of paranoia and the revelation of untold stories and mystery. Shardlake is shocked to be told by Thomas Cromwell of the plot against Anne Boleyn, and the motivation for the murders in the novel is revenge for the framing of Mark Smeaton as Boleyn's lover. As Sansom points out in his 'Historical note', 'It is generally accepted that the accusations of multiple adultery against Queen Anne Boleyn were fabricated by Cromwell for Henry VIII, who had tired of her' (Sansom 2007: 441–2). Thus the revelation of conspiracy and secret history in the novel, a staple of paranoid crime thrillers from Raymond Chandler to James Ellroy, is in fact the outlining of a contemporary historical orthodoxy, a kind of insight by hindsight. Compare, for instance, the way that Philippa Gregory's novel *The Other Boleyn Girl* problematically accepts and dramatises the accusations against Boleyn (de Groot 2008: 219–20).

Writers also congregate around particular issues, sites or events. For instance, for Victorian detective fiction the key site is the railway, as it represents the shock of the new in society and allows a meditation upon a city, London, on the threshold of modernity. In Jackson's *A Metropolitan Murder* (2004) the newly built railway is the scene of various killings. The novel introduces a social campaigner, Cotton, who acts to reveal the authentic Victorian London to the reader as he explores it in the same way that Webb provides the movement towards narrative conclusion by solving the crime.

Writers are interested in the nineteenth century as the crucible for the modern world in so far as they are interested in industry, photography, railways and mechanical modernisation, but they also see the past as a place of crime, spirituality, repressed sexuality, colonial tension and class hostility. The notion of the 'detective' novel derives from books published in the Victorian period, including short stories by Edgar Allan Poe, Dickens's *Bleak House* and Wilkie Collins's *The Moonstone* (1868), and from the development of the police force during the middle part of the nineteenth century, so Victorian crime fiction has a certain self-referentiality.

Historical fiction for men has also produced the key satirist of the form, George MacDonald Fraser. MacDonald Fraser's self-consciousness as an adventure novelist can be demonstrated by the fact that he contributed the entry on Sabatini to the *Dictionary of National Biography*, claiming that in *Captain Blood* he 'demonstrated his mastery of the art of blending fiction with soundly researched historical fact' (MacDonald Fraser 2004). His series of novels purporting to be autobiographies of the character Harry Paget Flashman (1975–2007) are popular and successful parodies of the historical colonial adventure novel. Flashman originally appears as a character in Thomas Hughes's *Tom Brown's Schooldays* (1857). In that novel he is a bully, cad and womaniser who is expelled from Rugby School for drunkenness. The Flashman novels, beginning with *Flashman and the Great Game*, follow his surprisingly successful trajectory after his expulsion. They are presented as the 'Flashman papers', a set of newly discovered manuscript memoirs in which an eighty-year-old Flashman looks back over his glittering career and gloats about how it was all a sham. After Rugby he joins the army and through a mixture of good horsemanship, luck and sycophancy gains the admiration of various important figures such as Lord Cardigan and the Duke of Wellington. This ability to impress his betters despite his selfishness, abject cowardice and avariciousness, traits which he keeps well hidden from the authorities but parades proudly to the reader, means that he is continually advanced and regularly decorated. In the opening novel of the series he makes his name in Afghanistan and India, and subsequent books see him despoiling the women and robbing the men of the United States, Central Europe and West Africa. As a character Flashman is not attractive; he is a foul-mouthed criminal bully and a vicious misogynist not above rape and the odd accidental murder. The novels recount his drinking, gambling, sexual rapacity and cowardice; they are sensationalist and scandalous, and Flashman's grubby ruthlessness is celebrated. However, the books also introduce the reader to the seedier side of the nineteenth century, recounting with some revisionist zeal the grim reality of empire. In undermining heroic accounts of imperial achievement the series suggests that heroism is foolish and that history itself generally celebrates those who have blundered into success.

HISTORICAL FICTION FOR CHILDREN

Historical novels specifically aimed at children and young readers have been part of the literary scene since the wide success of Frederick Marryat's 1848 *Children of the New Forest* (Butts 1997). As Maria Nikolajeva argues, such work rarely contains 'great historical events such as revolutions, military campaigns and battles; even when it does, the primary focus is not on kings and heroes but on ordinary people' (Nicolajeva 1996: 131). Marryat's book is exemplary in this matter, as it considers the Civil War from the point of view of children forced to hide from it in the New Forest.

History aimed at children tended, throughout the nineteenth century, to offer accounts of great events and important men. The *Boy's Own Book of Stories from History* (1850) claims to 'repeat stories from history, to divert and assist the young in their *plays*' (Bennett 1850: iii). This idea that history might be consonant with or at least provide the content for play, a kind of ludic historical imagination, suggests that history stories for children were both educational and helped sustain their games. Tales from history were educative, exemplary and something to be imitated to aid the development of the young mind. This association between play and history is developed in the work of G. A. Henty, whose 122 books for boys were hugely successful from around 1868–1902 (Arnold 1980: 17–28). A contemporary reviewer considered in 1892 that 'Wherever English is spoken one imagines that Mr Henty's name is known' (Arnold 1980: 25). Henty was an apologist for empire who wrote adventures for boys often set during key imperial and national events such as Clive in India, Wolfe in Canada or Drake's naval campaigns, amongst other historical settings. Much historical fiction of the nineteenth century worked in tandem with other cultural forces to shore up images of empire and the value of colonialism. Henty's books were used as educational adjuncts throughout the first half of the twentieth century in the United States, the United Kingdom, Canada and Australia, demonstrating the pedagogic use of historical novels for children (Arnold 1980: 19). Henty had intended his works to be educational, and they are additionally moralistic, heroic, conservative and nationalistic. He cites sources in his prefaces and footnotes, pointing out his use of particular accounts; this suggests that he is clearly deploying a model of 'authentic' historical fiction: 'all my history shall be absolutely unassailable' he claimed (cited in Arnold, 1980: 89). In the preface to his novel of Hannibal, *The Young Carthaginian* (1887), he claims to follow W. J. Law and the French historian Hennebert in his writing. The intention of the book is to educate, as when Henty himself was at school: 'I am sure I would have liked to know a great deal about this struggle for the empire of the world, and as I think that most of you would also like to do so, I have chosen this subject for my story' (Henty 2004: 2). He concludes, though, 'you will perceive that although our sympathies may remain with Hannibal and the Carthaginians, it was nevertheless for the good of the world that Rome was the conqueror in the great struggle for empire' (Henty 2004: 2). This clear sense of the imperative of civilisation and empire demonstrates how Henty's work was saturated with a particular type of imperial ideology. Henty mixes history with sensational adventure and derring-do; his heroes are boys who are swept up in events and become extraordinary through their achievements or resourcefulness. As he argues in *With Lee in Virginia*, 'Even in recounting the leading events in these campaigns, I have burdened my story with as few details as possible, it being my object now, as always, to amuse, as well as to give instruction in the facts of history' (Henty 1889: 2). The general sweep of his books is the nationalistic perfection of the British, and this is particularly achieved through military conquest and victory. The novels follow military campaigns and describe key battles in some considerable depth; they include maps, for instance, and in-depth accounts of conflict. Henty provides a template for twentieth-century historical fiction written by men for men; interested in valour and virtue, nationalistic, and approaching the past through the lens of military history.

A key interpretative strand for children's historical fiction is education. Lynda Adamson includes in her bibliography of children's historical fiction an appendix outlining the 'readability' of each book according to Edward Fry's graph (Adamson 1994: 319). Adamson's bibliography sees historical fiction for children as a useful educational adjunct: 'This annotated bibliography provides an easy reference to appropriate fiction which conveys historical ideas in a particularly meaningful way by adding the dimensions of character ... a basic list of books that will yield both a history lesson and a worthwhile reading experience' (Adamson 1994: xi). This dogmatic sense of the pedagogical potentiality of the historical novel explicitly asserts that the combination of fictional elements (character) and historical framework can be both entertaining and educational. Yet children's historical novels, just as much as those for adults, can introduce conflict, potentiality and confusion. Joan Aiken's illustrated counterfactual novel *The Wolves of Willoughby Chase* imagines an alternative England: 'The action of this book takes place in a period of English history that never happened – shortly after the accession to the throne of Good King James III in 1832. At this time, the Channel Tunnel from Dover to Calais having been recently completed ... ' (Aiken 1962: 6). In a less obviously counterfactual way, Rosemary Sutcliff's *The Eagle of the Ninth* takes as its starting point 'two mysteries', one about the disappearance of the Ninth Legion in AD 117 and the other the excavation of a wingless Roman Eagle in Silchester, to create an adventure story (Sutcliff 1954: foreword). This is an explicit attempt to fill in the gaps of history, to explain the unknown through fiction. Sutcliff's further Roman novels include *The Silver Branch* (1957) and *The Lantern Bearers* (1959); she was one of the first popularly successful female children's historical novelists, and her work particularly explores British history. *The Eagle of the Ninth* is also illustrated, and this visual element is one way in which historical fiction for children is differentiated from that for adults.

Philip Pullman's series of novels set in the nineteenth century (1985–94) are part of a cultural interest in Victorian sensationalism which ranges from the work of Sarah Waters to the crime fiction of Lee Jackson and Anne Perry. Key to these novels are issues of class mobility and the New Woman. Some historical novelists of Victorian England allow powerful women to be part of the set-up, like William Monk's wife in Anne Perry's detective series, or Jim Stringer's spouse, who is an active suffragette in Andrew Martin's railway novels. Both have a large influence on the action. More particularly, Pullman's Sally Lockhart and Lee Jackson's Sarah Tanner both represent socially mobile, proto-feminist figures who may be disapproved of by society (Sally is a single parent, Sarah a former criminal) yet are resourceful self-directing women with money, independence and agency who investigate crime relatively fearlessly. Sally Lockhart, brought up by her father, has an unorthodox background, as detailed in *The Ruby in the Smoke* (1985):

> she had been brought up by her father – oddly, in the view of various busybodies … her knowledge of English Literature, French, History, Art, and Music was non-existent, but she had a thorough grounding in the principles of military tactics and book-keeping, a close acquaintance with the affairs of the stock-market, and a working knowledge of Hindustani.
>
> (Pullman 1985: 10–11)

The novel dramatises her aunt's attempts to gain her a position, possibly as a governess, despite her lacking accomplishments. Sally is, in truth, very like the youthful protagonists of the novels of G. A. Henty or the adventure stories above; more complex but recognisably heroic in her virtues. The novel suggests that the 'normal' accomplishments associated with young women at the time are not practical and do not allow them to move in the 'real' world; the only way that a girl might gain agency is to act 'oddly', like a boy. When she finds that crying, or appearing weak, is useful she deploys the action, despite the fact that 'she disliked this intensely, but she had no other weapons' (Pullman

1985: 15). This is an implicit critique of the patriarchal society in which Sally finds herself, striving for progress yet socially backward. Pullman's historical thrillers, then, present a 'modern' heroine constrained in many ways by the past: 'the masculine viewpoint of the earlier historical novel has been challenged by contemporary writers in favour of the "her-story"' (Nikolojeva 1996: 131).

4

LITERARY FICTION AND HISTORY

This chapter considers manifestations of the historical novel as a prevalent, even unremarkable format. In particular it considers the ways in which the contemporary literary historical novel has folded various tropes of formal, historiographical and theoretical radicalism into a newly popular, relatively sanitised blend. The novels that we consider in this section have a global reach and market; they are successful on a worldwide scale. In particular, novels about the two world wars of the twentieth century have a resonance due to their subject matter which seemingly gives them significance and importance beyond the confines of their home country.

THE HISTORICAL NOVEL AS AN INTERNATIONAL FORM

From its inception as a recognisable genre, arguably, the historical novel was an international form; indeed, its success on a transnational scale meant that the novel in general became predicated upon a kind of cultural translatability. Whilst Scott might have thought of his audience as largely Scottish and British, his novels immediately became read, admired and mimicked throughout Europe, North America and the British Empire; his work reached Brazil, Australia and Russia, influencing writers from Alexander Pushkin to Alexandre Dumas, from James Fenimore Cooper to Marcel Proust. Scott's works spoke to newly emergent independent nation states and allowed the site of the historical novel to be a crucible for the discursive formation of states and races. History became crucially important to national self-definition, as Lukács argues in his discussion of Scott: 'The appeal to national independence and national character is necessarily connected with a reawakening of national history' (Lukács 1962: 25). The historical novel, then, might be seen as a tool for national self-definition, and to work globally as a form and locally in terms of the effect of its content. In modern critical and sociological terms, this has been defined as 'glocalisation', describing the interaction of the local with the international. The historical novel is part of the typology of nationhood and helps to define what Benedict Anderson terms the 'imagined communities' of countries (Anderson 2006).

At the same time, whilst Scott's form seems radical and influential, what of his content and, most particularly, his source material? Scott's novels, and all subsequent historical novels with a reach beyond their country of origin, provoke a secondary type of othering to that we first identified in Chapter 1. History is other, and made familiar through the illusions of fiction. The history of another nation is further distanced from the reader. What did Pushkin or Fenimore Cooper have in common with Edward Waverley and the people of the Scottish Highlands; what, more specifically, did they know about them other than was included in Scott's notes? This double othering inflects our reading of historical novels about other cultures and societies. A good example of this is Boris Akunin (real name Grigory Shalvovich Chkhartishvili), who is immensely successful in Russia and worldwide. His Erast Fandorin series of novels, set in the Romanov era, have been characterised as part of the *poshlost* in that country, nostalgia for a time before communism, similar to the *ostalgie* in Germany for the old partition. He is part of a new Russian 'mass culture fixated on pastiche versions of the dynastic past' (Anderson 2007). His novels dramatise a conscious and ideological use of hindsight:

Not a trace was left of Brilling's usual sardonic humour and a note of fierce determination had appeared in his voice. 'If the tumour is not surgically removed in the embryonic stage, then these romantics will give us a *révolution* that will make the French guillotine seem no more than a charming piece of idle mischief. You and I will not be allowed to grow old in peace, mark my words.'

(Akunin 2003: 77–8)

As Perry Anderson notes, 'hugely successful pulp, marketed as serious fiction and produced by writers from an elite background, would be an anomaly in the West ... In Russia it is a pattern' (Anderson 2007). Akunin's novels speak to a particular set of contemporary Russian concerns, but his work has been translated and attained a similarly massive global audience. What, then, might a Western audience make of the Fandorin series? Is the Tsarist context simply another set of generic tropes, along with the thriller-detective form? Does Akunin manage to key into a set of global stereotypes about pre-communist Russia? Furthermore, do historical novels cater to international audiences who might fetishise epochs from the history of another nation?

At the same time, the issue of how authors approach their sources is inflected by this nationalist paradigm. Is it the case that historical novelists may only write about 'their' history in so far as they have some kind of ethnographic, sociological, nationalist, geographical claim to a past? Clearly not, as writers have amply shown. However, it does tend to be the case, primarily, presumably, because of access to source material, or language problems, or lack of confidence, that historical novelists keep within their own national historical boundaries. Yet does this mean that 'history' is somehow inert and neutral, mere source material? Again, clearly not. However, this tension and dynamic infects our reading and understanding of historical fiction. The Australian writer James Bradley appears to have broken free of his country's past in *The Resurrectionist* (2006), setting his novel in the grim London streets of the early 1820s and specifically amongst the grave robbers servicing the various professional anatomists of the time. However, the novel inverts this for the last section, as one of them is transported to Australia for his crimes, and the novel becomes a meditation upon origin, a consideration of the relationship between mother country and colony. The inhabitants of the colony are formerly prostitutes, convicts, criminals and murderers, yet 'To laugh at them, or mock them, however, is no easy thing, for what lies in their pasts is there for all of us. And so we conspire not to enquire, nor to tell, as if by this silence we might forget what was and make a life without a past, as if this were a land without history, a country founded on the air' (Bradley 2006: 286). This is impossible, however: 'And yet the past is ever there' (Bradley 2006: 286). *The Resurrectionist* elegantly creates a dialogue about national character and self-definition through its historical setting, reclaiming 'British' history for a postcolonial audience.

However, when writers have written about other pasts they have sometimes done so problematically. If, to use L.P. Hartley's well worn phrase, 'the past is a foreign country', then there are various problems associated with visiting, invading, appropriating or annexing it. Engaging with 'foreign' history might lead to problematic encounters, as, for instance when colonial writers use the exotic otherness of fantasised histories. There might, though, be a virtue to engaging with contested history. This certainly has become the case as writers have begun to write back from the margins of sexuality, empire and class (see Chapter 6). This might lead to Hari Kunzru's very deliberate deconstructing of the British imperial novel in *The Impressionist* (2002). It definitely has led to the most delicate and sophisticated of meditations on the status of art, history and the writer, Orhan Pamuk's *My Name is Red/ Benim Adim Kirmizi* (2001/1998), which considers the profound issues associated with the interpenetration of the art of one civilisation by another: 'does illustrating in a new way signify a new way of seeing?' (Pamuk 2001: 33; Stone 2006). At the same time, if *all* the past is foreign then it surely does not matter if the reader has any connection with the history being fictionalised?

Within this context, a further pertinent question might be asked: is there such a thing as transnational, global historical literacy? Certainly some tropes like the First World War or the Holocaust might arguably have a kind of global resonance, whereas others are more specific and nationally considered. In a globalised media system with multidirectional transcultural information flows, what is the status of the historical novel? Can it open up inter-cultural dialogue or does it tend to homogeneity? Chapter 2 dealt in some ways with these issues, albeit in a Eurocentric way, up to the early parts of the last century. Yet since then issues of trans-nationality and cosmopolitanism in culture have become focused in ways hitherto unforeseen, particularly with the inception of particular forms of economic and cultural globalisation of which **postmodernism** is possibly a consequence or a driver. A good example of this newly globalised system is the author Salman Rushdie, discussed in Chapter 5, who is clearly an international writer addressing the histories of a particular set of areas such as India, Pakistan and Britain (Brennan 1997). To what extent, then, can and do historical novels address a transnational com-munity? Or, to turn the question around, to what extent are his-torical texts inextricably grounded in the moment and site of their inception and publication? Can they talk across cultures, geographies and histories? Certainly it would seem that in order to understand historical fiction it might be important to have a grasp of its original context, setting and moment. After this, though, novels (as Scott's demonstrate) might have a reach far beyond their primary instance and purpose.

That said, as has been argued, the audience of historical novels might often suffer the **authentic fallacy**, in which case historical empathy is rendered irrelevant anyway. Furthermore, the educa-tional element of historical fiction means that the reader approa-ches wishing to learn more about something unknown. It might be that, as Lukács argues, the motif of the historical novel is its demonstration of history as process, something which might speak to any nation and engender a sense of revolutionary potential irrespective of content (see Chapter 2). And finally, the innate alienness of historical fiction serves to suggest that having any prior awareness is of little consequence.

LITERARY FICTION AND HISTORY

For the moment, though, let us focus our discussion on British and what has been termed **Anglophone** writing. In 1984 when the influential literary journal *Granta* published their first 'Best of Young British Novelists' list historical fiction writing was generally absent, as it similarly was in 1994 when the second list appeared, but in 2004 many of the young writers featured took history as their subject. Similarly, since the nomination of Rose Tremain's *Restoration* and Kazuo Ishiguro's *The Remains of the Day* (the eventual winner) in 1989, the Booker prize has frequently recognised Anglophone historical fiction. Booker judge Natasha Walter noted the upsurge of interest in historical settings, particularly in novels by women, in a 1999 essay that lamented how these new fictions were over-researched and inert: 'can all this pretty detail substitute for the vigour of real imaginative engagement with a novelist's own times?' (Walter 1999).

Writing historical novels is no longer something to be considered vulgar, the preserve of romance writers, or guaranteed to tie one to a particular type of genre. 'That recent British and anglophone fiction has taken a historical turn has become an axiom of critical commentary,' writes Suzanne Keen (Keen 2006: 167), and she argues that, of all the sub-genres of the novel, the historical is the only one that has been widely, successfully and respectfully used by contemporary literary writers. Keen quotes Linda Duguid's judgement that historical fiction has 'become respectable, even intellectual' (cited in Keen 2006: 168). Of course, it might be argued that the literary turn to the historical form of the 1990s was merely a return; as Chapter 2 has suggested, the historical novel was clearly fundamental in developments of the novel throughout the nineteenth century, and the move by contemporary writers to use history is more a swing back to a mode which was bourgeois, middle-ranking and literary already. Furthermore, the key question for us to ask is how this type of literary historical fiction impacts upon the historical novel as a genre, rather than the other way round. Why has middle-ranking literary fiction developed a fascination with history? What does it mean for a sub-genre to become 'mainstream'? Can we consider historical novels to be 'serious literary fiction'?

The story of middle-ranking historical fiction over the past few decades is the 're-bourgeoising' of the genre, as a form that had been either experimental or non-literary became a site of normality for middle-class authors. A key example of this might be the British writer Julian Barnes. Barnes is a best-selling literary writer, whose work gestures towards the experimental. His 1984 *Flaubert's Parrot* considers literary memorialisation through the central character's quest to find the stuffed parrot that stood on Flaubert's desk whilst he wrote *Un coeur simple*. The character discovers at least three legitimate parrots, undermining the idea of certainty. The book also writes various different biographies of Flaubert, pointing towards the idea of complexity within narratives of a life (Bell 1993). Barnes's 1989 *A History of the World in 10½ Chapters* stitched together a variety of narratives, including an account of Géricault's painting 'The Wreck of the Medusa' and the story told by a woodworm on Noah's Ark (Buxton 2000). *England, England* (1998) presents a dystopia in which all the important bits of English national history and culture have been transported to a theme park on the Isle of Wight, and 'Old' England falls into bucolic despair, renamed 'Albion'. Barnes is able and willing to consider conceptual questions relating to history, memory and cultural product, and is obsessed with the ways in which literature and reality interact. At the same time his work is undemanding and certainly not radical in the ways of authors discussed in later chapters.

A similarly inert or politically neutral formal experimentation occurs in Rose Tremain's 1989 *Restoration*. Tremain's novel demonstrated the popularity and possibility of the literary historical novel. *Restoration* was one of the first literary-fiction historical novels to achieve critical, institutional and popular success. It won the *Sunday Express* Book of the Year award and was shortlisted for the Booker prize. Before the publication of *Restoration* it was unusual for a British literary novelist to approach history unless they were writers deploying the tropes of postmodern fiction or identity politics to interrogate and undermine it as a problematic and political discourse (see Todd 2006: 198–230 and Chapter 5). Florence King, reviewing the novel in the *New York Times*, argued that Tremain 'has restored the historical novel to its rightful place of honor after nearly two decades of degeneration into the sweet-savage imbecility of so-called historical romance' (King 1990), demonstrating the critical distaste for genre fiction and the sense of a rebirth of the 'serious' literary historical novel. *Restoration* was the first in a series of hugely successful prize-winning best-selling historical fictions, in particular Pat Barker's *Regeneration* trilogy (1991–95), A. S. Byatt's *Possession* (1990), Sebastian Faulks's *Birdsong* (1994) and Ian McEwan's *Atonement* (2001). These novels demonstrated a renewed literary interest in telling stories set in the past. These bourgeois novels clearly demonstrate the influence of postmodern style and form. They take the tools of postmodern **historiographic metafiction** and make them main-stream and popular. In so doing these novelists drew some of the political sting from such techniques, but each is still self-conscious enough in style and form to suggest an interest in questioning authority and legitimacy. These novels demonstrate the assertion made in Chapter 1, that the techniques of historical fiction *necessarily* imply a form that is self-conscious, complex and questioning. Novels such as *Restoration* are consciously 'literary' in so far as they eschew easy genre classifications, attempt density of style and complexity of theme. They sell well and are increasingly attended to within popular culture, as can be demonstrated by the interest in literary fiction shown by Oprah Winfrey and the Richard and Judy book club. They are what Richard Todd calls 'serious lit-erary fiction', books which appeal to a sophisticated general audience (Todd 1996: 3). They contrast directly with the genre, pulp or 'low' fiction discussed in Chapter 3.

Restoration is self-conscious in form. Robert Merivel, the flawed narrator, attempts to account for the 'messy constellation' of his life by providing five starting points, explaining that 'There was a beginning to the story, or possibly a variety of beginnings' (Tre-main 1989: 5). The novel also undermines historical taxonomisa-tion, as the title word is used as a thematic motif throughout the novel as well, of course, as very specifically meaning the time period after the return of Charles II in 1660. Tremain's thoughts on her own practice are illuminating, as they demonstrate her interest in self-deception and her motives for looking at the alien past:

> I suspect that many writers deceive themselves about why they write. My self-deception is that I create in order to understand and that the final end of it all might be wisdom. This means that I deliberately

seek out the strange, the unfamiliar, even the unknowable, as subjects for my novels and trust my imagination to illuminate them to the point where both I and the reader can see them with a new clarity. The writers I admire most seem to have this kind of goal: to comprehend experience distant from their own, in nature, place and time, and to let the extraordinary cast new light on the quotidian.

(Tremain n.d.)

Tremain here suggests that meditation upon the past is a tool for the reconceptualisation of the day-to-day. It allows a revelation about the contemporary. Tremain is both historian and fiction writer, conscious enough of her role to eschew straightforward authentification but deriving it nonetheless through her style and formal organisation.

The cover of her second historical novel, *Music and Silence* (1999), accentuates historical difference and contention. The cover splices together two portraits. The upper half is taken up with a detail from 'Christian IV' by Abraham Wuchters (1638), the lower half a detail from a portrait of Christian's second wife, 'Kirsten Munk' by Jacob van Doordt (1623). There is no attempt to merge the pictures, and therefore they are at some odds with each other. This awkward presentation foregrounds the central conceits of the book, particularly the setting up of various binaries (light–dark, music–silence, knowledge–ignorance, life–death). The novel is interested in such historical collage. Tremain presents a huge number of different narrators, from a variety of backgrounds and nations. Some of her inclusions are official (letters) or authored (private writings and diaries), where some are just the thoughts of children. She creates a melange in which her own third-person voice is often not given precedence. She therefore blends metafictional complexity with a traditional authoritative omniscient narrator. The novel is playfully aware both of its appeal to historical veracity and its own contingency: 'Peter Claire reads this second letter several times before closing it. He notes what versatile things words may be and how, contained within them, can reside other words, nowhere set down and for ever invisible to the eye, but having an existence just the same' (Tremain 2000: 264). Tremain allows her work a theoretical flexibility,

controlling and controlled, somehow contingent and authoritative, and this in turn achieves an odd kind of historical
dynamic. It allows for a type of **postmodern** historical fiction
whilst still giving the reader the comfort of the external arbiter
and organiser. Implicitly and stylistically indebted to John
Fowles, although without the compulsive textual game playing of
his *The French Lieutenant's Woman* (1969), Tremain is relatively
unusual in her desire and ability to inhabit these different types
of authoritative form.

WAR NOVELS

Tremain's factual subject, the seventeenth century, is one of several
canonical periods returned to by literary authors in contradistinction to those preferred by genre writers. The most significant historical events considered by literary novelists over the
past decades have been the two world wars of the twentieth century. Sebastian Faulks's 1993 novel *Birdsong* began a vogue for
literary historical novels about the trenches during the First
World War and the two world wars more generally. It was one of
the first of these types of novels to really deal with the grinding
horror of the trenches, the grimness and trauma which are now
familiar tropes. It seems clear that revisiting the well known past
of the two wars allows novelists to negotiate and understand
extremes of human behaviour, such as suffering, trauma, possibly
heroism, within a familiar set of tropes. Considerations of the
wars of the twentieth century became common during the 1990s
and demonstrated interest in traumatic historical events as a way
of exploring memory, loss and horror (MacCallum-Stewart 2006).

Birdsong has a sophisticated structure and is told from the point
of view of three chronological periods (1910, 1916–17 and
1978). The first two are a straightforward recounting of the
character Stephen Wraysford and his experiences before and
during the war. The third outlines the investigation of this story
by his descendant, Elizabeth, after she finds his journal. However,
far from being an account of the 'knowing' present, the 1978
story line is itself a historicised narrative. The character in this
time does not know things that the reader does, so a hierarchy of

knowledge is created. The modern sections are interleaved with those from the war period, and the movement between past and present is a way of conceptualising the relationship between past and present, between 'reader' of history and 'participant' in history. The novel therefore dramatises in the central character of Elizabeth the ways in which people in contemporary society understand their past. Through engagement with the personal and the revelatory, her experiences make her more whole. Elizabeth uses her past to understand herself through a type of empathy and experiential understanding.

The novel is as interesting, in many ways, for its meta-textual commentary on why people are interested in their past:

> What she described as a mild curiosity crystallized inside her to a set determination. Beginning with the contents of her mother's attic she would track this man down: she would make up for the lateness of her interest in him by bringing all her energy to the task. It would be one way, at least, of understanding more about herself.
>
> (Faulks 1994: 250)

When upbraided about her lack of knowledge Elizabeth wonders whether she learnt it at school: 'Perhaps they [other children] did. I don't seem to have been paying attention. It all seemed so boring and depressing, all those battles and guns and things' (Faulks 1994: 251). She is interested not in the details of history but in an empathic understanding of the past: 'But what was it *like*?' (Faulks 1994: 256). Elizabeth's exploration of the journals leads her to unexpected revelation: 'Again she had touched the past. It had stopped being history and had turned into experience' (Faulks 1994: 410). 'History' as taught at school is dull, whereas personal history, experience, can make that past live. This is **metonymic** for the relationship of the historical novelist to history. Novelists are important for their ability to take dry facts and information and invest them with fictional life, to somehow attempt to communicate what the past was *like*. Yet even within this the novel acknowledges its partiality as it concedes the unknowability of the horror of the war:

> No child or future generation will ever know what this was like. They will never understand. When it is over we will go quietly among the

living and we will not tell them. We will talk and sleep and go about
our business like human beings. We will seal what we have seen in
the silence of our hearts and no words will reach us.

(Faulks 1994: 422)

Pat Barker's *Regeneration* trilogy (1991–95) takes this sense of
unknowability and makes it the central motif of the narrative.
The novels follow the progress of a psychoanalyst, W. H. R.
Rivers, as he attempts to understand and to heal those traumatised
by trench warfare. Their ordeal in combat means that 'Rivers's
patients are, for the most part, stuck in time, in reliving one
particular moment of experience or trauma ... [they] suffer either
from amnesia or anamnesia, too little or too much memory'
(Brannigan 2003: 22–3). They struggle to live with what has
happened to them, either unable to speak or subject to horrific
nightmares making them relive the horrors. The use of a doctor of
psychoanalysis allows Barker to consider the ways in which horrific
experience and memory bleed into the present-day psyche: 'Rivers's
treatment sometimes consisted simply of encouraging the patient
to abandon his hopeless attempt to forget, and advising him to
spend some part of every day remembering' (Barker 1992: 26).
The personal past in *Regeneration* has physical consequences in the
present and must be understood and engaged with in order to
prevent confusion, chaos and illness.

The *Regeneration* novels include famous poets Siegfried Sassoon
and Wilfred Owen (and Rivers is also real). Barker praises the
fictional dynamic created by the interaction of the 'fictional'
characters with the 'actual': 'you find in some extraordinary way
that the fictional characters like Billy Prior actually seem to
acquire more energy from being in relationship to actual historical characters' (Barker 2000). She posits some kind of tension
between the real and the imaginary. However, fictional practice is
grounded in factuality: 'it was always very important to me that I
didn't change anything about the historical characters, that they
actually thought and said what I've said they thought and did
on a particular day' (Barker 2000). The natural habitat of the
novelist would seem to be what people think and do, but here
Barker cedes her ground to history. The facts of history and

biography give her a frame within which to work, or upon which to project.

Regeneration presents the war as an event of massive psychological significance which shifted the ways in which people conceptualised history and rationality. These novels by Faulks and Barker take the trauma of the war and fold it into their meditations upon memory and identity. In both instances the experience of combat leads to inability to articulate one's identity, a desire to not speak of things and to repress them. Historical events here become something to forget, something unable to be expressed, something that might wound or hurt the psyche.

As such, the war novels of the early 1990s recalibrated standard cultural tropes about the war but in the main did not particularly reorder them. Two final books to consider in this instance, though, did manage this in very different ways. Sebastian Barry's *A Long Long Way* (2005; also discussed in Chapter 6) undermined the standard Anglophone narrative of the First World War by considering it from an Irish perspective, demonstrating that for many who fought and were traumatised its function as part of a national mythos was far from clear. The novel challenges the historical orthodoxies inherent in Faulks's and to an extent in Barker's work. Ian McEwan's *Atonement* (2002) is a complex novel of the Second World War, and provides an extraordinary moment of metafictional self-consciousness at the end which undermines historical novel writing in many ways by demonstrating the authentic fallacy of the realist novel (de Groot 2008: 221).

A Long Long Way follows Willie Dunne, a member of the Royal Dublin Fusiliers, from his home town to the trenches of Flanders. Dunne lives through most of the great horrors of the conflict. Barry uses his central character to come at two key historical events with fresh eyes: the Great War and the 1916 Easter Rising in Dublin. The war experience of the ordinary Irish soldier is a relatively untold story, and Barry explores what it meant to be fighting for a cause that was not necessarily one's own. As well as an attempt to personalise what are now standard tropes such as the gas attacks, going over the top, the mud of the trenches, the novel is a **postcolonial** writing back of a familiar narrative. It is a clearly complex cultural entity of the sort described in the

opening of this chapter, asking questions about historical translatability and the hegemonies of knowledge sustained by fiction
about the past. The First World War is not part of the teleology
of Britain but the moment of the Irish Rebellion. Barry, an Irish
writer publishing with a British press (Faber & Faber), interrogates the historical myth that the war was a heroic sacrifice on
the part of those who fought. He points out that most of those
who were there had no desire to sacrifice themselves, and that
they were simply tools of a declining imperial power. Willie and
his regiment view the events in Dublin first-hand and his disquiet
at seeing a new kind of 'enemy' communicates clearly the utter
confusion of the time.

Timmy Weekes, an Englishman in the trenches, introduces the
soldiers to Dostoevsky. When asked how the Russian novelist
would have dealt with the trenches, he says, 'Dante is the chap
for this ... or Tolstoy.' 'Now, Tolstoy wrote about wars. But not
like this war. In his war you could still go home and fall in love
with a lady ... Well, maybe it i'n't so very different. Maybe not.
Anyway, they don't write books about the likes of us. It's officers
and high-up people mostly' (Barry 2006: 231–2). The novel
explicitly takes the experience of the ordinary soldier in the trenches
and shifts the focus of the historical novel. Furthermore, this section
suggests that in the past wars and history in general have been
considered in a romantic light, but that fictionalising will not be
possible for the current conflict. Barry is concerned here to reflect
upon the ways in which an event might be rewritten and recast
after the event, the ways that stories are told that become myths.
In contrast, the novel articulates the utter confusion which is
characteristic of the war experience: 'He didn't understand the
war in the upshot, and he had thought to himself a dozen times
and more that no one on earth understood it rightly' (Barry 2006:
282).

As a coda to this discussion of war novels it is important to
consider *Atonement*. Ian McEwan's book demonstrates the concerns
of the historical war novel combining with the mode of expression
and form of the serious literary **historiographic metafiction** discussed above. In doing so it fractures the fragility of the historical
novel by demonstrating its **authentic fallacy**. The story concerns

an event before the war in which Robbie Turner is falsely convicted of rape mainly owing to the flawed testimony of the young Briony Tallis. He is imprisoned and then goes to war, where he is taken from Dunkirk beach and returns to his love, Briony's sister Cecilia. Briony tracks the two of them down, and vows to begin the legal procedure necessary to exonerate Robbie. The final section, now set in 1999, has Briony visiting the Imperial War Museum reading room for the last time, checking the final details of her research. She is a historical novelist, passing her manuscript to an elderly colonel to check details like language, and writing to those who experienced Dunkirk. She sees her research as a movement towards veracity: 'Like policemen in a search team, we go on hands and knees and crawl towards the truth' (McEwan 2002: 359). However, she also cheerfully admits that she is not too bothered about details: 'If I really cared so much about facts, I should have written a different kind of book' (McEwan 2002: 360). However, in the final pages of Briony's narrative she tells the reader that the happy ending in which Robbie and Cecilia come back together is made up, as he died at Dunkirk and she in the Blitz. What becomes clear is that most of the two middle sections of a four-part book are her fiction; she has written the narrative to attempt to atone through fiction for her destructive lie, itself a fiction which devastated real lives. She is unable to publish the truth because of the threat of legal action from the actual rapist. The section draws attention to the innate dishonesty of historical fiction *per se*, and particularly in this case, suggesting that the historical novelist might always ignore the actuality of history in order to tell the story that they want to tell. Briony is cowardly until the end, not trusting the reader's fortitude:

> How could that constitute an ending? What sense or hope or satis-
> faction could a reader draw from such an account? Who would want to
> believe that they never met again, never fulfilled their love? Who would
> want to believe that, except in the service of the bleakest realism?
>
> (McEwan 2002: 371)

The self-serving element of Briony's narration is clearest here (Wells 2006: 124–5). Rather than represent accurately what happened, rather than feel a duty to history, she weakly suggests that her readership would not want the truth. Thus the novel reveals itself to the reader as a tissue of fictions and lies; as an exercise in atonement and egotistical comforting. The novel demonstrates the **authentic fallacy** through its formal arrangement. This fallacy works through the realist mode, as the reader tends to believe, even when it is narrated by a clearly unreliable narrator, the 'reality', authenticity and accuracy of the historical novel. Briony's additional section in *Atonement* points towards all historical fiction as being a romanticised version of events, a well wrought creation. Indeed, it is the 'bleakest realism' which tends to underpin this mimetic authenticity. The conundrum here relates to self-consciousness. If an historical novel is not self-aware, interested in undermining its own authority and legitimacy, then it might be failing in its duty to history, as it might open itself up to obfuscation and untruths. The modes of postmodernism might be seen to be necessary, indeed fundamental, to the project of historical novel writing.

History has become such a regular trope for literary novelists as to be almost unremarkable, but, as can be seen, this prevalence is relatively new. What emerges strongly from this chapter is that the techniques of postmodernism as articulated in Chapter 5 have become the techniques of the modern historical novel. Questioning the legitimacy of narrative and undermining authority are fundamental to the ways that contemporary novelists approach the past. Once again, this indeterminacy and dissident complexity are fundamental to the historical novel as a phenomenon or format.

5

POSTMODERNISM AND THE HISTORICAL NOVEL
HISTORY AS FICTION, FICTION AS HISTORY

This chapter explores how radical literary and historiographical theory of the 1960s and 1970s influenced the writing of historical fiction, and the ways in which this was both resisted by, and already innate within, the form. We address some key questions. How did experimental writing of the latter part of the twentieth century adapt the historical form to its own ends? How do the set of aesthetic strategies associated with postmodernism intersect with history, and what does this mean for the writer? How might formal experimentation be used in order to undermine the organisation of history?

POSTMODERNISM AND METAFICTION

Postmodernism is notoriously difficult to define. In general it might be characterised as a set of ideas and practices that reject hierarchy, stability and categorisation, 'a mood arising out of a sense of the collapse of all those foundations of modern thought which seemed to guarantee a reasonably stable sense of Truth, Knowledge, Self and Value' (Hutcheon 1989: 345). Postmodern theories, particularly following the ideas of Jacques Derrida, challenge our sense of centredness and order, suggesting instead that the world is innately unknowable and unstable. Postmodernism is articulated in Derrida's notion of 'play', the fact that systems are not stable structures but in a constant state of flux (outlined in Derrida 1967: 278–94). The disengagement of the signifier from the signified in linguistics has in turn led to a set of cultural theories interested in the lack of relationship between word and thing, and the gaps that this implies in representation, writing and communication. A further theory, based in the thought of Jean-François Lyotard, sees postmodernism as a movement which seeks to undermine 'grand narratives'. These are ordering ideological stories, totalising explanations that have attempted to systematise and control us. The postmodern condition, according to Lyotard, consists of politicised 'incredulity' towards the organisational and representational tyranny of these legitimating narratives (Lyotard 1984: xxiv). The disestablishment of such grand narratives means that postmodernism is a crisis of legitimation as well as representation.

'History' itself is a complex entity within these types of thinking, a grand narrative in need of undermining, and a key element of a disavowal of **Enlightenment** models of progress and civilisation. Often in postmodernism 'History' works as an example of how life is innately textualised and therefore questionable because signifier and signified do not map on to each other. Roland Barthes, in his 'Discourse of History' (1967), illustrates

> this narrative style of history, which draws its 'truth' from the careful attention to narration, the architecture of articulations and the abundance of expanded elements (known, in this case, as 'concrete details'). So the circle of paradox is complete. Narrative structure, which was originally developed within the cauldron of fiction (in myths and the first epics) becomes at once the sign and the proof of reality.
>
> (Barthes 1970: 154)

For the sceptic Barthes the style and manner of historical writing strive to mimic reality by deploying the tropes of fiction. What, then, of historical fiction within this framework? It seems that the type of novel which gestures towards 'historical' authenticity, but which consciously deploys fictional tropes to attain that quality, in some ways must demonstrate the gap between written text and truth. Barthes continues: 'In other words, in "objective" history, the "real" is never more than an unformulated signified, sheltering behind the apparently all-powerful referent. This situation characterizes what we might call the *realistic effect*' (Barthes 1970: 153). This careful **post-structuralist** disavowal of 'reality' in historical writing was part of what led to what has been called the '**postmodern turn**' in **historiographical** writing. Theorists such as Hayden White, Nancy Partner, Louis Mink, Alun Munslow and Keith Jenkins have conceptualised 'history' as a set of narrative tropes (Munslow 1997; Jenkins 2003). Hayden White, particularly, has been influential in his assertion that rhetoric and metaphor are integral parts of history writing, and that 'History' is a narrative form itself rather than an account of historical 'truth'. Such writers have interrogated the idea that historical writing might communicate anything to the reader about the 'past': 'the genuine nature of history can be understood only when it is viewed not solely and simply as an objectivised empiricist enterprise, but as the creation and eventual imposition by historians of a particular narrative form on the past' (Munslow 1997: 2). Keith Jenkins has argued that 'it frees us up from being held in thrall to commonsensical rigid designations if we see that terms like "the past" and "history" are, like other terms, *empty signifiers*' (Jenkins 2003: 35). The past is something that we impose order and meaning upon, but which is ultimately unknowable: 'Since "the past", by definition, does not exist, surely we can "know" it only by way of representations' (Chase 1996: 67).

What is interesting for students of fiction is the ways in which this new theorising of 'History' has drawn attention to historical writing's innate literariness, and its adherence to a mode we might describe as 'realist' and narrative. Historical writing which attempts to present a known past perpetuates what Robert Berkhofer calls 'the illusion of realism' (cited in Jenkins 2003: 45). It is important that scholars recognise 'history not as an **epistemology** but as an aesthetic' (Jenkins 2003: 49). Historical writing, and indeed all the ways in which we understand and engage with the past, are innately partial. Importantly, though, postmodern historiography argues that this situates 'History' squarely within the framework of the imagination: 'For texts are not cognitive, empirical, epistemological entities, but speculative, propositional invitations to *imagine* the past *ad infinitum*' (Jenkins 2003: 49). Jenkins's idea that through an engagement with historical texts the reader is invited to '*imagine*' a set of multiple pasts suggests a way of approaching history and particularly the reading of 'evidence' as something clearly fictional, in so far as we understand fiction as something which is held in opposition to concrete 'fact'.

What does all this mean for the novels we are interested in? First, it suggests that 'History' has come under some attack as a way of legitimating particular versions of the past. Second, the 'literariness' of history has led to a resurgence of interest in fictional forms and the ways they represent the past. Indeed, this conceptualising of the fictionality of the factual past has led some scholars to argue for the educational and historiographic value of writing historical stories or imagining timelines (Slotkin 2005; Ferguson 2000). The ways in which postmodern historiography has troubled our understanding of how 'History' is written and constructed point towards a crisis of representation that postmodern historical novelists have manipulated. Postmodern novelists of the past have developed and evolved this indeterminacy. Indeed, the very insubstantiality inherent in our relation to 'History' has provided them with a set of tools for challenging legitimating narratives and locating radical dissent. A key example of this might be John Fowles's clear attack on the Marxist cyclical view of history in *The French Lieutenant's Woman* (discussed below): a view of the past which, in his opinion, is overly deterministic. The decentring of the central master narratives of historical fact has allowed authors to explore a variety of issues, from the problem of unreliable narratives (Kazuo Ishiguro's *The Remains of the Day*, 1993) to marginalised and hitherto unwritten histories (Sarah Waters's *Tipping the Velvet* (1998)), to 'What if?' and counterfactual scenarios (Robert Harris's *Fatherland*, 1992). The understanding that 'History' is simply the interpretation of a tissue of quotations and texts has given greater force and impetus to those who represent that past through quotation, text and fictional prose. Indeed, it might be argued that historical fiction has always problematised the writing of and understanding of history (de Certeau 1992; White 2005).

Historical novels are keenly interested in the interaction between what is 'known' and what is made up, querying, for instance, the deployment of varieties of quoted 'evidence', which is often literary, therefore highlighting the innate textuality of history, to frame a persuasive narrative, and the use of the realist mode to present a story which is clearly fiction. All these are elements of the contemporary postmodern historiographic critique. Historical fiction points towards its own insubstantiality. As the character Villanelle, herself a text, as she is named after a type of French poem, in Jeanette Winterson's 'historical' novel *The Passion* (1987) famously repeats, 'I'm telling you stories. Trust me' (Winterson 1987: 40). The central paradox of historical fiction, the consciously false realist representation of something which can never be known, seems to prefigure the postmodern crisis in historical writing. Indeed, the practices with which this book opened, that the historian's job is to explain the otherness of the past, whilst the novelist explores the differences of the past, seem to no longer be so distinct. Both novelist and historian are using trope, metaphor, prose, narrative style to interpret and render a version of something which is innately other and unknown.

I am going to use the model described by Fredric Jameson as a means of locating a further discussion of the aesthetics of postmodernism as it might relate to the historical novel. In 1983 Jameson described postmodernism as a 'cultural reaction to high modernism, a rebellion against the canonical, the **reified** monuments one has to destroy to do anything new' (Jameson 1996: 186). It was an aesthetic mode interested in melding high and mass culture, in celebrating kitsch, and in interrogating narrative linearity. Jameson goes further, suggesting that the term 'postmodern' is 'a periodizing concept whose function is to correlate the emergence of new formal features in culture with the emergence of a new type of social life and a new economic order' (Jameson 1996: 187). 'Postmodern', then, is a modal descriptor bridging culture and socio-economic states; through an analysis of the tropes of postmodernism we can begin to see a 'new moment of capitalism' (Jameson 1996: 187). He particularly outlines two different elements of postmodern culture and society that are of importance to our present discussion: pastiche and schizophrenia.

For Jameson, pastiche is 'speech in a dead language' (Jameson 1996: 188). Where parody mocks the original, assuming 'the feeling that there is a linguistic norm' which can be mocked, pastiche recognises that 'the very possibility of any linguistic norm ... would vanish, and we would have nothing but stylistic diversity and heterogeneity' (Jameson 1996: 188). Jameson's conceptualisation of the postmodern aesthetic is that it blankly mimics: 'in a world in which stylistic innovation is no longer possible, all that is left is to imitate dead styles, to speak through the masks and with the voices of the styles in the imaginary museum' (Jameson 1996: 190). Jameson's account of schizophrenia is derived from the work of psychoanalyst Jacques Lacan. In this theorisation it occurs psychoanalytically at the breakdown of the relationship between signifier and signified, or a lack of appreciation of the 'interrelationships of material signifiers' (Jameson 1996: 195). For Lacan we *understand* due to time. Through language we 'have what seems to us a concrete or lived experience of time' whereas the schizophrenic 'is condemned to live a perpetual present' without personal identity 'since our feeling of identity depends on our sense of the persistence of the "I" and the "me" over time' (Jameson 1996: 195). Due to the breakdown in signification and representation demonstrated by Derrida, and through the development of a late type of capitalism, contemporary society finds itself in the position of the schizophrenic, unable to appreciate the passing of time because of the corruption of language.

This ahistorical condition is the consequence of late consumer capitalism. Postmodernism is an apolitical, culturally schizophrenic expression of our inert, morally neutral economic state which has led to a bleeding of legitimation and a concomitant anxiety:

> the way in which our entire contemporary social system has little by little begun to lose its capacity to retain its own past, has begun to live in a perpetual present and in a perpetual change that obliterates

traditions of the kind that all earlier social formations have had in one way or another to preserve.

(Jameson 1996: 201)

This nightmarish 'perpetual present' means that all institutions and organising discourses have begun to come undone as they are demonstrably disengaged from anything real. We live, for Jameson, in a world of surface and echo, unable to properly remember or create anything new. The postmodern world is schizophrenic, then, in its inability to sense time actually passing and its perpetual presentness.

How does this work in practice? Ultimately all historical fiction might be said to be **deferred** in its workings, as its subject materials are distanced and othered from the experience of the reader. If pastiche is 'speech in a dead language', might the historical novel be a fictional pastiche of history in so far as it imitates history but is never *actually* history? This raises legitimacy issues, particularly about whether the historical novel is as 'real' as other fiction. If, as Hayden White suggests, all historians play with rhetoric and metaphor in constructing their narratives, then all historical fiction is predicated upon fictionalised 'versions' of the past. The historian attempts to legitimate power structures by creating truth and writing the dead, but this activity is innately corrupted and seeking to represent the other (or the explanation of the other of history that we have discussed briefly already) reveals the fiction of history (de Certeau 1992: 11). All historical novels are, ultimately, pastiche reworkings and reimaginings of interpreted and unsubstantiated factual narratives. It is no coincidence that Fredric Jameson centres his discussion of postmodernism on a critique of E. L. Doctorow's *Ragtime* (1977), a historical novel (see Baker 2000: 123–52). Such writings are artefacts of Jameson's 'perpetual present', imitating a past which never existed. This may not impact upon the material experience of reading such a novel, but it has important implications for the study of the form. Furthermore, it suggests ways in which the genre might be differentiated from other types of fiction.

In the case of books which mimic particular literary styles, such as novels that engage with novels, the genre becomes a form of pastiche in which the source material is not historical evidence but other fiction. It is common particularly for postmodern historical writers to engage with cultural narratives of particular periods, as is clearly the case in A. S. Byatt's *faux* Victorian style in *Possesssion* (1991), or in Hari Kunzru's suggestion that his novel *The Impressionist* (2002) was

> largely a game I was playing with orientalism, with a Merchant Ivory view of India, and with the history of the British novel, which is so wrapped up with ideas of a British male self coming to full presence or knowledge in the mystical mirror of the East. The book is an anti-*Kim*, but also plays around with *A Passage to India, Heart of Darkness, Hindoo Holiday* and others.
>
> (Kunzru 2006)

Kunzru suggests that his version of Anglo-Indian history in the novel was a response to a cultural discourse (Orientalism), to modern versions of the past (Merchant Ivory's films of the 1980s) and to novels of India by Rudyard Kipling, E. M. Forster and Joseph Conrad that are now generally considered part of an imperialist mode of writing. He is echoing and pastiching but, it might be argued, to political effect and purpose. Jameson's model of pastiche has been attacked by, among others, Linda Hutcheon who argues that postmodern imitative techniques have been particularly effective for those excluded by dominant cultural ideology (Hutcheon 1988: 22–36 and see discussion in Chapter 6). As some critics have argued, postmodern fiction represents the 'heterodox historical moment' and allows 'marginalised people to emerge as equal historical subjects and narrators' (Thomas Docherty and Robert Holton, cited in Baker 2000: 123). That certainly seems to be the case with *The Impressionist*, which uses its historical novel form to attack fixed centralised identities and undermine imperial truths, manipulating the collage rather than dully and dumbly imitating. That said, as we noted at the beginning of the chapter, the debate still rages.

To continue our discussion of Jameson, if pastiche is the keynote stylistic mode of postmodernism then what of the schizophrenic anxiety provoked by the destruction of linguistic certainty? In her book on the subject Patricia Waugh defines **metafiction** as 'a term given to fictional writing which consciously and systematically draws attention to its status as an artefact in order to pose questions about the relationship between fiction and reality' (Waugh 1984: 2). This would seem to demonstrate Jameson's model of schizophrenia but, again, is a less bleak interpretation of the set of symptoms. Books in this category, for Waugh, are self-reflexive and fragmented. Their writers seek complexity and archness, and this is in many ways due to an awareness within society 'of the function of language in constructing and maintaining our sense of everyday "reality"' (Waugh 1984: 3). If the world is seen to be constructed through language, and the very assuredness of this language as a means of disclosing actuality has been questioned, then issues arise relating to how it is possible to describe or communicate anything accurately or truthfully. Metafictional writing, for Waugh, is historically particular, and begins in the mid-1960s: 'Contemporary metafictional writing is both a response and a contribution to an even more thorough-going sense that reality or history are provisional; no longer a world of eternal verities but a series of constructions, artifices, impermanent structures' (Waugh 1984: 7). In order to express this, novelists began to turn away from traditional methods that 'correspond to this ordered reality', in particular those relating to chronology, the omniscient narrator and questions of narrative linearity (Waugh 1984: 7). Metafiction is a type of writing which demonstrates the play of the linguistic and representational system and the loss of assurance in articulation. It effectively challenges the realist mode:

> Metafictional deconstruction has not only provided novelists and their readers with a better understanding of the fundamental structures of narrative; it has also offered extremely accurate models for understanding the contemporary experience of the world as a construction, an artifice, a web of interdependent semiotic systems.
>
> (Waugh 1984: 9)

Waugh's *Metafiction* draws upon the literary and cultural theories of Jacques Derrida, Michel Foucault and Roland Barthes in particular, post-structuralist and **deconstructionist** critics who suggest that language is indeterminate and therefore meaning is constantly deferred. She points to Alain Robbe-Grillet, John Fowles and B. S. Johnson among others as examples of novelists who have subverted and attacked mainstream methods in order to experiment with narratives and forms that consciously interrogate the action of reading and writing. In particular, the work of Roland Barthes sought to demonstrate that the text held a multiplicity of meanings waiting to be triggered not by the author but by the reader:

> We know now that a text is not a line of words releasing a single 'theological' meaning (the 'message' of the Author-God), but a multi-dimensional space in which a variety of writings, none of them original, blend and clash. The text is a tissue of quotations drawn from the innumerable centres of culture. Once the Author is removed, the claim to decipher a text becomes quite futile. To give a text an Author is to impose a limit on that text, to furnish it with a final signified, to close the writing. In the multiplicity of writing, everything is to be *disentangled*, nothing *deciphered*; the structure can be followed, 'run' (like the thread of a stocking) at every point and at every level, but there is nothing beneath: the space of writing is to be ranged over, not pierced; writing ceaselessly posits meaning ceaselessly to evaporate it, carrying out a systematic exemption of meaning. In precisely this way, literature (it would be better from now on to say *writing*), by refusing to assign a 'secret', and ultimate meaning, to the text (and to the world as text), liberates what may be called an anti-theological activity, and activity that is truly revolutionary since to refuse to fix meaning is, in the end, to refuse God and his hypostases – reason, science, law.
>
> (Barthes, 1977: 146)

Barthes moves from linguistic analysis to a clear sense that the undermining of fixed meaning is heretical, revolutionary and new. He argues for a decentring of meaning, and the substitution of the importance of the author for the power of the reader to make a text happen. Barthes's formulation is therefore radical in its attack on the various structures which might attempt to order, control and repress. In particular, the authority of the semi-divine 'author' is disestablished as the source of legitimate meaning. This leads to the empowerment of the reader through engagement with a text. Writing is liberated, and has the power and opportunity to free those involved in it, not simply from imaginative chains, but from the physical oppression of the state, of science and of religion. In contrast with Jameson, Barthes argues for the opportunities and the political potential of this state of affairs.

Linda Hutcheon sees historical fiction as the clearest artistic expression of postmodernism. Indeed, in its 'rethinking and reworking the forms and contents of the past' such writing is 'paradigmatic' for the aesthetic workings of postmodernism (Hutcheon 1988: 5). What Hutcheon terms 'historiographic metafiction' is characterised by contrariness, and in this self-reflexiveness, subversiveness, and particularly in its meditation upon history and identity, is found the key expression of postmodern sensibility (Hutcheon 1988: 5). Hutcheon argues that such writing is 'not just another version of the historical novel' (Hutcheon 1988: 5), yet it is clear that it is an evolution of such writing, albeit one which is heavily influenced by theoretical models and new styles. Whether such postmodern fictions are strictly historical novels is a moot point; certainly their practice has instituted a new narrative approach that feeds back into contemporary historical novel writing (see Chapter 4). Hutcheon's reliance on Georg Lukács's modelling of the historical novel form is compelling. She demonstrates that his key definitions suggest that the historical novel and historiographic metafiction might inhabit different, although surely overlapping, territory (Hutcheon 1988: 113–15). However, we might quibble with her confident assertions. The postmodern historiographic metafictions that she writes about take their experimental purchase from their new understanding of history, no doubt, but they also take their formal ability to interrogate realism and to highlight their own metafictionality from the mature, sceptical set of generic rules already in place for historical fiction.

Is there a relationship between the historical novels of Scott and the fictions of postmodernism? Certainly there has been a shift in conceptualisations of 'History' itself, and the purposes and virtues of such a style of writing. Postmodern writings using the past may not strictly be 'historical novels' but they are a highly influential way of meditating upon history through fiction, and as such they demand our attention. What, particularly, Hutcheon and Waugh point out is that from the 1960s onwards the mode of writing fictional histories shifted (Hutcheon 1988: 115). For Hutcheon the key elements of historiographic metafiction are its ability to implement provisionality and problematise knowledge:

> The interaction of the historiographic and the metafictional foregrounds the rejection of the claims of both 'authentic' representation and 'inauthentic' copy alike, and the very meaning of artistic originality is as forcefully challenged as is the transparency of historical referentiality.
>
> (Hutcheon 1988: 110)

Such types of fiction emphasise intertextuality, contradiction, self-consciousness and problems of narrative. The form 'destabilizes received notions of both history and fiction' (Hutcheon 1988: 120). For Waugh, metafiction demonstrates that the novel as a form has become aware of its own innate artificiality, that it is a construction of a type of reality:

> Indeed, it could be argued that, far from 'dying', the novel has reached a mature recognition of its existence as *writing*, which can only ensure its continued viability in and relevance to a contemporary world which is similarly beginning to gain awareness of precisely how its values and practices are constructed and legitimized.
>
> (Waugh 1984: 19)

This self-consciousness, relatively shorn from its radical roots, is now a commonplace in fiction (see Chapter 4). Indeterminacy and narrative self-consciousness demonstrably seek to draw attention to the problematic mimetic quality of narrative, and articulate a clear suspicion of attempts to provide a 'truthful' image of the world and its past. Such practice began in the 1960s as a consequence of authors digesting the work of various theorists, and was clearly an extremely radical set of innovations. It also signalled the integration of a new set of literary tropes with which to write, and these ideas have some profound implications for fiction generally and for historical novels particularly. Yet it must be argued that the concepts which Waugh and Hutcheon celebrate in historiographic metafiction have been present in historical novels since their inception: self-consciousness, indeterminacy, the problematising of ordering narratives. At the same time, we might quibble that many historical novels have a conservative agenda, seeking to close off debate and dialogue, and that to read them as dissident is to read against the grain, a decidedly post-structuralist approach.

JOHN FOWLES: METANARRATIVE AND PASTICHE

We can trace the key elements of postmodern metafiction, and their implications for historical novels, by considering an early example of the practice: John Fowles's *The French Lieutenant's Woman* (1969). Fowles's novel is set in 1867 and concerns the relationship between Charles Smithson and Sarah Woodruff, who meet in Lyme Regis and become attracted to each other, with problematic consequences. Fowles consciously echoes the prose and style of various Victorian novelists, in particular Thomas Hardy. The book is a pastiche of a particular style. Each chapter begins with a series of epigrams, clearly meant to situate the novel within a variety of epistemological discourses such as Marxism, history, Victorian poetry and culture, or religion. On the final page of the novel Fowles uses the epigram of the chapter, a prose line from Victorian poet Matthew Arnold, to interpret the entire novel. This demonstrates his interest in the meaning of the paratextual intertexts and how they might influence a reading of the book itself. These paratextual intertexts, along with a series of footnotes, situate the novel within a set of historical and textual contexts, acting in the same way that all authorial signposts do in historical fiction. They frame the narrative but also invoke questions of authenticity, directing the reader to consider how historical evidence is presented to make a particular case. But, in this case, they also subtly demonstrate how Fowles is stylistically echoing and invoking a series of literary forebears. They add to the effect of collage that the historical novel form constantly deploys.

Charles is a palaeontologist, and his interest in Lyme is the presence of the Undercliff, an area rich in fossils. His interest in fossils leads him to the work of Charles Lyell, whose scientific observations about geology undermined the global chronology of the Church and ushered in a new perspective on the history and age of the world. Charles is therefore a scientific rationalist. Charles is also a closet Darwinian, interested in the question of evolution, and of a form of scientific history. As Darwin had concluded in *On the Origin of Species* (1859):

> There is grandeur in this view of life, with its several powers, having been originally breathed by the Creator into a few forms or into one; and that, whilst this planet has gone cycling on according to the fixed law of gravity, from so simple a beginning endless forms most beautiful and most wonderful have been, and are being evolved.
>
> (Darwin 1996: 396)

Darwin here articulates a type of historical activity that he terms 'evolution', a continual cycle moving towards an imagined, possibly divine, perfection of some kind (Beer 2000). *The French Lieutenant's Woman* is keenly interested in various such grand or **metanarratives**. The order promised by discourses like Science (Darwinian evolution), Marxism, Religion and Literature are all important to the content and form of the novel. These ways of explaining the events of the past, as part of evolution, as part of the class struggle, as a movement toward forgiveness and salvation, or as a set of imaginary textual concerns and generic developments, are all consciously invoked by and represented by various characters. Ultimately the striving to impose order of any kind is undermined by the indeterminability of the book. This is clear in its refusal to adhere to any type of system and in its disavowal of structuring elements. By questioning the explaining metanarratives Fowles strives to demonstrate the indeterminacy of the world, its brilliant and bleak chaos: 'the river of life, of mysterious laws and mysterious choices, flows past a deserted embankment' (Fowles 1996: 445; Acheson 1998: 46–7). Though he is concerned with science, religion, gender relations and fiction, it is clear that Fowles's great subject in his novel is history itself and our relation to it. The text suggests that any engagement with the past is governed by innumerable different types of discourse, and is subject to various distancing interventions. What we are given of the past is a set of narratives and stories which cannot explain events or render truth. And if they try, without recourse to commenting upon their own practice, we should be suspicious of them.

Fowles's imitation of the Victorian novel, in particular its association with an omniscient narrator and a very proper rationalism, is broken up by his very conscious deployment of metafictional tropes. These range from the invocation of historical events such as the diegetically unknown publication of Karl Marx's *Das Kapital* in 1867 to the clear location of a character who is supposedly the 'author' within the novel's formulation. Fowles in his character as 'narrator' is keenly interested in the relationship between then and now, suggesting that he knows the ancestors of various of the characters and that he lives in one of the houses in the novel. The 'narrator' appears in a railway carriage, contemplating Charles whilst he sleeps. This 'metafictional deconstruction', to use Waugh's term, illustrates the artificiality of the narrative and in doing so attempts to undermine the ways in which systems such as realism, science and religion impose legitimacy, mimesis and order upon society and the text. This 'narrator', Fowles's avatar in the novel, but not to be confused with the *actual* author, concludes his twelfth chapter with the words 'Who is Sarah? Out of what shadows does she come?' (Fowles 1996: 96), and the opening to the next chapter begins:

> I do not know. This story I am telling is all imagination. These characters I create never existed outside my own mind. If I have pretended until now to know my characters' minds and innermost thoughts it is because I am writing in (just as I have assumed some of the vocabulary and 'voice' of) a convention universally accepted at the time of my story: that the novelist stands next to God. He may not know all, yet he tries to pretend that he does. But I live in the age of Alain Robbe-Grillet and Roland Barthes; if this is a novel, it cannot be a novel in the modern sense of the word.
>
> (Fowles 1996: 97)

It is not a 'modern' novel; it is a 'postmodern' one. This moment of self-consciousness undermines the 'convention' of the Victorian novel and points to the erosion of at least two kinds of authority: religious and authorial. The god-novelist is decentred and the novel acknowledges its own fragility as a constructed artefact. This is clearly demonstrated by the fact that Fowles gives the story three different conclusions, highlighting the lack of clear edges to the story and its innate fictionality. To repeat Waugh's manifesto for metafictional practice: 'reality or history are provisional; no longer a world of eternal verities but a series of constructions, artifices, impermanent structures' (Waugh 1984: 7). By using the form of his novel to expose this, Fowles attempts to subvert the controlling patterns of science, historical progress and history. He demonstrates how the overtly realist novel is a false construct, attempting to present an authoritative version of things it cannot hope to successfully pull off. The 'narrator' challenges the reader:

> So if you think all this unlucky (but it *is* Chapter Thirteen) digression has nothing to do with your Time, Progress, Society, Evolution and all those other capitalized ghosts in the night that are rattling their chains behind the scenes of this book ... I will not argue. But I shall suspect you.
>
> (Fowles 1996: 99)

Having already mentioned Roland Barthes, the narrator here is consciously aware of his own intertextuality. The reference to the 'unlucky' chapter is a throwaway joke or allusion to the artificiality of the novel's structure, and the idea of the 'suspect' reader invokes the famous lines of Charles Baudelaire's modernist poem *Les Fleurs du mal*. These lines are themselves famously used in that most intertextual of poems, T. S. Eliot's *The Waste Land:* 'Hypocrite lecteur, – mon semblable, – mon frère!' ('Hypocrite reader, – my copy, – my brother!'; 'Au lecteur', Baudelaire 1857: l. 40). The fact that the reader might actually *believe* the narratives of 'Time, Progress, Society, Evolution' and have some kind of actual investment in them makes them worthy of suspicion. The chapter, and indeed the novel, interrogate the idea of omniscience and suggest that a kind of ethereal, undefined freedom is preferable to the constraints of master narratives or, indeed, of master narrators.

Fowles's historical fiction, therefore, deploys metafictional elements in order to demonstrate the problem of realism and to suggest new ways in which novels might begin to mean. His work interrogates history by challenging the entire set of concerns which underpin the 'novel': author, reader, realist style, mode of communication, formal organisation. In doing so he shows how the writing of historical novels can bring into question the legitimacy of multiple institutions and discourses, and demonstrates the aesthetic range and power of the form.

UMBERTO ECO, *THE NAME OF THE ROSE* AND DETECTIVE FICTION

Much postmodern fiction dramatises the search for a truth which self-evidently cannot be found; the signifier cannot relate to the signified. The obsession with linguistic immanence, the unremarked chaos of the world and the complication of textual evidence has led many postmodern authors to use the figure of the detective or investigator in their work. The idea of the scholar-as-detective has proved especially attractive to authors: 'Literary critics make natural detectives,' claims a character in A. S. Byatt's *Possession* (1991: 238). The analogue between scholarship, in particular the approach of the academic historian, and the investigator is the search for palpable truth through deductive reasoning. The historian-hero-investigator is a regular figure in popular culture, from Indiana Jones to Robert Langdon in *The Da Vinci Code* (de Groot 2008: 49–57). In Robert Harris's *Archangel* the historian is explicitly compared to the investigator: Fluke Kelso, the acacemic hero, finds 'an aesthetic pleasure in the sheer detective work of research' (Harris 2000: 55). The historian here is seen as someone who seeks solutions through the arrangement of evidence and the stories of witnesses; but who also needs to be careful about believing the wrong thing. The detective as historian often 'presupposes the existence of one prior, correct version of the past, at which it is possible to arrive by a careful process of recovery, and to which it is imperative to owe allegiance' (O'Gorman 1999:

20). However, the story of the detective novel is often that of the detective's search for truth, rather than the story of the crime itself. Tzvetan Todorov concluded that there were two interlocking stories, with one absent:

> The first, that of the crime, is in fact the story of an absence: its most accurate characteristic is that it cannot be immediately present in the book ... The status of the second story is, as we have seen, just as excessive; it is a story which has no importance in itself, which serves only as a mediator between the reader and the story of the crime. Theoreticians of detective fiction have always agreed that style, in this type of literature, must be perfectly transparent, imperceptible; the only requirement it obeys is to be simple, clear, direct. It has even been attempted – significantly – to suppress this second story altogether.
>
> (Todorov 1977: 46)

Todorov here points to a series of absences and narratives which are somehow hidden or unseen. This has led many detective novels to mourn the fact that meaning is generally absent and that life is chaotic. Postmodern detective fiction, such as that by Paul Auster or Jorge Luis Borges, for instance, emphasises the strangeness and futility of the attempt to discover the solution to the crime (Marcus 2003: 250).

Umberto Eco's novel *The Name of the Rose* (1980) combines the scholar-detective trope and the detective-historical fiction format (see Chapter 4). The novel demonstrates how the historical detective novel at once clearly upholds generic values but allows the innovative literary writer to actively undermine and attack notions of 'truth', decipherment and order. The novel concerns the investigation by a monk of a set of murders taking place in a remote monastery in 1327. It is written by one of the protagonists, Adso, whose translated narrative eventually reaches a scholar, who publishes it. *The Name of the Rose* clearly plays with generic tropes. The central character is the monk William of Baskerville, referencing both Arthur Conan Doyle's *The Hound of the Baskervilles* (1902) and the logician William of Ockham whose tenet **Ockham's razor** informs Sherlock Holmes's logic. More profoundly Eco uses the genre to reflect on the nature of knowledge, the systems of knowing that are deployed by societies and, ultimately, to consider that the world is chaotic and not subject to any collecting principle (McHale 1992: 147–64).

Ultimately, despite the ordering systems and epistemologies that the book presents, represented formally by such techniques as the organisation of the text according to the Christian day (from Matins to Compline), the situating of a map of the monastery at the beginning of the novel, and the action taking seven days, the world is seen to be destructive and disordered. As Eco pointed out in his 1984 'Postscript', 'this is a mystery in which very little is discovered and the detective is defeated' (cited in Marcus 2003: 257). Eco is clearly indebted to the labyrinthine fictions of Jorge Luis Borges and the narrative innovations of Alain Robbe-Grillet, writers who used the detective format to question and undermine knowledge systems (Marcus 2003: 253–6). The framing narrative of the lost manuscript is a key trope for Gothic novels, including prototype detective novels such as Robert Louis Stevenson's *The Master of Ballantrae* (1889) and James Hogg's *Confessions of a Justified Sinner* (1824). Eco's characteristically sly self-consciousness prefaces the framing narrative with the epigraph 'Naturally, a manuscript', referring simultaneously to the setting of the book in a learned abbey, the plot relating to a lost text, and the novel's literary ancestry (Eco 1984: v). The novel includes many other Gothic elements such as a dark forbidding library, secret passageways, cemeteries, the abbey setting. Gothic tropes offer a way of understanding the chaos of the world which is combated by the rationalism of William, but the spectral element of the Gothic is the creation of a fear of the loss of order which the final destruction of the library demonstrates. The framing of the narrative by suggesting that it is being transcribed from a lost manuscript is also an echo of the famous historical fiction of Alessandro Manzoni, whose *Betrothed* (1823) begins with the author's frustration at having to 'transcribe this story from this scratched and faded manuscript' and his eventual realisation that 'the sequence of events [could] be taken from the manuscript and the language recast' (Manzoni 1997: 4, 5). Both novelists use their approach to suggest an authenticity to their work whilst simultaneously pointing to the partiality of historical evidence.

A good example of this is found in the enigmatic title of the book. It gestures towards meaning, literally the discovery of the 'name' and what the 'rose' is, but the reader is never actually allowed to discover what this might mean. The final words of the 'past' narrative express the regret of Adso remembering his story that he cannot come to knowledge of what happened. 'Of the rose of the past, we have only its name,' he writes, although he does so in Latin ('stat rosa pristina nomine, nomina nuda tenemus'; Eco 1983: 502), once again introducing a deferral of meaning, as the reader would either have to translate or miss the reference. The use of untranslated Latin throughout the text is a way of creating levels of knowledge and disclosure, of playing academic tricks on the reader. Adso's quote strongly suggests the distance that the past has from the present, and the inability of memory to connect the two. He says of telling his own story: 'it is a hard thing for this old monk, on the threshold of death, not to know whether the letter he has written contains some hidden meaning, or more than one, or many, or none at all' (Eco 1983: 501). The past is a foreign country, known only through words that make little sense, and constantly moving out of reach. William's final lament bitterly recognises this: 'I have never doubted signs, Adso; they are the only things man has with which to orient himself in the world. What I did not understand was the relation among signs ... I behaved stubbornly, pursuing a semblance of order, when I should have known well that there is no order in the universe' (Eco 1983: 492).

'THE SOUND OF GHOSTS LAUGHING SADLY': MAGICAL REALISM AND HISTORY

There are other, similarly international, types of metafictional querying of the discourses of the past. Indeed, the dynamism of fictional approaches to history during the 1980s and 1990s once again demonstrates the potentiality of the historical fiction as form. Colombian Gabriel García Márquez's novel *One Hundred Years of Solitude* (*Cien años de soledad*) was originally published in Argentina in 1967, and therefore is contemporaneous with John Fowles's narrative experimentation. García Márquez's purpose is very different from that of Fowles, although, in many ways, his anti-realist impetus has similar motivations. García Márquez is the key exponent of what is known as **magical realism**, a style much associated with Latin American writers of the 1970s and 1980s. Magical realism adds to the European tradition of realism elements such as myth, magic, mysticism and nature: 'a narrative style which consistently blurs the traditional realist distinction between fantasy and reality' (Williamson 1987: 45). As such it provides a querying of the representational strategies of realism much as postmodern narrative techniques do. The style's 'ironic interplay' of seemingly fantastical and realist tropes means that it [magical realism] undermines itself continually: 'In spite of its ostensible fusion of fantasy and fact, magical realism is conceived as a wilfully specious discourse that inevitably betrays its hallucinatory character in the very act of its being read' (Williamson 1987: 47). Magical realism is therefore a type of metafiction, a self-conscious style which draws attention to itself and, quite consciously, points to the speciousness of realism. In its very uncertainty, in the lack of explanation of strange and wonderful things and, indeed, the embedding and effacement of such things within the narrative as if they were straightforward, magical realism subverts fiction in the same way that metafiction points to fiction's artificiality.

One Hundred Years of Solitude concerns the Buendía family and how their fortunes intertwine with the town, Macondo, which they founded in a marshy area of an unnamed South American country. The Buendías undergo multiple experiences from the clearly magical (a plague of insomnia, the ascension to heaven of a girl known as Remedios the Beauty) to the non-specifically political (a civil war, a massacre of striking workers). Michael Wood has argued that the keynote of the novel is loneliness, solitude and doom, 'the sound of ghosts laughing sadly', and he notes that the novel is written in a 'retrospective future tense', somehow invoking nostalgia whilst also introducing melancholy (Wood 1987: 38, 39). García Márquez's novel obsesses on ghostliness and the idea of the past inhabiting the present. The spectres in the novel are not warnings or manifestations but somehow physical renderings of the past (one ghost is woken up by being urinated on, for instance; García Márquez 1978: 216). These spectral shadows are mournful presences with no polemic or educational virtue, they simply infect the present. The founding of Macondo, for instance, is due to Jose Buendía's need to leave his home town in order to avoid the guilt that a ghost continually reminds him of.

Historical movement is measured in abstract terms in the novel, such as through social and technological progress, represented by the coming of the railroad, the invention of the electric light bulb or the imposition of government on the community. *One Hundred Years of Solitude* provides an ephemeral, playful, epic, dynastic history which explores through the development of a family and a town the creation of a set of identities. The novel's technique is conceptual, impressionistic and insubstantial: it 'contains all History, synthesizing it in symbolic episodes' (Gullon 1971: 30). Slowly the magic of community and self-determination is lost as the village becomes isolated and forgetful. At one point the matriarch Úrsula sighs, 'the world is slowly coming to an end and those things [magic] don't come here any more' (García Márquez 1978: 154). Later this affects her in a physical way: 'once again she shuddered with the evidence that time was not passing, as she had just admitted, but that it was turning in a circle' (García Márquez 1978: 272). Towards the end of the novel the town's introspective nature leads to alienation and loneliness: 'The indolence of the people was in contrast to the voracity of oblivion, which little by little was undermining memories in a pitiless way' (García Márquez 1978: 280). Rather than develop as a place and, by extension, as a nation, the town is doomed to circularity. This is demonstrated by the recycling of names as each new generation of Buendías is named after the first.

As Williamson argues, the degeneracy of Macondo is due to its 'progressive evasion of history' (Williamson 1987: 61). The novel condemns the town, isolated and introspective, never to break its cycle. **Metonymically** Macondo is Latin America, doomed to fail repeatedly through history, to be marginal and ejected. At the conclusion of the novel the town's isolation leads to its obliteration. The final Buendía, Aureliano Babilonia, begins to decipher mysterious documents that have been kept in the family house for decades, and as he reads the prophecy of Macondo's end the settlement is beset by a fearful biblical wind that tears it apart, 'because races condemned to one hundred years of solitude did not have a second opportunity on earth' (García Márquez 1978: 336). The inhabitants of the village have not made any impression on history, and their inaction has led to their destruction. The conclusion of the novel is bleak and mysterious, seemingly prophesying or accounting for a dreadful inertia that is punishable by being totally forgotten. The people of Macondo are slothful and introverted, and they are finally destroyed as a consequence. The solitude of the novel's title is therefore a state of isolation and a concomitant loss of agency and direction.

Indian-British writer Salman Rushdie similarly deploys a variety of semi-fantastical magical elements to undermine and question historical narrative in *Midnight's Children* (1981). The novel follows the life of Saleem Sinai, born in 1947 on the stroke of independence in India (hence a child of midnight). Like *One Hundred Years of Solitude* the novel follows a loose allegory for the history of the newly freed country in order to comment upon and engage with paradigms of nationalism. The novel is dynamic, anti-linear, and interested in the binary relationship between chaos and order (Gurnah 2007: 97). By following the modern history of India, from war to terrorism, and analysing the hangover of empire, the novel queries the formation of nationhood. Rushdie cited *One Hundred Years of Solitude* as instrumental in his writing of *Midnight's Children*, and critics have suggested that he took from García Márquez 'a theory of fantasy which is referred to colonialism' and 'the presence of the magical in the everyday' (Gurnah 2007: 100). Furthermore, the complexity of the novel's reference points demonstrates its interest in multiplicity: 'Though Saleem Sinai narrates in English ... his intertexts for both writing history and writing fiction are doubled: they are, on the one hand, from Indian legends, films, and literature and, on the other, from the West – *The Tin Drum*, *Tristram Shandy*, *One Hundred Years of Solitude*, and so on' (Hutcheon 1989: 65). Rushdie's subsequent novel *Shame* (1983) similarly used magical realist techniques to explore the violent history of Pakistan. Magical realism, then, at the level of style and narrative, seems to be implicitly anticolonial and politicised through its engagement with questions of order, rationality and enforcement. In its rejection and interrogation of ways of marshalling 'reality' it celebrates complexity, hybridity and exploration of otherness. In a very clear sense Rushdie challenges traditional modes of relating 'truth', particularly those associated with the writing of history and especially the history of nation.

Rushdie suggested in his writing on the novel that he wished to demonstrate 'the provisional nature of all truths, all certainties', and pointed up the partialness of his novel: '*Midnight's Children* is far from being an authoritative guide to the history of post-imperial India' (Rushdie 1991: 12, 23). In contrast to many of the characters in historical novels, Saleem thinks that he is central to India's development, a **metonym** for the nation. The novel, though, explicitly challenges historical narratives and undermines models of progress and the mythmaking of nationhood. Indeed, the unreliability of the novel's narration is the point for Rushdie. His words here demonstrate for us the ways in which all post-modern fiction of this kind strives to undermine rational, logical, positivist ways of thinking about consciousness:

> History is always ambiguous. Facts are hard to establish, and capable of being given many meanings. Reality is built on our prejudices, misconceptions and ignorance as well as our perceptiveness and knowledge. The reading of Saleem's unreliable narration might be, I believed, a useful analogy for the way in which we all, every day, attempt to 'read' the world.
>
> (Rushdie 1991: 25)

Rushdie here elides history, fact, reality and perception. Indian history, nationhood and identity in the novel are all unreliably defined, because they are all reliant on the interpretation of multivalent 'facts'. In her work on metafiction Waugh cites the **uncertainty principle** of physicist Werner Heisenberg to argue that 'it is impossible to describe an objective world' (Waugh 1984: 3). This idea of ambiguity is what Rushdie is illustrating here. The world is simply a set of discourses and pieces of evidence which we read and interpret in particular ways.

History, for these writers, is a key discourse to trouble, to fragment and rupture, because of its proto-realist, nationalist, evidentiary striving for objectivity. Magical realism, or at least the infusing of narratives with mystical and mythical elements, is often deployed by writers of historical fiction with a view to undermining mainstream models, to creating a sense of ephe-merality, and to critique ideas of nationhood, identity and story-telling itself. In its attack on the supposed legitimacy of the realist mode it is part and parcel of the metafictional-postmodern project and its desire to undermine larger totalising narratives. Magical realism tends less harshly and possibly less consciously (and, one might argue, less pompously or obviously) than meta-fiction to introduce melancholia, bleakness and sadness into the novel form.

'TAP-DANCING ON THE EDGE OF THE ABYSS': PROBLEMATISING POSTMODERNISM THROUGH HISTORY

One problem with postmodernism as a set of approaches might be that it does not allow for a politically engaged set of writings. Indeed, postmodern historiography, and postmodernism in general, have been attacked for their refusal to allow for progressive change, and their attempts at rendering culture and society poli-tically inert (Jameson 1996; Eagleton 1997). Angela Carter's comment on this is characteristically abrasive and specific: 'a whole lot of the post-modernists were sort of tap-dancing on the edge of the abyss' (cited in Day 1998: 12). This brilliantly cap-tures the worrying sense of postmodernism being about overt display for its own sake, and the possible disaster – the slip into darkness – that it might facilitate in its narcissism. In particular, for **feminists** the possible illusions of postmodernism were obvious: in attacking grand narratives such thinking shut down the possibility of political progress and programmatic change. However, as Waugh argues, postmodernism and feminism share certain concerns, intending 'to disrupt traditional boundaries' particularly between the dominant and marginal in culture, and this overlap suggests common ground, particularly 'leading to an unprecedented aesthetic self-consciousness and awareness of the problematic situation of the contemporary writer in relation to historical actuality and fictional tradition' (Waugh 1989: 6; Anderson 1990).

Diana Wallace argues that certain feminist postmodern historical novels 'contest the idea of a single, unitary and linear history. They emphasize the subjective, fragmentary nature of historical knowledge' (Wallace 2005: 202). A good example of this is Margaret Atwood's *Alias Grace*, which interweaves contradictory narrative, quotations from contemporary sources and fictional characters to present a clearly feminist postmodern interpretation of the trial and subsequent reputation of a notorious murderess.

Atwood attacks various discrepancies in the case, highlights problems concerning mental illness and suggests that the 'facts' of the matter are extremely hard, indeed almost impossible, to establish. Her contention is that the public arraigning of Grace Marks since her imprisonment in 1843 was part of the workings of an aggressive dominant patriarchy. She writes, 'I have of course fictionalized historical events (as did many commentators on this case who claimed to be writing history)' (Atwood 1997: 547). Atwood's conscious stylisation of undecidability here shows how the lessons of postmodernism might politically problematise 'reality' and history.

More conceptually, Angela Carter's own 1984 novel *Nights at the Circus* goes some way to illustrating how the various modes of metafiction and allied postmodern techniques might be deployed to create a state of indeterminacy which in itself is challenging, interrogative and deeply politicised. Carter was a very committed feminist, an astute literary critic and extremely politically aware as a novelist. She argued for a committed writing, claiming that 'narrative is an argument stated in fictional terms' (Sage 1996: 50). For Carter art was a way of understanding the world and as such it was of vital importance. At the same time, she had a clear sense of the time in which she was writing as somehow contributing to her ability to conceptualise indeterminacy and to write revelatory, hopeful work: 'The sense of limitless freedom that I, as a woman, sometimes feel is that of a new kind of being. Because I simply could not have existed, as I am, in any other preceding time or place. I am the pure product of an advanced, industrialised, post-imperialist country in decline' (Carter 1997).

This sense of the 'new' woman that is made possible through the development of history is something which imbues *Nights at the Circus*, with its central character the circus *aérialiste* Fevvers, who claims to have been not born but hatched. 'Is she fact or is she fiction?' those about her ask, and the journalist sent to expose her wonders whether she has a navel, that definer of the physical body's identity as human (Carter 1994: 7; Botting 1999). Fevvers compares herself to the family of the progenitor of Western history: Helen, the daughter of Leda, raped by Zeus as a swan, who provokes the Trojan War and all that follows (Carter 1994: 7). Yet she also claims to be originless, and creates herself through her performances on-stage and off: 'the central part of the novel turns upon the circus ring, where identities (and the boundaries between male and female, animal and human) are blurred, inverted, reformed' (Bannock 1997: 201).

Nights at the Circus is set in 1899, 'as the last cobwebs of the old century blow away', and its musing on history and subjectivity demonstrates how the postmodern novel might help articulate the indeterminacy of self (Carter 1994: 39). By demonstrating how definitions of gender, sexuality, anthropocentrism and class are all social and cultural constructs, Fevvers shows how one might create an identity through manipulating the various performances of selfhood, gesturing towards a space of unmediated possibility away from definition and oppression. Fevvers's refusal to be originated, her celebration of matrilineal orders and non-traditional family units, and her desire to create herself, all involve a key element of agency and transgression. She is aware and able to challenge social and cultural norms. Indeed, she desires to do so, and in enacting her own identity she demonstrates how legitimating discourses of self are mere constructs created to hold people in place. However, it is Walser, the rational male journalist, who loses his personality in the circus:

> Walser's very self, as he had known it, departed from him, he experienced the freedom that lies behind the mask, within dissimulation, the freedom to juggle with being, and, indeed, with the language which is vital to our being, that lies at the heart of burlesque.
>
> (Carter 1994: 103)

For all Carter's worry about tap-dancing her concern here is to suggest that within performance lies the kernel of 'self'. Theatre, for Carter, is threatening and subversive because it allows us to play with identities and show them to be unreal. The ways in which self is defined, through masks, through dissimulation, through language, might be put off and transformed within the theatre, and shown to be just an act.

Fevvers's desire is for all women to experience the freedoms she has invoked for herself:

> And once the old world has turned on its axle so that the new dawn can dawn, then, ah, then! all the women will have wings, the same as I ... she will tear off her mind forg'd manacles, will rise up and fly away. The dolls' house doors will open, the brothels will spill forth their prisoners, the cages, gilded or otherwise, all over the world, in every land, will let forth their inmates singing together the dawn chorus of the new, the transformed –
>
> (Carter 1994: 285)

The echoing of literary history ('mind forg'd manacles' is from William Blake's poem 'London') and revelatory religious apotheosis make this a writing-back of both; an answer to male histories, both religious and textual. Fevvers takes what has been and changes it to allow her and her sisters freedom. There is a certain irony at play here. Carter's novel celebrates a potentiality which has not come true; it argues for a limbo-like transformative space which is not yet at hand. Fevvers's companion Lizzie is the real agent of historical change, a Marxist spy who foments revolution. ('It's going to be more complicated than that,' she replies to Fevvers's idealistic vision; Carter 1994: 286.) The novel is trapped in its historicity at times, striving to textually represent the possibility of social and cultural change whilst having to acknowledge that the ideals of 1899 are still not satisfied. Yet the very invocation of the possibility of spaces of difference, change and what has become defined as **queerness** demonstrates Carter's faith in the potential to move towards something new and hitherto unthought of: a type of history without oppression and control, but expansive and dynamic. The fault lines opened by the postmodern and post-structuralist interrogations of truth, history and realism might be explored by politically astute writers interested in representing possibility. In doing so, they implicitly interrogate two of the words used in the title of this book, 'historical' and 'novel', in order to create something new. But as has been argued throughout, this problematising of the contemporary self in the face of the historical is something which is innate to the genre.

This indeterminate space of possibility is also invoked by Jeannette Winterson in her novels *The Passion* (1987) and *Sexing the Cherry* (1989), which both use historical framework to make political points about identity and selfhood. Winterson similarly involves narrators who challenge anthropocentrism. Venice-dwelling Villanelle in *The Passion* has webbed feet, and *Sexing the Cherry*'s grotesque giant Dog-Woman can hold a dozen oranges in her mouth at once. Winterson is far more formally interrogative than Carter, undermining her versions of history in ways that are similar to those deployed by magical realists. Temporality in both books is interrupted, played with and broken up. In the novels, both of which take place in recognisable historical periods and meditate on the workings of history, Winterson highlights the indeterminacy and insubstantiality of chronological understanding:

> The future is foretold from the past and the future is only possible because of the past. Without past and future, the present is partial. All time is eternally present and so all time is ours. There is no sense in forgetting and every sense in dreaming. Thus the present is made rich. Thus the present is made whole.
>
> (Winterson 1987: 62)

Winterson's conscious undermining of history, her interleaving of past and present narratives, her playful interrupting of chronologies, is seen by Laura Doan and Sarah Waters as evidence of her radical purpose in writing:

> Winterson regards the past more as a useful site to rewrite, and thereby intervene in, history-making ... what appears as a mapping of the past in Winterson's work is in effect the postmodern appropriation of the trappings of history.
>
> (Doan and Waters 2000: 24)

Like Carter, Winterson uses the 'trappings of history' to comment upon and undermine history itself. As with all the writers considered in this chapter, the past is a place of deep conflict, and the ways in which our relation to that past is formulated, expressed and represented are problematic, difficult and nebulous. Winterson's appropriation of historical form and content, and her subsequent creation of a new space of experiment and freedom, demonstrate the ways in which through deploying postmodern aesthetic approaches writers might begin to reform and intervene in contemporary life. For Carter and Winterson writing about history allows the undermining of contemporary norms and the disrupting of models of identity, be they sexuality or gendered. As we will see at greater length in the next chapter, this interrogation and challenging of history has given writers the opportunity to deploy the form politically irrespective of a postmodern context.

6

CHALLENGING HISTORY

So far, the account of the historical novel that has been articulated has emphasised its strangeness as a form, and its possibility for involving complex and dissident readings. The historical novel fundamentally challenges subjectivities, offering multiple identities and historical story lines. Far from being a rigid, ordering structure History seems to provide a set of potentialities and possibilities. From its beginnings as a form the historical novel has queried, interrogated and complicated fixed ideas of selfhood, historical progression, and objectivity. This became something that was explicitly undertaken in political fashion in postmodern fiction, but had been characteristic of the genre before that. This final chapter considers further ways that historical fiction might be a disruptive genre, a series of interventions which have sought to destabilise cultural hegemonies and challenge normalities. The chapter considers how the concepts of the former chapters like the fragmentation of narrative voice, pastiche, the unravelling of genre have been applied in contemporary writing. Whilst some critics of the postmodern historical novel like Fredric Jameson see it shorn of political significance, indeed actively destructive, the work considered in this chapter mitigates against this reading. Historical fiction, the chapter suggests, provides a space for political intervention and reclamation; for innovation and destabilisation. The chapter is in many ways about how historical fiction can report from places made marginal and present a dissident or dissenting account of the past. However, in some of the later sections we see how alternative readings and writings of the past can be used to support a reactionary agenda. In particular, though, we look at revisionist views of history that reclaim the past on behalf of a variety of unheard voices. We also look at the ways that History is challenged, both by the telling of dissident stories and by the positing of alternative realities.

The chapter, then, looks at how historical fiction has been used to challenge the mainstream. In particular we look at how accepted history has been disputed and how untold atrocities have been uncovered in a fictional context. This demonstrates how the historical novel can advocate ideological positions, mourn a lost history or attack the mainstream version of events for polemic and political purposes. However, as has been argued throughout, such conflicted histories have been central to the form since its inception. These reconsiderations of past events have significance for present identity, particularly national, and therefore these novels suggest the ways in which the historical novel might make a clear contemporary political intervention. This, though, has been queried by some critics, as the discussion of E. L. Doctorow's *Ragtime*, below, shows.

CONFLICTED NATIONAL HISTORIES

Historical novelists have been long interested in the discussion of nation creation; from Scott onward the substantiation of a sense of national identity has been part of the historical writer's purpose and mode of working. However, such writing has equally been concerned with the destruction, querying or troubling of the foundational myths of history. This is particularly obvious if we consider three particular examples: the United States, Ireland and Australia. Each of these countries has a modern history rich in foundational myth: the old West; the Easter uprising of 1916 and its aftermath; the Outback and the pioneering spirit. These narratives of national creation have been repeatedly questioned by novelists seeking to rethink the ways in which nations, and therefore national identity, are constructed. Obviously the historiography of each of these countries is significantly debated, and, particularly in the case of Ireland, the significance of particular events and historical occurrences is still conflicted; these novels merely use the space created by such dissonance to situate their practice.

Cormac MacCarthy's influential and ambiguous *Blood Meridian or The Evening Redness in the West* (1985) tracks the unnamed 'kid' in his horrifically violent journey through frontier America and Mexico in 1849. The 'kid' joins a group called the Glanton gang, who historically existed, and some of the book is based on one of the gang's memoirs. They are a loose collection of mercenaries who undertook scalping expeditions on the Mexican–American border, hunting down and killing Indians for profit. Written in a dry, unflinching style, the novel undermines the myths of the American west by reminding the reader that the amoral nation was founded upon death, violence, rape and domination. The book is almost unbearably graphic in its violence and horror, including hangings, death by starvation, scalping and various gun battles. It is clearly a historical novel in its use of source materials such as diaries and newspapers. The novel's discussion of a particular historical moment is an attempt at demystifying it, undermining an earlier, romanticised image. 'This looks like the high road to hell to me,' says a soldier at one point, and this sense of the bloody and sinful within the nation's past is key to the novel's purpose (MacCarthy 1990: 45). MacCarthy therefore uses his novel to interrogate the sense of a nationhood forged in pioneering, instead seeing America as party to vicious, violent territory grabbing and aggressive annexation. This is something commonly undertaken by the modern western film, for instance. Other key historical novels to explore historical–contemporary Americanness in similar probing fashion are E. L. Doctorow's *Ragtime* (1977), Don DeLillo's *Libra* (1988), Nathaniel Hawthorne's *The Scarlet Letter* (1850) and even James Fenimore Cooper's *The Last of the Mohicans* (1826). For Fredric Jameson *Ragtime* suggests the final empty joke of the postmodern engagement with history, an empty set of representations concerned only with the textualised idea of the past rather than its reality, 'the historical novel as postmodern artifact, a monument to the waning of content and the primacy of the image' (Shiller 1997: 539). Yet, as has been argued in the previous chapter, the novel as interrogative mode of historical enquiry is a reading which is as valid as Jameson's. As the examples discussed here suggest, through their consideration of history as malleable text and complex entity novels can point to a new and politically dissident reading of the past and the present. Indeed, the historical novel's self-awareness is part of its generic make-up, a fundamental element of the form.

Throughout the 1990s James Ellroy and Walter Mosley reinvigorated the hard-boiled crime genre, writing significant novels reclaiming the history of Los Angeles and, like McCarthy, rewriting the myths surrounding the formation of nationhood and American identity. Their approach to genre fiction deconstructs the genre formally, stylistically and in terms of content. Both novelists use their historical settings to comment ironically upon the present and also to reveal the rotten underbelly of the American twentieth century. Their work demonstrates the generic self-awareness inherent in the historical and its ability as a form to subvert.

James Ellroy's hard-boiled historical novels take a very familiar genre, the *noir* thrillers of Dashiell Hammett, Jim Thompson and, most of all, Raymond Chandler, and wrench them apart. His 'LA Quartet' (1987–92) presents the violent, corrupt, racist Los Angeles of the 1940s and 1950s. Ellroy shows the reader that the central idealisations of American life such as Hollywood, music, the press, politics, the police, the city, nationalism are grimy, violent and filthy. Even linguistically his books destroy order, using slang and distorting syntax until the reader is disorientated. Ellroy's writing works to undermine iconic figures such as Howard Hughes, Frank Sinatra and Martin Luther King by portraying them as paranoid, violent, sex-obsessed, drug-peddling, power-crazed horrors. Ellroy uses his historical fiction to point to an inherent violence in America that is given a conservative sheen by the actions of nostalgia. In idealising the past society misses this. The revealing of the viciousness beneath the patina of respectability in American institutions comes to its baroque conclusion in his political 'secret history' trilogy *American Tabloid* (1995), *The Cool Six Thousand* (2001) and due to conclude in 2009 with *Blood's a Rover*. *American Tabloid* covers the period 1958–63 and includes the Bay of Pigs invasion and the assassination of John F. Kennedy. Ellroy prefaces it with these words:

> America was never innocent. We popped our cherry on the boat over and looked back with no regrets. You can't ascribe our fall from grace to any single event or set of circumstances. You can't lose what you lacked at conception.
>
> Mass-market nostalgia gets you hopped up for a past that never existed. Hagiography sanctifies shuck-and-jive politicians and reinvents their expedient gestures as moments of great moral weight. Our continuing narrative line is blurred past truth and hindsight. Only a reckless verisimilitude can set that line straight.
>
> (Ellroy 1995: 5)

Ellroy's writing here attempts to attack all idealised versions of the American past in fiction and film, a past that 'never existed'. He argues against destructive realism, the 'reckless verisimilitude' that never looks below the shiny surface. It is not possible to look into the past to learn truth but to understand the chaos and grimness that is the present. Ellroy continues, 'It's time to demythologize an era and build a new myth ... to embrace bad men and the price they paid to secretly define their time' (Ellroy 1995: 5). Like McCarthy, Ellroy goes back to the foundational myths of contemporary society in order to destroy them and expose their innate falsity and hypocrisy.

More overtly politically, Walter Mosley presents the reader with an unseen, previously marginalised historical Los Angeles in his Easy Rawlins novels. Mosley puts his 'black detective narrator in a previously invisible textual location', setting his stories in the black suburb of Watts during the 1940s and 1950s and reclaiming a black post-war *noir* experience (Berger 1997: 281; Cochrane 2000). Part Chester Himes's flawed hero, part Raymond Chandler's maverick private eye, Easy Rawlins is a complex, transgressive, engaging and lean creation (McCracken 1990: 168). *Devil in a Blue Dress* (1990) is his initiation into the murky criminal interface between white and black worlds. Rawlins aspires to be his own man, to own property, to have a good job, but is constantly undermined by outside social forces beyond his control. The only way to shirk the implacable definition white America has prepared for him is to go outside of normal social interaction, to live beyond the law whilst appearing to be the very model of propriety. *A Red Death* (1991) is the sequel to *Devil in a Blue Dress*. It continues Mosley's reinvigoration of the genre, but it also extends and develops the *noir* novel. *A Red Death* moves from the relatively simple genre paradigms and moral simplicity of *Devil in a Blue Dress* to consider communism, civil rights, espionage, government corruption and an increasingly complex sense of national/racial identity. Whilst *Devil in a Blue Dress* gestures towards a preoccupation with wider issues than the genre novel was able to deal with (racism, government corruption, paedophilia, interracial relationships, mortgages), it is still in thrall to its formal plot concerns. *A Red Death* eschews such a generically narrative-led approach for a wide-ranging meditation on Americanness. It is the imperative to live outside of social norms that provides the backdrop to *A Red Death* and begins the sequence of events that leads inexorably towards death and guilt. Easy Rawlins has become a better person: attending college courses, helping the community out, enjoying the sunshine, going to church. Yet the government will not allow him to be, and the Internal Revenue Service (IRS) comes calling about the apartment blocks of which he is the (anonymous) owner. Forced to become an FBI informer, he infiltrates the First African Church to spy on a Jewish communist dissident and find some missing persons. He also has various people pursuing him for various reasons, suicidal tenants, church deacons dying during fellatio, house repossession and a growing political conscience to deal with. The plot sprawls to eventually encompass prostitution, betrayal, the Holocaust, African nationalism, manufacturing industry and the status of the black man in 1950s America. Mosley integrates important concepts with street language, moving from violence to tenderness with assurance. The relationship between black and white becomes more nuanced and complicated, although there are still racist institutions, policemen and IRS agents, and Easy is trapped in a society that oppresses him because of his colour. In the left-wing Jew Chaim Wenzler we are presented with a man whom Easy trusts and comes to love. African nationalism is considered briefly. Easy ends up friendless, loverless, nearly hopeless; he has won back his reputation and his money but in the process sacrificed nearly everything, forced to betray and spy just to keep his status as a struggling but comfortable member of society.

Mosley's novels write about black experience within a generic format, challenging first a white history as well as the fictional culture which marginalises black writing. He offers an alternative History, as well a separate literary history, and although critics have argued that his approach is somewhat 'muted' and ambivalent (Berger 1997: 281) the novels' metacritical element, interrogating their genre and the history they write about, enables them to be texts which challenge and subvert the format of the historical crime novel. He challenges what is effectively a white form and undermines it through his reorganisation of its tropes and his rewriting of the *actual* historical period which white *noir* fiction covered. The Rawlins novels intentionally interrogate boundaries of race, genre and culture in order to query the dominant modes. As McCracken argues, whilst popular fiction generally has a transgressive potential, 'the use of that potential for a particular project requires a sophisticated narrative which can relate the symbolic and the social for liberation rather than domination' (McCracken 1990: 174).

Irish novelists have often used historical fiction to consider nationalism through analysis of key events, in particular the uprising of 1916 and its aftermath. Sebastian Barry's *A Long Long Way* (2006; also discussed above, in Chapter 4) is a revisionary account of the First World War. Barry considers how the war was not for those who fought it:

'Now, Tolstoy wrote about wars. But not like this war. In his war you could still go home and fall in love with a lady ... Well, maybe it i'n't so very different. Maybe not. Anyway, they don't write books about the likes of us. It's officers and high-up people mostly.'

(Barry 2006: 232)

The character speaking, an Englishman, considers that the subject of a novel is emphatically not the common soldiers. Barry's book clearly refutes this. The intertextual reference to Tolstoy, a historical novelist whose idea of history seems elitist now, is common for a historical novelist, a self-referentiality which can be traced throughout the genre. The people Barry depicts fighting the war are Irish, pressed into service to protect a nation that is not their own. Willie Dunne, the naive-innocent hero, is part of a unit which is gassed, attacked, and mostly destroyed. At one point they are sent back to Ireland to put down the uprising, Irish troops used against Irish rebels. One of the rebels attempts to take him prisoner, calling him 'Tommy' (Barry 2006: 92) before being shot by an officer. The defence of the Post Office is described by Dunne as 'a most queer moment of ill-fitting likelihood' (Barry 2006: 87), and the sense of unreality continues through this section:

> 'Step back in, Private,' called the captain. 'Don't parley with the enemy.'
> 'What enemy?' said Willie Dunne. 'What enemy, sir?'
> 'Keep back away, or I will shoot him.'
>
> (Barry 2006: 88)

Later Willie asks a dying Irish rebel if he is German: 'We're all Irishmen in here, fighting for Ireland' (Barry 2006: 92). Barry's novel queries the glory and honour of the war effort, presenting it as an event alienated twice from the characters; through class (it is not their war) and nation (it is fought for another country). Another account of the Irish uprising and subsequent civil war is Roddy Doyle's *A Star Called Henry* (1995). Doyle's novel follows a man who becomes an IRA gunman in the rebel army before his eventual disillusionment with the cause:

> Another martyr for old Ireland.
> I was going. I couldn't stay here. Every breath of its stale air, every square inch of the place mocked me, grabbed at my ankles. It needed blood to survive and it wasn't getting mine. I'd supplied it with plenty.
>
> (Doyle 2000: 342)

Henry realises he is expendable, a tool used by others to further their own ends. Similar to Barry, Doyle sees the uprising and subsequent civil war critically, returning to this most celebrated event in Irish history in order to re-examine what happened then and what it means now. Both writers are concerned with the interrogation of received opinion and, through a consideration particularly of the narratives of those marginalised from the historical story (the working classes), a recalibration of significance.

Finally in this discussion of writers returning to key national events, Peter Carey's *True History of the Ned Kelly Gang* (2001) looks at one of the enduring myths of colonial Australia. The novel takes the standard generic form of manuscripts 'discovered', a set of letters and accounts prepared for Kelly's daughter. It includes, for instance, cuttings from newspapers (with her mother's additional notes giving 'truer' information; Carey 2001: 349–56) and scraps about the cultural transmission and creation of the Kelly myth (Carey 2001: 404). This self-consciousness about historiography is postmodern in its analysis of the ways in which history is 'created', but it similarly militates against this by demonstrating the subjective construction of the past. Furthermore, the self-consciousness is something which has been part of the historical novel throughout its manifestation. Carey similarly acknowledges a key generic trope when he accentuates the importance of intertextual historical romance narrative: Kelly reads and rereads R. D. Blackmore's *Lorna Doone* (Carey 2001: 403), for instance. The novel is told in Ned's stream of consciousness voice, particularly with his unpunctuated vernacular. It presents Kelly as worked upon by authority, as dignified and fair but continually attacked by weaker, vain authority figures. For much of the time Kelly's voice is not mediated by historians (or 'authors') but strives to tell the 'truth'. The working and labouring classes celebrate Ned, partying for the birth of his daughter, for instance: 'We proved there were no taint we was of true bone blood and beauty born' (Carey 2001: 387). Again, class is crucial in the construction of a dissident, alternative historical reading.

The novel suggests Kelly is a **metonym** for Australia, and constructs a national identity through perseverance, humour and desire for liberty; but this is troubling:

What is it about we Australians, eh? he demanded. What is wrong with us? Do we not have a Jefferson? A Disraeli? Might not we find

someone better to admire than a horse-thief and a murderer? Must
we always make such an embarrassing spectacle of ourselves?

(Carey 2001: 419)

The novel rehabilitates Kelly, warts and all, suggesting a foundational myth or national characteristic which is not an 'embarrassing spectacle' but forthright, dissident, alert and strangely
noble. At the same time, the desire to complicate through historical
fiction the understanding of key elements of the past that manifest
in contemporary national identity demonstrates the political
perspective and potentiality of the form.

HISTORY FROM THE MARGINS

As has been argued, historical fiction has been used to quarrel
with particular historical narratives. Historical novels have often
been used to reinsert communities into the past, rescuing them
from the marginal positions to which they have consciously been
consigned. This is the case in the former examples with the
working classes, for instance. The following sections further consider novels that present a dissident voice. In particular we will
concentrate on Toni Morrison's presentation of slaves' narratives,
Sarah Waters' revisionist lesbian reclamation of the Victorian
novel and Chinua Achebe's profound intervention in his country's
history. We will also analyse Hari Kunzru's response to E. M.
Forster in *The Impressionist* and consider the importance of colonial
history to contemporary identity.

Race and the loss of history

An extremely important and influential example of the ability of
historical fiction to voice an alternative, disquieting and destabi-
lising past is Toni Morrison's novel of American slavery, *Beloved*
(1987). As Kimberly Chabot Davis argues, the fictional return to
the legacies of slavery has the effect of reinvigorating a contemporary culture allegedly historically moribund and politically
inert (Chabot Davis 2002: 727). Novelists interested in the 'particular
concerns of marginalized communities haunted by a history of

oppression' use historical fiction to 'insist on the political urgency of rewriting history from the perspective of the disempowered' (Chabot Davis 2002: 728). Chabot Davis's point, discussing this trend of historical engagement, is that in returning to voice the marginalised and the oppressed novelists have found ways to explore the trauma of the past and also to add political urgency to their work. Dedicated to 'Sixty million and more', the estimated number of those who died in the slave trade, *Beloved* is a shocking and disturbing text (Morrison 2006: 3). The central character, Sethe, kills her own daughter in a fit of lunacy and despair whilst living on a slave plantation. Her story mirrors the case of Margaret Garner, who killed her daughter and attempted suicide when caught after escaping in Kentucky in 1856. The novel recounts the lives of Sethe and her family after they have escaped from Sweet Home plantation, but uses flashback and storytelling to return repeatedly to the events of that time.

Beloved is not a comfortable novel, and its version of history is shot through with sexual abuse, violence, child murder, torture, haunting, loss and despair. It presents the past as something where horrors happen, and as a place to be escaped. The characters in the novel attempt to suppress their traumatic past. However, it resurfaces as ghostly hauntings, or dreams, nightmares and visitations. Paul D., for instance, places his memories in a 'tobacco tin lodged in his chest'; when he arrives at the location of the novel 'nothing in this world could pry it open' (Morrison 2006: 133). Sethe's repression of her memory results in a ghostly visitation and the arrival of a new daughter, Beloved, whom she believes to be an incarnation of the child she killed. Through love and sadness the central characters attain a kind of acceptance and a way of forgetting, or at least being able to look forwards rather than backwards: 'me and you, we got more yesterday than anybody. We need some kind of tomorrow' (Morrison 2006: 314). The novel explores various ways of facing, understanding and living with the horrific events in the past. Much as the characters in the novel need to learn to support each other as a community in order to live with what has happened to them, American society needs to face its horrors so that it might eventually understand them and face them. More than most historical fictions *Beloved* dramatises the ways in which the past can haunt and inhabit the present, how in particular the violences of history are still being dealt with in the present. Morrison's novel rebuts the nostalgic versions of the American past found in such historical romance fictions as Margaret Mitchell's *Gone with the Wind* (1936). Mitchell's text expresses a strong sentimental fondness for the traditions of the past which have been destroyed by, among other things, the Civil War; the beauty and harmony of a society based upon slavery have been upset by a conflict undertaken to end it. *Beloved* demonstrates how historical novels can engage in political rewriting, outline the traumas of the past, rescue the marginalised and give voice to those who were silenced.

Gay and lesbian historical fiction

One of the key phenomena of the past twenty years has been the new visibility, popularity and reach of the gay and lesbian historical novel, both popular and literary, as evidenced, for instance, in the award of the Booker prize to Alan Hollinghurst in 2004 for *The Line of Beauty*. Historical novels involving gay and lesbian characters are not particularly new. Mary Renault's *The Persian Boy* (1972) narrates the story of Alexander the Great through the eyes of his slave and lover Bagoas, for instance. Gay and lesbian writers have explored particularly female social networks and lesbian relationships from Sylvia Townsend Warner's *The Corner that Held Them* (1948) to Doris Grumbach's *The Ladies* (1984). Fiction by gay and lesbian authors utilising the past has often been interested in the recovery of a hidden genealogy of sexuality (Doan and Waters 2000) or, as in the case of Edmund White's influential *A Boy's Own Story* (1982), have consisted of confessional **Bildungsroman** accounts of coming out.

Gay and lesbian historical fiction has regularly been interested in the creation of alternative histories or the reclaiming of marginalised narratives, particularly through the queering of either the physical or the trope of the archive:

> the queer archive, in its very existence and operation, brings about
> the *queering* of the concept of the archive – and the queering of

history, truth, evidence and authority, traditionally understood – where 'queering' involves a destabilisation that is conceived as necessarily subversive, and practically deconstructive.

(Mitchell 2009)

Gay and lesbian historical fiction deploys the archive in order to challenge heteronormative models of historiography, therefore articulating a sense of identity created *against* the mainstream archive, *without* that archive and constructed *despite* that archive. Such novels query/**queer** the notion of 'evidence' and in doing so interrogate the ways that the past and that history have been written and constructed.

This challenge to the physical tropes and discourses of straight history concurs with the mission that Laura Doan and Sarah Waters outline for lesbian historical fiction. In their influential article about lesbian historical fiction Doan and Waters argue that such writing has allowed authors to 'identify a lesbian tradition that has been both routinely overlooked by the historical record and calculatedly expunged from it' (Doan and Waters 2000: 17). This reclamation, however, is problematic. Doan and Waters suggest that writers eschew the search for a genealogy of sexuality because it becomes limiting in its reliance on mimicking heteronormative structures. Instead, through an interrogation or a 'jettisoning of generic structures altogether' (as is found in the work of Jeanette Winterson), writers might use history to illuminate 'the queer identities and acts against which modern lesbian narratives have defined themselves' (Doan and Waters 2000: 25). Lesbian historical fiction might allow the creation of a new set of possibilities, outside of (or at least not defined by) patriarchal, heteronormative bounds and historiographic limits. This argument militates against much criticism of historical fiction by querying the relationship between then and now. Doan and Waters argue that historical fiction should not help articulate a contemporary identity but, rather, might allow the complexity of varying identities to be possible (see also Bravmann 1997).

Sarah Waters's trilogy of Victorian novels (*Tipping the Velvet*, 1998, *Affinity*, 1999, *Fingersmith*, 2002) moved lesbian historical fiction into the mainstream of publishing and reading. It explores the unvoiced history of lesbian identities, as well as moving in the conclusions to point to ways to avoid, challenge or interrogate the types of identity formation that have been made available by a society wishing to order and constrain. *Fingersmith* ends with Maud admitting to Sue that she is now writing pornography, having been bound to curate her uncle's library of such writing in the earlier part of the novel. However, the writing of this erotic fiction then becomes a site of rebellion: 'It is filled with all the words for how I want you ... ,' she explains to an indignant Sue (Waters 2003: 547). As Mitchell argues, the 'pornography collection is, then, imaginatively resignified as a hidden history of female pleasure and desire – rather than a means of the objectification, imprisonment and abuse of women' (Mitchell 2009). In *Tipping the Velvet* the potentiality of dissidence is represented in two ways at the conclusion. First the idealised socialist fair in London's Victoria Park points to a new set of possibilities for all human beings. More important is the central character, Nan's, disavowal of the various 'types' of identity she has performed and worn throughout the novel in favour of a new, honest, scary unknown: 'Oh! I feel like I've been repeating other people's speeches all my life. Now, when I want to make a speech of my own, I find I hardly know you' (Waters 2002: 471). Even more than this, the structure of *The Night Watch* (2006), which is told backwards, means that in the midst of the early happiness of relationships is the understanding on the part of the reader of their destruction and subsequent bitterness. This novel is Waters's most formally challenging to date, and the 'reverse linearity is a way of dissenting and disrupting the hierarchies of normal historical knowledge' (de Groot 2008: 224).

Tipping the Velvet opens in conversational, personalising fashion: 'Have you ever tasted a Whitstable oyster? If you have you will remember it ... Did you ever go to Whitstable, and see the oyster-parlours there? My father kept one; I was born in it' (Waters 2002: 3). Quite apart from immersing the reader in the narrative, and assuming a conspiratorial (sensual) connection, the opening has a metanarrative aspect. The novel has been concerned with 'histories', a term which is used in relation to characters' pasts but which is also used technically by the boyish Dickie.

Dickie's 'history' has been told to and reprinted by a prototype sexologist concerned with 'perversion' and alternative sexual identities: 'It has been written by a man, in an attempt to explain our sort so that the ordinary world will understand us' (Waters 2002: 311). Nan is physically struck by this book by her unpleasant patroness Diana, who draws blood. The telling of a story, or one's 'history', becomes a more or less scientific articulation of identity, a statement of intimacy, a way of explaining, and something that might harm one. Nan moves through various recognisable stages of lesbian identity, from first infatuation to bored cynicism, before meeting Florence, who is importantly somehow undefinable in her gender and sexuality. In her happiness and attempt to explain herself to Flo, Nan tells her story. 'I took a breath. "Have you ever," I said, "been to Whitstable … ?" Once I began it, I found I could not stop' (Waters 2002: 430). Effectively, then, the entire 'history' of the novel has been Nan's confession to Flo, her account of the ways that she developed into what she is 'now'. This has the effect of bringing the narrative into the present, as if there has been an inevitability about the story as told, emphasised by the various *faux*-sensation-novel ominous sentences about what is going to happen next. However, in the diegetic moment of the novel the future now hangs in the balance, and Florence goes off to think about it and judge. The sense of inevitability is lost here and Nan appears finally to act rather than react to circumstances, to choose her future. The novel then allows her a glimpse of what she might become if she rejects her past in the person of her first love, Kitty, who arrives to ask for her back, and she commits to a future which is unclear but full of potential: 'Besides, I don't think it is an endless task. Things are changing' (Waters 2002: 391). They have a child, the son of Flo's former love, and live with Flo's radical brother, and in this strangely potential family unit is seen the possibility of a more hopeful future.

Nan travels through Victorian England from innocence to understanding and finally to a kind of quiet acceptance of herself, her sexuality and, most important, that her love for Flo is far more important than any of these other things. Throughout the first two **picaresque** sections of the novel Nan encounters a selection of possible lesbian identities. She begins her story in Whitstable as a girl obsessed with the music hall singer Kitty Butler. She becomes part of Butler's entourage, her lover and, eventually, her partner on stage in her male impersonation act. Nan regularly uses her acting skills in her life, either to get what she wants or sexually, or to give people what they want. The novel foregrounds issues of performance and drag and as such is a dramatisation of some of the central ideas of **queer theory**, in particular those articulated by Judith Butler. Butler argues that parody of heterosexuality, specifically drag, demonstrates how all sexual identities are constructs that might be interrogated and undermined. This happens in the possibilities that Nan's new career opens up to her, from the ability to live with Kitty to the newness of London. Furthermore, after her break-up with Kitty Nan impersonates a man in order to keep from harm in London and begins to make money as a 'renter', performing sexual acts for money with men who think she is a boy. Nan intentionally preys upon these men as a kind of revenge on the man who stole Kitty from her. This kind of 'perverse' complication of already complex identities (repressed homosexual Victorian man serviced by unacknowledged transvestite) points to a grim dynamism in historical sexual identities. It is unclear if Nan feels herself empowered by her ascendancy over the men or whether the episode is a bleak comment on the horrors of the unsatisfied and unfulfilled desire felt by them. She is then taken in by a powerful lesbian woman whose friends dress at costume parties as historical 'archetypes' such as the Ladies of Llangollen, Sappho or Marie Antoinette. During this period she often wears a dildo, mimicking and also mocking maleness but also rendering the masculine redundant at a sexual level. What the novel points to is that gender, sexuality and identity are all in a state of some flux, and that this dissonance is hardly a 'modern' phenomenon. Waters has argued that the historical period of her work is integral to what she is doing: 'I think we have a duty to take history seriously – not simply to use it as a backdrop or for the purposes of nostalgia. This, for me, means writing a fiction with, hopefully, something meaningful to say about the social and cultural forces at work in the period I'm writing about' (Waters 2006). Her work reinserts a set of lesbian narratives into history whilst simultaneously raising the possibilities of something entirely new, or at least of a way of avoiding the mistakes of the past in favour of a potential future.

Alan Hollinghurst's *The Line of Beauty* is very different in its version of historical fiction, but it similarly involves a protagonist who is rejected by society that he clings to and who is seen in the end to be better than it. It is a novel of education, echoing particularly Dickens, but also about ageing, gaining a personal history for oneself and through that an understanding. It very heavily echoes Evelyn Waugh's *Brideshead Revisited*, with the middle-class cuckoo in the rich nest mainly observing and becoming a keeper of secrets. The book follows the protagonist Nick as he becomes attached to the family of a boy he lusts after at university and discovers their various secrets and strangnesses. The father of the family is a Conservative MP, and the plot follows the rise and fall of Thatcherism and the increasingly apparent social vileness of that particular project. Tonally the book echoes Henry James, the writer Nick is studying for his PhD, in allowing the elegant characters just enough rope to hang themselves:

> 'What would Henry James have made of us, I wonder?' she went on.
> 'Well ... ' Nick chewed it over. He thought she was rather like a high-minded aunt, proposing questions with virginal firmness and ignorance ... He said, 'He'd have been very kind to us, he'd have said how wonderful we were and how beautiful we were, he'd have given us incredibly subtle things to say, and we wouldn't have realized until just before the end that he'd seen right through us.'
>
> (Hollinghurst 2004: 140)

The book sees history as a place for revelation, as a backdrop for self-articulation, and, ultimately (as in Edmund White's *Farewell Symphony*, 1997), as a place of sadness and melancholia. Nick receives the news of his lover Leo's death from AIDS on the day of the 1987 election, and Hollinghurst directly contrasts and frames his narrative with the historical events of the 1980s as the decade grows old and weary. The novel itself has a formal notion of historicising, as it is the sequel to Hollinghurst's ground-breaking *The Swimming Pool Library* (1988), which was told in the 'now'. In the 'sequel' the 1980s have become history and understandable not in the moment but as being in the past, framed by hindsight and illness. Nick finally achieves a kind of separatist self-awareness when he is thrown out by Gerald the MP: 'he was seeing the history of his action, and seeing it as Leo himself had seen it, but distant and complete' (Hollinghurst 2004: 400). Ironic and complex, the novel again dissociates itself from any types of available identity, and particularly the ways of behaving that are being offered by a society demonstrably vituperative and corrupt (Mitchell 2006: 51). Of course, this book has argued throughout that historical fiction in general tends to query the commonplaces of **historiography**, and it follows therefore that gay and lesbian historical writing has found the form conducive to the more general cultural work of the queer project.

Women on the margins

One physical aspect of the reclaiming of the past, and the creation of an alternative (fictional) archive, is evidenced in Sylvia Townsend Warner's *The Corner that Held Them* when it was reprinted in 1993 by the feminist publishing house Virago. The novel had been out of print for decades, and its republishing demonstrates a desire to reclaim and recall lost texts by female writers. The reclaiming and creation of an alternative literary history was a politicised means of asserting a feminist agenda. Virago was particularly influential during the 1970s and 1980s in reprinting the works of key forgotten or marginalised women writers; as such it was a key part of second-generation Anglo-American feminist attempts to reclaim literary history. Elaine Showalter's *A Literature of their Own* (1977) and Sheila Rowbotham's *Hidden from History* (1973) influenced the introduction of particular lists such as Virago Modern Classics and the Virago Reprint Library. The press was founded in 1973 by Carmen Callil, Rosie Boycott and Marsha Rowe to publish books by and about women. A 'virago' originally meant a strong or warlike woman; after a while it became a shrewish scold. This double meaning suited the press, which was interested in reminding the patriarchal literary establishment that their stranglehold over publishing was at an end.

This reclamation of what was a term of insult figures the purpose and activity of the press. The reprinting of works such as Townsend Warner's novel and Radclyffe Hall's *The Well of Loneliness* (1928; published by Virago in 1982) demonstrates the ways that fiction could be used politically, and also how the act of reclaiming a writer might also reinvigorate particular ways of thinking about history through literature. Virago's work is about reclaiming a marginalised literary history through the use of textual signifiers, in this case books.

George Eliot's formulation in *Middlemarch* that 'the growing good of the world is partly dependent on unhistoric acts' (Eliot 1871 IV: 371) was in part an attack on a kind of patriarchal history that ignored or marginalised the actions of women. Historical fiction has often sought to explain the experience of those on the margins, and, in particular, to deal with the grim lives of women. Particularly, these novels demonstrate the ways that patriarchy ignores, violently controls or represses the desires of women, be they aristocrats or beggars. Sandra Gulland's *The Many Lives and Secret Sorrows of Joséphine B.* presents an historically visible woman, although one considered only for her relationship with the French military leader and emperor Napoleon. Gulland's account of the life of the empress Joséphine is written as a diary and is *faux* naive and direct in its presentation of the growth of the character. Gulland makes use of editorial footnotes to confirm or explain historical details; she also includes a chronological timeline of Joséphine's life and a bibliography. The novel gestures generically towards diary, autobiography and life-writing, suggesting a desire for personal revelation and understanding which is implicitly denied Joséphine in the wider social context. The scholarly apparatus also works to reinsert Joséphine back into the historical mainstream. Furthermore, the content of the novel undermines the romance of the couple in the popular imagination, suggesting instead that the marriage was unequal, unpleasant and unwanted: 'I am married. Again. My husband is not the man I dreamt of as a little girl, not my *grand amour*, and certainly not the king the fortune-teller had foretold. Only Buonaparte, strange little Napoleone. Now Napoléon' (Gulland 1995: 431). Rather than being the passionate relationship of cliché, the marriage between Napoleon and Joséphine is something which she neither seeks nor enjoys. Joséphine is a female character constrained by history to act in particular ways, and through her self-revelatory writing the reader is able to understand further the oppression of patriarchy.

A similar anti-romantic historical novel is Arthur Golden's *Memoirs of a Geisha* (1997), an account of an orphaned girl sold to a brothel. Whilst it ends relatively straightforwardly with the girl, Sayuri's, eventual escape to New York and love of a sort, the novel dramatises the horrors and restrictions of a particularly aggressive patriarchal society and in doing so points to the continued marginalisation, silencing and subjugation of women. Historical novels have often focused on the lack of options available to women within such constraining and ordering social ideologies and structures, and, in particular, have highlighted how prostitution and sex work have often been forced upon women because they are allowed no alternatives. Emma Donoghue's *Slammerkin* (2001) makes this connection plainer, in similar fashion to Atwood's *Alias Grace*, by fictionalising the true story of Mary Saunders, a girl executed for murder in 1764. *Slammerkin* is a novel about women who have nowhere to go and therefore become prostitutes. They are the flotsam of male history, forgotten and unloved. It is a novel of the ordinariness and inescapable grimness of life as a woman in a historical society. Donoghue rehearses the facts about poor women on the margins of society forced into selling their bodies, raped and abused, many frozen to death or hanged. There is an absence of 'history' as a process or liberating discourse rather than as a crushing horror. These types of novel are the antithesis of the romance fiction discussed in Chapter 3, although they have a deal in common with the feminist impulses of some of that work, such as that of Catherine Cookson, and also with the postmodernist fictions of Margaret Atwood, discussed in Chapter 5. They work within a particularly feminist vein of writing which is revisionist, recalling the ways in which women were oppressed. They are also comparative, in so far as they work by exposing the patriarchal exoskeleton of a historical society in order to suggest that such ideological effects still exist, albeit possibly unseen.

Anti-colonial fiction and identity

Other writers have used the opportunity afforded by the historical novel to concentrate on and respond to the cultural, political and social legacies and mechanisms of empire and colony. Much of this work has been written in the light of the critical writings of Edward Said and other theorists of **postcolonialism**. Postcolonialist theorists study work produced both by those under colonial rule and by the colonialists themselves; they furthermore analyse reactions to the collapse of colonialism and also interrogate contemporary Western attitudes to other cultures. Postcolonial theory discusses the state of being colonised and analyses how cultures respond to the process of subjection and marginalisation.

In his famous work *Orientalism* (1978) Said analysed the ways that culture serviced and sustained empire during the nineteenth century. He argued that what he termed 'Orientalism' is a way of describing and analysing the way that the West looks at the East. It therefore constructs a caricatured binary to sustain the economic, epistemic and cultural importance of Europe and further to contain the anxiety and unease provoked by the otherness of the East. In particular, Orientalism was a means for the West to constrain the East within particular narrow structures:

> Taking the late eighteenth century as a very roughly defined starting point Orientalism can be discussed and analyzed as the corporate institution for dealing with the Orient – dealing with it by making statements about it, authorizing views of it, describing it, by teaching it, settling it: in short, Orientalism as a Western style for dominating, restructuring, and having authority over the Orient.
>
> (Said 1977: 3)

On this account Orientalism (and indeed *Orientalism*) is to some degree an institutional construct. It is ratified and created by institutional forces like law, culture, religion and education. The language of this Orientalism reveals the way in which the West constructed and thought of the Orient. In no way does it describe the reality of the East, but rather an interpretation which is based upon tradition, justified expressions of bigotry, power, ideology and anxious fascination: 'these representations [of the Orient] rely upon institutions, traditions, conventions, agreed-upon codes of understanding for their effects, not upon some distant and amorphous Orient' (Said 1977: 22). In particular, Orientalism is something which is produced and sustained through cultural artefacts: 'Orientalism is premised upon exteriority, that is, on the fact that the Orientalist, poet or scholar, makes the Orient speak, describes the Orient, renders its mysteries plain for and to the West' (Said 1977: 20). It is a set of assumptions about the Orient which in itself produced and simultaneously supported a view of the East. So the Orient is timeless, strange, racially stereotyped, feminine, degenerate. Without this cultural support, Said argues, imperialism would have been hamstrung:

> without examining Orientalism as a discourse one cannot possibly understand the enormously systematic discipline by which European culture was able to manage – and even produce – the Orient politically, sociologically, militarily, ideologically, scientifically, and imaginatively during the post-Enlightenment period.
>
> (Said 1977: 3)

For Said, then, the imagining and writing of colony, and the economic and ideological implications performed and reiterated with this writing, was as important as the administering of an imperial legislature. The discourse of Orientalism was crucially important to the creation and sustaining of empire. In his later book *Culture and Imperialism* Said demonstrates at length how cultural products, in particular the novels of Jane Austen, Charles Dickens and Joseph Conrad, might be 'implicated in the rationale for imperialist expansion' (Said 1993: 100).

Postcolonial theory has many component parts which we do not have the space to investigate here, but of further interest to our investigation is the work of Homi Bhabha. Bhabha has two concepts that are important to our discussion of historical fiction: 'ambivalence' and 'mimicry'. Bhabha, like Said, argues that a central purpose of colonial discourse is to construct the subject of colonisation as savage and uncivilised, and through this to justify the invasion and continued occupation and administration of empire. However, Bhabha argues that this objective is never fully attained. This is because colonial discourse pulls in two directions: first, to make the colonised strange and other and therefore outside Western culture and civilisation; second, however, this construction of knowledge about the Orient in itself makes the colonised knowable and understandable. The more the West knows about the colonised the less the distance between the two sides. Bhabha argues that Western presentations of the East are constantly sliding ambivalently between similarity and distance. Bhabha further argues that by teaching the colonised their language the colonisers had to face the threat of resemblance. This threatened to collapse the binary distinctions that colonial discourse was grounded upon. The discourse of colonisation is therefore constantly embattled and in a state of flux, according to Bhabha, it is constantly problematised.

How are these theories articulated in historical fiction? One problem here is that the notion of history in relation to the postcolonial is vexed. The colonised subject was often conceptualised outside of imperial history; certainly the relationship of the colonial individual to a discourse which has 'systematically excluded the reality of colonized experience' is complex (Ashcroft 2001: 99). Ashcroft argues that one of the ways that post-colonial people are able to approach such authoritative discourses as history is by approaching them through liminal modes: 'writing in the marginal space between literature and history, which may authorize otherwise forbidden entries into the intellectual battlefield of European thought' (Ashcroft 2001: 99). By troubling, attending to the local, and writing-back or rewriting history, post-colonial authors might introduce a 'political contestation of imperial power' (Ashcroft 2001: 100). This interrogation is fundamentally something that 'works through, in the interstices of, in the fringes of, rather than in simple opposition to, history' in order to reveal its fragmentary nature: 'an entry into the discourse which disrupts its discursive features and reveals the limitations of the discourse itself' (Ashcroft 2001: 100). In order to explicate this the remainder of this section will look at three distinct types of postcolonial historical fiction: that which engages directly with the action and legacy of empire; that which politically writes-back and mimics the dominant culture of empire; and that which, in a more contemporary context, interrogates the fictions of empire to demonstrate their moral bankruptcy. Each of the examples we discuss here is concerned with troubling the mainstream accounts of the past, and with using fiction to challenge orthodoxy; they are, additionally, interested in giving a voice to figures marginalised by the imperial project (itself a concept problematised by the theorist Gayatri Chakravorty Spivak; see Spivak 1988).

Chinua Achebe's trilogy *Things Fall Apart* (1959), *No Longer at Ease* (1960) and *Arrow of God* (1964) represents a profound intervention into the historical genre, an account of the troubles of Nigeria after independence from empire, an ambiguous foundational national epic, and an articulation of masculine identity. Each novel explores a significant portion of Nigeria's history, and, more polemically, his work gives a voice to the African which many Western writers had denied: 'I would be quite satisfied if my novels (especially the ones I set in the past) did no more than teach my readers that their past – with all its imperfections – was not one long night of savagery from which the first Europeans acting on God's behalf delivered them' (Achebe 1977: 45). The coda 'with all its imperfections' signals Achebe's characteristic ambivalence; his characters are hardly saintly, and their actions range from arrogant to murderous. It is clear from his words here that his work, particularly his historical fiction, is keenly politically engaged and revisionist. He wishes to retell the story of the past from a different perspective, particularly where that perspective has no textual or historical referent.

Things Fall Apart is an account of the Umuofia leader Okonkwo, his family and his village during the late nineteenth or early twentieth century. It presents an account of the lives and customs of the tribe, and recounts the complex and often contradictory impact that Western colonialism has on their ways of life. Okonkwo asks, 'Does the white man understand our custom about land?' and his friend Obierika answers:

> How can he when he does not even speak our tongue? But he says that our customs are bad; and our own brothers who have taken up his religion also say that our customs are bad. How do you think we

can fight when our own brothers have turned against us? The white man is very clever. He came quietly and peaceably with his religion. We were amused at his foolishness and allowed him to stay. Now he has won our brothers, and our clan can no longer act like one. He has put a knife on the things that held us together and we have fallen apart.

(Achebe 1996: 124)

Particularly Okonkwo and his peers object to the imposition of Christianity. At the same time, the novel shows faction within the tribe, and suggests that change, be it historical, social, cultural, cannot be navigated or controlled. Intolerant Christian converts kill a sacred python, attack the native religion and eventually unmask one of the *egwugwu* (the village gods) at a ceremony. In retaliation the *egwugwu* burn a church to the ground. This leads to the village leaders being imprisoned, and Okonkwo's eventual despairing suicide when he realises that his clan will not go to war to preserve their identity. The unnamed District Commissioner, a coloniser, hears of this suicide and decides at the end of the novel that it will make an interesting paragraph in his racialist anthropological work *The Pacification of the Primitive Tribes of the Lower Niger*.

The novel therefore takes the colonial history of Nigeria and demonstrates how the rights, traditions, customs, religions and lives of the native peoples were traduced by Western imperialism. It complicates and nuances the reader's historical understanding of the country and its historical manifestation. *Things Fall Apart* demonstrates quite ruthlessly the historical process of colonisation, in so far as it shows the changing of the lives of those living in colonised areas. The District Commissioner's book *The Pacification* is just the kind of Orientalist project that Said argues 'represented' the Africa to the West. It does not understand the locale, but simply wishes to present the savagery of the native peoples in order to maintain the power structures of empire.

The other novels in the trilogy demonstrate the historical consequences of colonisation, from the destruction of tribal customs to the personal tragic cost of the colonial encounter. The two subsequent novels dramatise different reactions to the new circumstances. Ezeulu, in *Arrow of God*, is a priest who directly confronts Christian missionaries in the 1920s. His ruthless zealotry leads to a famine in his village and thence directly to the villagers' conversion. Obi, Okonkwo's grandson in the near-contemporary *No Longer at Ease*, finds that rejecting the traditional lifestyles for a 'mission-house upbringing and European education' (Achebe 1987: 64) abstracts him from his country and leads him to selfishness, meanness and base behaviour. Obi is regularly compared to his grandfather, now erroneously recalled as he 'who faced the white man single-handed and died in the fight' (Achebe 1987: 48). Achebe demonstrates how communities misremember and how this can be in itself a destructive process. In reading Okonkwo's death as somehow sacrificial Obi's family pander to a generalised short-sighted tendency in the novel to bemoan the travails of the nation as being the fault of external forces. The trilogy sees the complexity of Nigerian history during and after colonisation and traces the violently corrosive impact of empire.

Imperial powers have been constantly critiqued in historical fiction, for instance France in Assia Djebar's and Jules Roy's writings on Algeria, and Mongo Beti on Cameroon. These novels all have very different purposes, contexts and political trajectories but they share a desire to present alternative histories, querying and attacking the legitimacy of official colonial narratives of the past. One of the key postcolonial strategies that Achebe deploys in the novel is that of 'writing back'. He regularly uses quotes from Western sources in his writing. In doing so he appropriates them, often misquoting them, and therefore he takes their itera-tive power as the agents of British culture for his own. This is a politicised form of mimicry (Ashcroft 1989; Creasy 2007). As the Kenyan novelist Ngugi wa Thiong'o argues, 'Language, any lan-guage, has a dual character: it is both a means of communication and a carrier of culture' (wa Thiong'o 1994: 439). Writing in English is a problematic and difficult political exercise (Achebe 2003). Achebe uses the language of British literature and culture as a means of interrogating and critiquing it, yet he was brought up to speak the language, so it has an ambivalent significance for him as part of his heritage, and this mixed inheritance is some-thing that the figure of Obi similarly wrestles with. The title of his first novel comes from W. B. Yeats's poem 'The Second

Coming'. On the one hand the allusion gives the novel a certain authority, but Obierika's words quoted above disrupt this: 'He has put a knife on the things that held us together and we have fallen apart.' Yeats's poem had claimed 'Things fall apart; the centre cannot hold;/Mere anarchy is loosed upon the world' (Yeats 1990: 235, ll. 3–4). Obierika is much more interested in community: 'we', not 'things', have fallen apart. Throughout the African trilogy Achebe misquotes and reconstructs T. S. Eliot, Tennyson, the King James Bible, Keats and Shakespeare, among others, and this disrupting of British culture is intentional, although obviously the Irishman Yeats is himself a colonised subject, demonstrating the innate complexity of this kind of approach. Often writing back is deployed as a means of cultural reparation and levelling. Within the context of the historical novel it does signify this, but it also demonstrates a desire to bring figures from the margins to the centre and to dissent from the authoritative narrative of the past. At the same time using language, history and cultural references in a different setting makes them something new, uses them to create something owned by the writer, and therefore challenges hegemonic models of cultural capital.

Examples of politicised writing back are multiple, but within this particular context we might consider the South African J. M. Coetzee's rewriting of *Robinson Crusoe* (*Foe*, 1986) and the Australian Peter Carey's take on *Great Expectations* (*Jack Maggs*, 1997). A kind of writing back is undertaken by Walter Mosley in his appropriation of the white detective genre, discussed above. Furthermore, the reconsideration of the hidden lives of famous characters or literary figures in historical fictional form is common, from Scott's representation of Shakespeare in *Kenilworth* (1821) to Julian Barnes's new angle on the life of Arthur Conan Doyle in *Arthur and George* (2005). However, in postcolonial discourse the rewriting or reconsideration of key components of a dominant colonial culture is part of a questioning and interrogation of that society; it seeks to undermine, engage and challenge (see Sanders 2005). This kind of rewritten fiction, not just anti-colonial fiction, but all appropriative writing, might be suggested to be a subgenre of the historical novel in so far as it takes as its past topic fictional narratives from history. These are works of alternative literary historical fiction, using the tropes of a cultural rather than an actual 'past' as the site of conflict and debate.

Jean Rhys's *Wide Sargasso Sea* (1966) is a rewriting of Charlotte Brontë's novel *Jane Eyre* (1847). *Jane Eyre* tells of how Jane and her lover Mr Rochester are not allowed to marry because of the existence of his Creole first wife, whom he has hidden in the attic of his house for several years:

> He lifted the hangings from the wall, uncovering the second door: this, too, he opened. In a room without a window, there burnt a fire, guarded by a high and strong fender, and a lamp suspended from the ceiling by a chain. Grace Poole bent over the fire, apparently cooking something in a saucepan. In the deep shade, at the farther end of the room, a figure ran backwards and forwards. What it was, whether beast or human being, one could not, at first sight, tell: it grovelled, seemingly, on all fours; it snatched and growled like some strange wild animal: but it was covered with clothing, and a quantity of dark, grizzled hair, wild as its mane, hid its head and face.
>
> (Brontë 1847: 321)

The woman is animalistic, mad, degenerate, unholy. She becomes wild and savage, finally burning down the house. She has no human selfhood, no voice other than a demoniac laugh and some indistinct grunting. She has been made this way by her treatment, Rhys suggests in her text. *Jane Eyre* has been seen to perpetuate many racist and imperialist assumptions about native peoples. For instance, Rochester portrays the West Indies as exotic and intoxicating:

> I found her a fine woman ... tall, dark, and majestic. Her family wished to secure me, because I was of good race; and so did she. They showed her to me at parties splendidly dressed. I seldom saw her alone, and had very little private conversation with her. She flattered me, and lavishly displayed for my pleasure her charms and accomplishments. All the men in her circle seemed to admire her and envy me. I was dazzled, stimulated: my senses were excited: and being ignorant, raw, and inexperienced, I thought I loved her.
>
> (Brontë 1847: 332)

He is led to folly by the exotic other which occludes his view of reality. This land drives him out of his senses, and he falls into the clutches of the evil natives. At one point, the only thing that saves him from lunacy is a 'wind fresh from Europe', the 'sweet' breeze of civilisation (Brontë 1847: 347).

Rhys's novel attempts to give a voice to the marginalised figure of Rochester's wife Antoinette. It is therefore part of a distinct project to recover or revoice the marginalised native voice, to give that voice consequence. This is both postcolonial and feminist, and it is significant that the most famous work of feminist scholarship on the Victorian period is Sandra Gilbert and Susan Gubar's 1979 *The Madwoman in the Attic*, itself about the marginalisation of women in *Jane Eyre*. Rhys critiques *Jane Eyre*, attacking the way that the text constructs a view of the West Indies, and criticising the representation of Bertha Mason. *Jane Eyre* is hardly an overtly colonial text, so Rhys points out the subtle, ingrained imperialism innate in writing from the imperial centre (that centre that 'could not hold' in Achebe). Rhys remembers that whilst reading *Jane Eyre* she had become 'vexed at her portrait of the "paper tiger" lunatic, the all wrong creole scenes, and above all by the real cruelty of Mr Rochester' (Howells 1991: 104). She gives Mason a self, an identity and a voice. She rewrites the colonial, canonical text. However, the novel is narratively complex: it also gives Rochester another version of events. So there are various conflicting viewpoints, and this questions the whole nature of representation: can one version of events be legitimated as real and true? All of literary history is therefore put into a state of flux, subject to negotiation and interrogation.

Rhys attacks the latent Orientalism of Brontë's novel by presenting a far more complex version of the Caribbean and of the main characters. She suggests that Rochester was a self-serving libertine who took advantage of the colonies for profit and power. The relationship between him and Antoinette is importantly based upon finance. It is an intensely sexual relationship, and Rhys suggests that it is Rochester's worry that he is succumbing to the exotic charms of the Caribbean (East in the terms of Orientalism) that drives him to reject his wife. He attempts to marginalise her, to construct her and contain her. He renames her in order to be able to further define and control her, as she says, 'You are trying to make me into someone else, calling me by another name' (Rhys 2000: 121). Rochester cannot accept her foreign nature, and his desire for her, and so chooses to reject her and humiliate her, to make her mad and then lock her up, constrain and control her: as he says, 'She'll not laugh in the sun again. She'll not dress up and smile at herself in that damnable looking glass. So pleased, so satisfied' (Rhys 2000: 136). There is an intense violence about the way Rochester treats his wife, a barely repressed destruction, that is analogous to the violation and oppression practised by English colonialism. Rhys critiques the representation of the West Indies in canonical English literature, and thus attacks the construction of an Orientalist caricature. She rewrites canonical literature, by giving a voice to the oppressed, and positing an alternative story for those consigned by history to the margins.

British historical fiction has often shown an ambivalence to the legacy of colony, for instance demonstrated by the complicity of Scottish doctor Nicholas Garrigan with the dictator Idi Amin's administration in Giles Foden's *The Last King of Scotland* (1998). The book demonstrates the clear blame associated with the British in the aftermath of empire. Contemporary, rather than historical, fiction has represented the consequences of empire and, in the United Kingdom, with the impact of an increasingly multicultural society. Half-historical accounts such as Zadie Smith's *White Teeth* (2000) or, more challengingly, Hanif Kureishi's semi-autobiographical *The Buddha of Suburbia* (1990) have considered questions of national identity, the disintegration and consequences of colonialism, and the struggle for multicultural identity (Tew 2007: 158–90). Fictional accounts of imperial episodes, from the Crusades, through first colonisation and the wars of conquest, do exist, but they are generally found in popular genre fiction such as the Sharpe series by Bernard Cornwell (mainly set in India), which offers a very uninflected version of events.

However, authors have begun to combine the critical approaches outlined by Said to historical fiction writing as a way of challenging and deconstructing various myths and narratives. Hari Kunzru's

The Impressionist (2002) fills colonial India and Africa with ethnographers, anthropologists, Christian missionaries and racist imperial administrators in order to express contempt for the project of empire. Key to the novel's interest to our discussion is that, like most historical fiction, it gestures towards mimetic realism whilst clearly undermining this style of writing: 'I never thought of it as a realist book and it is very interesting to me how much writing about it treated it as an attempt to write a realist narrative' (Kunzru 2002). The novel puts ideas of ambivalence, mimicry and recognition into play and builds a compelling set of complicated relationships. The central character, accidental son of an English officer and an Indian woman, moves through seven distinct phases of identity. He takes on various external characteristics in order to survive; these are both racial and gendered, demonstrating the fluidity of identity: 'Bobby is a creature of surface. Tissue paper held up to the sun. He hints at transparency, as if on the other side, on the inside, there is something to be discovered. Maybe there is, maybe not. ... Stitch a personality together' (Kunzru 2002: 250). The novel follows the protean protagonist through India and thence to Oxford, Paris and Central Africa, as he strives actually to find himself. He has a final revelation when watching a stage impressionist and realises that in switching between selves he has lost contact with something innately *him*:

> The man becomes these other people so completely that nothing of his own is visible ... In between each impression, just at the moment when one person falls away and the next has yet to take possession, the impressionist is completely blank. There is nothing there at all.
>
> (Kunzru 2002: 419)

The novel interrogates identity and nationality, and articulates a series of debates about what happens in various contexts when native peoples either mimic, perform or are English. It is about the disarticulation of identity within a colonial context, the ways that gendered selves might be worn and the dangers of being defined by the discourses of others. It is a writing back, too, a serious intervention into a cultural discourse of empire and an attempt at rewriting or recalibrating the ways in which the historical and fictional past might be represented, as discussed in Chapter 5:

> The Impressionist is largely a game I was playing with orientalism, with a Merchant Ivory view of India, and with the history of the British novel, which is so wrapped up with ideas of a British male self coming to full presence or knowledge in the mystical mirror of the East. The book is an anti-Kim, but also plays around with A Passage to India, Heart of Darkness, Hindoo Holiday and others.
>
> (Kunzru 2006)

Kunzru positions himself as writing fiction that responds to that of others. It is a conversation or a dialogue with historical texts (including films of colonial books), demonstrating their problematic representation of India. However political, though, the novel concludes relatively inertly. *The Impressionist* ends with a protagonist who is either beyond identity or literally selfless: 'For now the journey is everything. He has no thoughts of arriving anywhere. Tonight he will sleep under the enormous bowl of the sky. Tomorrow he will travel on' (Kunzru 2002: 481). The end of identity and the escape from a defining history, it seems here, are a kind of blankness. Historical fiction written about colonial periods, or from a postcolonial perspective, then, writes back, articulates alternatives, interrogates and intervenes, but it should not simply be characterised as dialogic, more considered as another set of dynamic and complex reactions to problematic and traumatic events that enable the writers to point to the very insubstantiality of the discourse of history itself.

As a way of considering how history might actively be physically challenged, we move finally to thinking about the writing of alternative, or counterfactual, history. What if? history is interested in mapped spaces of otherness, in presenting actual substitute realities rather than challenging or reinterpreting what is commonly accepted to have occurred. The historical scholarship in this field, and the fictional, explore ideas of potential or of possibility. We finish the chapter by considering a novel that has spawned an entire tourist industry and that has also been challenged in the courts for its version of truth, and which provides an interesting test case for the influence of the historical novel on the popular imagination.

ALTERNATIVE HISTORIES AND INTERVENTIONS

Counterfactual history, also known as 'What if' historiography, has become increasingly formalised in recent years. As an academic pursuit it emphasises the contingent and rejects totalising and overdetermined structures such as Marxist analysis. What if? or counterfactual history was not the preserve of the academy until the 1990s with the publication of Geoffrey Hawthorn's *Plausible Worlds* (1991), Niall Ferguson's collection *Virtual History: Alternatives and Counterfactuals* (1997) and *What If?* edited by Robert Cowley (1999). Counterfactual history is iconoclastic and, its proponents argue, a necessary corrective to overly proscriptive and prescriptive models of history:

> History is properly the literature of what did happen; but that should not diminish the importance of the counterfactual. What-ifs can lead us to question long-held assumptions. What ifs can define true turning points. They can show that small accidents or split-second decisions are as likely to have major repercussions as large ones.
>
> (Cowley 2001: xi–i)

Academic What if? history posits that we understand historical casuality better if we eschew determinism and consider the alternatives as they might have been thought of by those at the time: 'counterfactuals should be those which contemporaries contemplated' (Ferguson 2000: 87).

Counterfactual thinking has a wider and less formalised manifestation than Ferguson's very careful theorising allows. It keys into popular cultural imaginative tropes of the 'road not travelled', enacted in films from *It's a Wonderful Life* (Frank Capra, 1946) to *Sliding Doors* (Peter Howitt, 1998). Indeed, such representation of the importance of particular choices to the life of the protagonist are in the background of nearly every 'classic' film narrative, structured as they generally are around particular crises that demand choice be made. Counterfactual history allows an alternative historical space to be imagined, suggesting that actual time might be in a state of flux. The counterfactual gestures towards the idea that history is about a set of individual, personal choices. There is some academic snootiness about counterfactuals. E. H. Carr called alternative history a 'parlour game', E. P. Thompson went further ('unhistorical shit') and nearer contemporaries such as Tristram Hunt have similarly decried the 'insidious' approach (Ferguson 2000: 4, 5; Hunt 2004). Yet its prevalence as a cultural trope cannot be ignored. Robert Harris's comment in the Author's Note to his counterfactual novel *Fatherland* suggests a conflation of Ferguson's cautious approach and a historical imagination quite prepared to run with ideas: 'Where I have created documents, I have tried to do so on the basis of fact' (Harris 1992: 386). This contrasts with the author's responsibility to history as outlined by Ian McEwan:

> The writer of a historical novel may resent his dependence on the written record, on memoirs and eye-witness accounts, in other words on other writers, but there is no escape: Dunkirk or a wartime hospital can be novelistically realised, but they cannot be reinvented.
>
> (McEwan 2006)

McEwan's sense of the past is forensic and evidentiary; Harris's counterfactual fictionalising is unhistorical. The counterfactual as a historiographic model and a cultural trope resonates, but in its problematising and undermining of the 'actual' presents both historian and novelist with moral problems. Certainly the historical novel rarely adheres to chronicle, such as happens in David Peace's *GB84* (2005), or docuhistory and fiction as 'faction', such as in Truman Capote's *In Cold Blood* (1966) and Kate Summerscale's *The Suspicions of Mr Whicher* (2008). A further paradigm is provided, that of Dan Brown, who when defending his novel *The Da Vinci Code* against a charge of plagiarism argued that 'A novelist must be free to draw appropriately from historical works without fear that he'll be sued and forced to stand in a courtroom facing a series of allegations that call into question his very integrity as a person' (*Guardian* 2006). Brown here further elides the relationship between 'fact' and 'fiction', suggesting that historical novelists should be able to cherry-pick whatever they wish; they have a responsibility to history, but not to the writers of that history.

What if? history comes in a variety of guises, and is prepared to question and interrogate the factuality of the past in order to challenge assumptions. What if? historical novels, then, are kind of historical novels squared, in so far as they fictionalise something which is already being fictionalised. Essentially all historical fiction is to some degree What if? writing, particularly if it concerns actual figures, and counterfactual novels effectively enshrine this slightly more formally. They flag the liberties that the historical novel takes with the historical record by more obviously asking the reader to forget what they know. As such they are strange cultural phenomena, inhabiting a literary grey area and lacking the legitimacy of the historical novel proper. What if? novels are exercises in reconsideration that work as imagination reorderings and, as such, challenge the standard assumptions of the popular historical imagination. Also in this category are those novels that happily take actual information and elaborate, as is the case in the majority of Peter Ackroyd's fiction, such as *Hawksmoor* (1985), *The Last Testament of Oscar Wilde* (1983) and *Milton in America* (1997). The basic unit of the counterfactual sub-genre is the positing of an alternative reality in order to explore particular sets of historical phenomena. Harry Turtledove's *Ruled Britannia* (2003) is set in 'Elizabethan' England but suggests that the 1588 Spanish Armada has been a successful invasion. The protagonist is William Shakespeare, who is asked to write a play to rouse the British and also one to celebrate Philip of Spain. The action takes place in standard grimy Elizabethan London but also in the theatre. The novel is a good example of the What if? narrative as a popular, even pulp, genre, and also demonstrates the sub-genre's obsession with real historical characters and important people. Turtledove's narrative uses an 'olde worlde' idiom in dialogue but also integrates Shakespeare's plays as intertexts throughout. The novel demonstrates that even at a popular level historical fiction is keenly interested in intertextuality or at least in reanimating older texts. The Shakespeare quotation also sets up a hierarchy of knowledge and an echo of 'actuality'.

Thomas Harris's two novels *Fatherland* (1992) and *Archangel* (1998) both in their way posit counterfactual arguments. *Archangel* suggests that Stalin had children; *Fatherland* that the Nazis did not lose the Second World War. In his What if? narratives Harris explores how history is made, how it works, and how those involved in it articulate their historical awareness. The novels are both extremely interesting for their representation in fiction of the figure of the historian (de Groot 2008: 49–53). In *Fatherland* the detective Xavier March becomes historian, piecing together the story through archival research and eye-witness accounts: 'It kept him going, his blessing or his curse, this compulsion to *know*' (Harris 1992: 95). The search for truth, fragmented and compromised though it may be, compels Harris's protagonists. The past for the professional historian Fluke Kelso in *Archangel* is alive and important. The Russia Kelso finds himself in is haunted by it, formed by it, broken by it:

> go back to New York, Dr Kelso, and play your games of history in somebody else's country, because this isn't England or America, the past isn't safely dead here. In Russia, the past carries razors and a pair of handcuffs.
>
> (Harris 2000: 167)

Harris's theme is this constant possibility of the violent intervention of the past in the present. He lectures his companion, 'Unless you understand that, you can't begin to understand Russia. You can't make sense of the present unless a part of you lives in the past' (Harris 2000: 233). The villains in *Archangel* want to 'bring the past back to life' (Harris 2000: 417), to turn the clock of history back (the scenario of Steve Berry's 2004 book *The Romanov Prophecy* outlines a similar story line). Aptly, for a book so steeped in Marxist-Leninist context, the novel is interested in the cyclical nature of history. The new Russia is compared to the Wiemar republic, waiting for its Hitler to arrive, the Messiah the old communists are looking for.

Similarly to them, as they point out, Kelso believes in the myth of objective historical truth. He is searching for truth, a detective of history. Happy to attend and speak at conferences, he nevertheless has lost his academic way, and has no taste for the archive or the library any longer. Instead he searches for the holy grail, for a document that will vindicate him: 'all the while hoping that one day he would produce something worthwhile – something true and big and definitive – a piece of history that would explain *why things happened as they did*' (Harris 2000: 193, italics original). Harris's previous non-fictional work on the Hitler diaries gives us a context here for this search for the historical philosopher's stone, an artefact that will explain, that will render the complexities of the truth straightforward (Harris 1987). Perhaps the Rosetta stone is a better comparison, a means to translate and understand a seemingly incomprehensible history. Of course Kelso doesn't find such a thing; what he does find is more complex, more plastic, more human. It doesn't solve anything, or explain anything. What if? history in this example is a possibility, a potential within the known facts rather than an alternative history. It adds to what we know but it doesn't explain it, it merely adds another context into the mix. As a character in *Fatherland* comments, 'The historian's mission. To bring out of chaos – more chaos' (Harris 1992: 241).

Fluke Kelso himself elaborates on this in his conference paper, which can be read as a paradigm not only for this novel but for historical fiction in general. The conference he attends is entitled 'Confronting the Past', convened to mark the opening up of the former communist archives. The academic framework, therefore, is a reclamation of the past, as finally the truth can be known, after decades of ideological whitewash. This is an opportunity to revisit and find out what actually happened rather than what you have been told. History is the plaything of the confident and well trained academic, rather than something that plays with him, although, later, Kelso will pinpoint the time at which he 'loses control' of proceedings and he is back to being played with by events. Kelso's research paper is anecdotal, presumptive, lacking analysis. In fact, it reads like narrative fiction rather than history. He tells the tragic story of those related to or close to Stalin, all of whom died early, died in suspicious circumstances or went mad. Using this human information as a platform, Kelso points out that despite the massive archives of the era that are being opened, 1.5 million files, we cannot know the gap between what happened and *why*. He reminds his audience:

> We can also see the death lists that Stalin signed. And we have his appointments book. So we know that on the eighth of December, nineteen thirty-eight, Stalin signed thirty death lists containing five thousand names, many of them of his so-called friends. And we also know, thanks to his appointments book, that on the very same evening he went to the Kremlin movie theatre and watched, not Tarzan this time, but a comedy called Happy Guys.
>
> But between these two events, between the killing and the laughter, there lies – what? Who? We do not know. And why? Because Stalin made it his business to murder almost everyone who might have been in a position to tell us what he was like ...
>
> (Harris 2000: 70, italics original)

Kelso's point, and the point of the novel, is about the subjective quality of 'history' as opposed to historical 'fact'. He puts much faith in oral testimony, as those who know someone intimately can tell us why things happen, but he also points out a fundamental gap between the known fact and the lived experience. We can trace movements and events but the human factor of motivation, interest, personality is something that can never be recovered by the historian. This gap, this tension and dynamic between the actuality of History, what can be to some extent uncovered, and the experience of life in History, is what historical fiction explores. The key motif for the historical novelist is the exploration of the phrase *'there lies – what? Who? We do not know'*. A text that doesn't acknowledge this historio-fictional gap is either actual narrative history or biography.

Fatherland is What if? fiction with a scope far beyond that of *Archangel*. The central conceit is that Germany did not lose, or really win, the Second World War, but that it made peace with Britain in 1944 and now exists as the Greater German Reich in 1964. Hitler lives and reigns, and in this context a detective story is presented to us, although one which is as much about history and documentation as it is about crime and intuition. The novel meditates on the ways that history can be used and created ('FOR ANY NATION, THE RIGHT HISTORY IS WORTH 100 DIVISIONS'; Harris 1992: 240). The central character, Xavier March, is obsessed with a search for truth, for what will become 'historical' truth by the end of the novel: 'And there was something else, the instinct that propelled him out of bed every morning into each unwelcoming day, and that was the desire to *know*' (Harris 1992: 95). He is detective-historian: March visits the Reichsarchiv to research his case and finds key documents that, when read in the correct way, direct him toward the 'truth'.

What he discovers is the covering up of the Final Solution and the extermination of the Jews. 'History' has happened, and its terrible events must be found out eventually. The word 'holocaust' is even used in the novel, in reference to Stalin (Harris 1992: 212). March and his American journalist companion discover 'unbelievable' details that will 'change history' (Harris 1992: 334). The enormity of the Holocaust is embedded in the novel, and as readers we feel the visceral shock of history despite our hindsight. We know that this has happened but coming to it if as it were new recasts it, shows once again the horror. Harris reproduces many actual documents and materials relating to the Holocaust, and in their measured terms the economical logic and horrific size of the extermination are revealed. Yet he also troublingly invents documents, maps and memoranda, interleaving them with real ones. Fiction imposes into a world of evidence that it should not have any right engaging with here. The notion of a central 'truth' relating to the events of the 1940s is to an extent undermined through this fictionalising. Whilst the entire novel is obviously a fabrication, this uneasy relationship between 'actual' historical events and 'fictional' ones is troubling to a reader. Should proving and discovering the Holocaust be material for a thriller? Should the events of the Holocaust be presented as fiction, as narrative? Are there some historical events and facts that need to be left alone, and is it the case that we can approach them only obliquely, as in this 'What if?' mode? These are the kinds of questions that counterfactual fiction provokes, but, similarly, they should be prompted by all historical fiction in its ability to question, challenge, undermine and problematise 'history'. Indeed, these ethical issues are those that were raised in Chapter 1, and Harris's very new kind of historical novel highlights how the form can provoke and ask very difficult cultural questions.

Similarly concerned with the consequences of actions in the 1940s, Philip Roth's *The Plot against America* (2005) is a counterfactual novel suggesting that the famous pilot Charles A. Lindbergh stood against Roosevelt for the presidency in 1940 and won, thus delaying America's entry into the war and introducing homeland persecution of Jews. Roth provides a chronology at the end 'as a reference for readers interested in tracking where historical fact ends and historical imagining begins' (Roth 2005: 364), and this idea of 'historical imagining', a fictionalising improvisation within the framework of history, is suggestive. Roth's novel considers the impact of the wider political on the personal. He uses the day-to-day experiences of his protagonists to demonstrate the nowness of what was to become history:

> And as Lindbergh's election couldn't have made clearer to me, the unfolding of the unforeseen was everything. Turned wrong way round, the relentless unforeseen was what we schoolchildren studied as 'History', harmless history, where everything unexpected in its own time is chronicled on the page as inevitable. The terror of the unforeseen is what the science of history hides, turning a disaster into an epic.
>
> (Roth 2005: 113–14)

Roth's 'terror of the unforeseen' makes history, and the writing of historical fiction, possibly, a way of understanding and dealing with the horrors of potentiality, of not being an individual with agency but someone prey to the inevitable chaos of history. At the same time he allows a **metonymic** everyman quality to those he writes about, an interest in the common man's experience as it relates to and is part of the wider historical sweep:

> 'Because what's history?' he asked rhetorically when he was in his expansive dinnertime instructional mode. 'History is everything that happens everywhere. Even here in Newark. Even here on Summit

Avenue. Even what happens in this house to an ordinary man – that'll be history too someday.'

(Roth 2005: 180)

Roth also deploys his counterfactual narrative to take a look at the grimier side of American attitudes to Jews, suggesting that the teleology of united nationhood usually thought of in relation to the war was fragile and brittle at best. The use of the counterfactual form allows Roth to reflect on how we understand history as 'what was the case', and how this is distinct from actually experiencing history.

Alternatives and historical conspiracy fiction

The most significant alternative positing or reconceptualising of history in the past two decades, however, comes in a novel which is set in the recognisable contemporary world. Dan Brown's *The Da Vinci Code* (2003) is a thriller in which an investigative academic reveals the historical truth behind the Catholic Church's conspiracy of silence regarding various key events. These concern Jesus's marriage, around eighty further gospels relating his mortal life, his subsequent blood line, his divinity, and the equal importance of celebrating the feminine in the rituals of the early ministry. By unlocking a series of clues and interpreting a range of texts and pieces of evidence, Robert Langdon demonstrates that the Church has consistently suppressed information which suggests things contrary to its patriarchal, oppressive teachings. Brown's novel, therefore, argues that 'centuries of established history' are wrong, that 'Nothing in Christianity is original' and that the Church is based upon the 'greatest cover-up in human history' (Brown 2003: 164, 232, 249). Indeed, as one of the academic characters in the book argues, 'It was all about power ... Christ as Messiah was critical to the functioning of the Church and State' (Brown 2003: 233). Building on the work of various experts, theologians and academics, Brown's novel presented history as something which might be challenged, changed and in thrall to the desires of power rather than the needs of truth. The alternative history posited in this novel is actually 'history' in so far as it is the 'reality' of things which has allegedly been obfuscated by faction. *The Da Vinci Code* presents a revision of history, a challenge to the established truths (de Groot 2008: 55–7).

The book has sold multiple millions and been translated across the world. It has spawned imitations, tourism, lawsuits and a minor publishing industry refuting, supporting and guiding the reader through the novel. The text's success demonstrates the popularity of historically led thrillers and furthermore that audiences are interested in works that challenge traditional epistemologies and knowledge traditions. Simon Cox's *second* companion to the book was written specifically for a new phenomenon, the 'Dan Brown tourist' interested in the 'cult and phenomenon' of the author (Cox 2006: 10, 13). The Louvre in Paris, for instance, scene of some of the action, has a standing exhibit on the novel. *The Da Vinci Code* has suffused culture to the extent that it now dictates the sceptical ways in which individuals might approach the past. Cox articulates the attraction of Brown's text in his assertion that 'I am proud to call myself an alternative historian – a historian of the obscure, as the BBC once called me' (Cox 2006: 13). This sense of presenting alternatives, of revising the mainstream or undermining the assumptions of society, is key to the attraction of Brown's novel.

Brown's book is part of a sub-genre of historical thriller novels that might be defined as 'conspiracy fiction' (see Knight 2000). These novels work to suggest that what we assume about the past, particularly relating to states, religions or events, might be in a state of flux. They posit other events, ways of interpreting history, and, in most cases, argue that if you have the key to a particular set of knowledges you will be able to see other, more problematic workings beneath the official narratives. These novels share a concern with undermining the official narratives of the Roman Catholic Church in particular, either by suggesting that it has been involved in conspiracy throughout its manifestation or by arguing that it is the puppet organisation of a much more shadowy collective like the Templars, the Freemasons or the Illuminati. Steve Berry's *The Third Secret* (2005) posits, in similar fashion to *The Da Vinci Code*, a shadowy Church attempting to protect and suppress the 'truth' about particular religious information conveyed to children in a 1917 vision of the Virgin Mary. The 'third message', a set of revelations which 'bore the cryptic mystery of a poem, the meanings subtle and open to interpretation', has been suppressed by the Church (Berry 2000: 51). The actual message allows for female priests, non-celibate priests, homosexual relationships and birth control. Berry's later novel *The Templar Legacy* (2006) similarly attempts to question the myths surrounding the life and death of Christ, postulating a lost fifth gospel that bears witness to a resurrection 'not literal, but spiritual' (Berry 2006: 460). Jesus dies and is born again in the hearts of his apostles and nowhere else, according to the testimony of Simon (the apostle Peter). This, therefore, undermines the entirety of the Church: 'There's no elaborate crucifixion, no empty tomb, no angels announcing the risen Christ. That's fiction, created by men for their own benefit' (Berry 2006: 461). Other examples include Michael Cordy's *The Miracle Strain* (1997; renamed *The Messiah Code* to pick up on the success of Brown's novel) in which the DNA and blood of Christ become a cure for modern disease, a similarly paranoid conspiracy novel which posits an 'alternative reality' in which history is different from that which we are sure of (Cordy 2005: 541). A sophisticated development of this type of novel is Kate Mosse's *Labyrinth* (2005), which interweaves a historical narrative with a contemporary grail conspiracy thriller, in a similar vein to Byatt's *Posession*. These novels came as part of a cultural secularism that might also be traced in Philip Pullman's *His Dark Materials* trilogy (1995–2000).

The conspiracy novels suggest that the past is wrong, or at least what society has been told is wrong. In short, that 'History' is a conspiracy designed to marginalise the truth of events. They are also keen to deploy particular codes, to suggest that with the right cryptographic-historical imagination and ability with dead languages the scholar can open the lock of lies and reveal the truth. Similarly to Eco's William of Baskerville, they are witness to academic, theological and intellectual suppression in the name of order and stability. The historian is an interpreter of signs and a solver of clues, a detective who with impeccable logic seeks to pull the scales from society's eyes. These fictions are counterfactual in so far as they posit a set of events, consequences and facts which run counter to the mainstream. By their very nature these historical novels point to their insubstantiality, the fact that they are fiction. At the same time, their Author's Notes underline their authenticity and, most important, the ambiguity of sources and narratives; the kinds of historical lacunae which allow the authors creative wriggle room. Finally, it is here, in the gaps of history, in the spaces between knowledges, in the lacking texts, within the misunderstood codes, that historical novelists work, and it is the very insubstantiality of the past that allows them to introduce their version of events.

Glossary

Anglophone

Written in English but not necessarily British in origin.

Authentic fallacy

The concept that readers of historical novels want to believe that what they are reading is somehow real or authentic, provoked often by the realist or mimetic mode of writing.

Bildungsroman

A novel which tells the story of the journey and life of the youthful narrator.

Deconstruction

A set of philosophies associated with Jacques Derrida in which language becomes destabilised; this in turn leads to the 'decentring', as there is no centre or origin, no presence. Instead there is a proliferation of meaning, multiplicity, dispersal.

Deferred

The principle, from Derrida, that because language has no immanent signification within it all meaning is put off or deferred. All signs mean because of their relationship to other signs, rather than anything particularly innate within them, and so their meaning is constantly articulated via other shifting boundaries.

Enlightenment

The period from the mid-eighteenth century in Europe in which rationalism, secularism and empiricism became the founding principles of society.

Epistemology

Set of knowledges or ways of knowing.

Eurocentric

An attitude which considers all issues from the point of view of Europe.

Feminist

A set of principles, philosophies or ideas which express a desire for female liberation and equality.

Historiographic metafiction

A term coined by Patricia Waugh to refer to novels which were self-conscious and interested in their own representation of the past.

Historiography

The theory or methodology of History and particularly the writing of History.

Magical realism

A type of writing, generally associated with Latin America, in which fabulous things happen within a realist framework.

Marxist

Applying the principles and theories of Karl Marx to history or the study of culture. Generally interested in seeing history as a series or cycle moving towards the emancipation of the proletariat.

Metafiction

Fiction which is self-referential and self-conscious; it might also have a **metanarrative**.

Metonymic

A word or term which signifies alone but also might stand for a broader set of ideas.

Modernism

A literary and cultural movement which during the late nineteenth and early twentieth centuries emphasised experimentation, fragmentation and innovation.

Noir

Type of film and writing which accentuates shadow, darkness, and ambiguity; generally associated with crime or thriller forms.

Ockham's razor

The philosophical principle that the simplest solution is invariably the best or that the simplest answer is usually the right one.

Picaresque

An episodic novel, romance or story following the travels and adventures of a particular character and charting their eventual journey towards self-knowledge and understanding.

Postcolonial

A set of practices, theories or writings associated with the desire to articulate an identity in the face of imperial oppression; or 'postcolonial', the period after colonisation.

Postmodernism

Postmodernism is a theory that rejects hierarchy, stability and category. It attacks grand narratives that have attempted to systematise and control us. It attacks our sense of centredness and stability, suggesting instead that the world is innately subjective and unstable. Postmodernism is interested in Jacques Derrida's notion of 'play', the fact that systems are not stable structures but in a constant state of flux.

Postmodern turn

A trend in historiography which emphasised the linguistic element of all history (as narrative) and therefore which suggested that 'truth' in historical inquiry was an impossible, and ill advised, end to aim for.

Post-structuralist

Post-structuralism posits that the way we understand the world is through a series of arbitrary discourses, languages and codes that are seen as culturally and politically constructed.

Queer theory

Queer theory theorises and analyses the construction and representation of gay and lesbian people in literature and society. In particular the notion of 'queerness' in literary theory has been developed to mean ways in which the normative discourses of culture and society might be challenged, interrogated or unbalanced. Queer theory is particularly interested in destroying the binary opposition of heterosexual/homosexual, in encouraging a more complex and subtle approach to sexuality and identity. Instead of the 'traditional' heterosexual/homosexual binary model, Queer theorists are interested in blurring the distinctions between 'distinct' models of sexuality.

Reformation

The turn in European theology and religious life away from the Catholic Church towards the new teachings of Protestantism; the 'reforming' of the corrupted Church during the period $c.$ 1517–1648.

Reified

Marxist term which refers to the process whereby subjects become objects, and vice versa, as something which is abstract comes to have actual (economic) value.

Uncertainty principle

Werner Heisenberg's theory of particle physics which generally is interpreted as meaning that the observer is never able to totally measure the value of an entity.

Whig history

A type of historiography which represents the past as progress towards an enlightened society; this is particularly exemplified in the institutions of parliamentary democracy and the development of personal liberty. The term was coined by Herbert Butterfield in *The Whig Interpretation of History* (1931).

Bibliography

Achebe, Chinua (1977) *Morning yet on Creation Day*, London: Heinemann

Achebe, Chinua (1987) *No Longer at Ease*, London: Heinemann

Achebe, Chinua (1996) *Things Fall Apart*, London: Heinemann

Achebe, Chinua (2003) 'The African writer and the English language' in Isidore Okpewho, ed., *Chinua Achebe's Things Fall Apart*, Oxford: Oxford University Press, pp. 55–67

Acheson, James (1998) *John Fowles*, Basingstoke: Macmillan

Adamson, Lynda G. (1994) *Recreating the Past: A Guide to American and World Historical Fiction for Children and Young Adults*, Westport CT: Greenwood Press

Adkin, Mark (1998) *The Sharpe Companion*, London: HarperCollins

Aiken, Joan (1962) *The Wolves of Willoughby Chase*, London: Cape

Ainsworth, W. Harrison (1844) *Windsor Castle*, Leipzig: Tauchnitz

Akunin, Bois (2003) *The Winter Queen*, trans. Andrew Bromefield, London: Weidenfeld & Nicolson

Allardice, Lisa (2006) 'Uncharted waters', *Guardian*, 1 June 2006, http://books.guardian.co.uk/hay2006/story/0,1787355,00.html (accessed 12 May 2008)

Anderson, Benedict (2006) *Imagined Communities*, London: Verso

Anderson, Linda (1990) 'The re-imagining of history in contemporary women's fiction' in Linda Anderson, ed., *Plotting Change: Contemporary Women's Fiction*, London: Arnold, pp.129–41

Anderson, Perry (2007), 'Russia's managed democracy', *London Review of Books*, 25 January, available at www.lrb.co.uk/v29/n02/ande01_.html (accessed 10 July 2008)

Arnold, Guy (1980) *Held Fast for England: G. A. Henty, Imperialist Boys' Writer*, London: Hamish Hamilton

Ashcroft, Bill, ed. (1989) *The Empire Writes Back: Theory and Practice in Post-colonial Literatures*, London: Routledge

Ashcroft, Bill (2001) *Post-colonial Transformation*, London: Routledge

Atwood, Margaret (1997) *Alias Grace*, London: Virago

Baker, Ernest A. (1968) *A Guide to Historical Fiction*, New York: Argosy-Antiquarian

Baker, Stephen (2002) *The Fiction of Postmodernity*, Edinburgh: Edinburgh University Press

Bannock, Sarah (1997) 'Auto/biographical souvenirs in *Nights at the Circus*' in J. Bristow and T. L. Broughton, eds, *The Infernal Desires of Angela Carter*, London: Longman, pp. 198–201

Barker, Pat (1992) *Regeneration*, London: Penguin

Barker, Pat (2000) Interview in 'The making of *Regeneration*', DVD extra, Artificial Eye

Barnes, Julian (2006) *Arthur and George*, London: Vintage

Barry, Sebastian (2006) *A Long Long Way* London: Faber

Barthes, Roland (1970) 'The discourse of history', trans. Peter Wexler, in Michael Lane, ed., *Structuralism: A Reader*, London: Cape, pp. 145–55

Barthes, Roland (1977) *Image, Music, Text*, trans. Stephen Heath, London: Fontana

Baudelaire, Charles (1857) *Les Fleurs du mal*, available online http://fleursdumal.org/poem/099

Beer, Gillian (2000) *Darwin's Plots*, Cambridge: Cambridge University Press

Bell, William (1993) 'Not altogether a tomb – Julian Barnes: *Flaubert's Parrot*', in David Ellis, ed., *Imitating Art: Essays in Biography*, London: Pluto, pp. 149–73

Bennett, Mary (1850) *The Boys' Own Book of Stories from History*, London: Nelson

Berdoll, Linda (2004) *Mr Darcy Takes a Wife*, Naperville IL: Sourcebooks

Berger, Roger A. (1997) '"The black dick": race, sexuality, and discourse in the LA novels of Walter Mosley', *African American Review*, 31: 2, pp. 281–94

Berry, Steve (2005) *The Third Secret*, London: Hodder

Berry, Steve (2006) *The Templar Legacy*, London: Hodder

Botting, Fred (1999) *Sex, Machines and Navels: Fiction, Fantasy and History in the Future Present*, Manchester: Manchester University Press

Botting, Fred, and Dale Townshend (2004) 'Introduction' in Botting and Townshend, *Gothic: Critical Concepts in Literary and Cultural Studies*, London: Routledge

Bourdieu, Pierre (1993) 'The field of cultural production, or, The economic world reversed' in *The Field of Cultural Production*, ed. Randal Johnson, New York: Columbia University Press, pp. 29–73

Bradley, James (2006) *The Resurrectionist*, London: Faber

Brannigan, John (2003) 'Pat Barker's *Regeneration* trilogy: history and the hauntological imagination' in Richard J. Lane, Rod Mengham and Philip Tew, eds, *Contemporary British Fiction*, Cambridge: Polity, pp. 13–26

Bravmann, Scott (1997) *Queer Fictions of the Past*, Cambridge: Cambridge University Press

Brendan, Mary (2008) *The Virtuous Courtesan*, London: Mills & Boon

Brennan, Timothy (1997) *At Home in the World: Cosmopolitanism Now*, Cambridge MA: Harvard University Press

Brontë, Charlotte (1847) *Jane Eyre*, London: Smith Elder

Brown, Dan (2003) *The Da Vinci Code*, London: Bantam

Buckley, J. A. and Williams, W. T. (1912) *A Guide to British Historical Fiction*, London: Harrap

Burstein, Miriam Elizabeth (2007) 'The fictional afterlife of Anne Boleyn: how to do things with the Queen, 1901–2006' in *Clio*, 37, pp. 1–27, accessed through Literature Resource Centre, 27 August 2008

Butterfield, Herbert (1924) *The Historical Novel: An Essay* Cambridge: Cambridge University Press

Butts, Dennis (1997) 'How children's literature changed: what happened in the 1840s?', in *The Lion and the Unicorn*, 21:2, pp. 153–62

Buxton, Jackie (2000) 'Julian Barnes's *Theses on History (in 10½ Chapters)*', *Contemporary Literature*, 41:1, pp. 56–86.

Byatt, A. S. (1991) *Possession*, London: Vintage

Campbell Barnes, Margaret (1949) *Brief Gaudy Hour*, London: Macdonald

Carey, Peter (2001) *True History of the Ned Kelly Gang*, London: Faber

Carr, E. H. (1984) *What is History?* Harmondsworth: Penguin

Carter, Angela (1994) *Nights at the Circus*, London: Vintage

Carter, Angela (1997), 'Notes from the front line' in *Shaking a Leg: Collected Writings* available online (www.nytimes.com/books/first/c/carter-shaking.html)

Cartland, Barbara (1971) *The Little Pretender*, London: Hurst & Blackett

Cervantes, Miguel de (1620) *The Historie of Don Quixote*, trans. Thomas Shelton, London: Blounte

Chabot Davis, Kimberly (2002) 'Generational hauntings: the family romance in contemporary fictions of raced history', *Modern Fiction Studies*, 48:3, pp. 727–36

Chakrabarty, Dipesh (1992), 'Postcoloniality and the artifice of history: who speaks for "Indian" pasts?' *Representations*, 37, pp. 1–26

Chase, Bob (1996), 'History and poststructuralism: Hayden White and Fredric Jameson' in *The Expansion of England: Race, Ethnicity and Cultural History*, ed. Bill Schwarz, London: Routledge, pp. 61–91

Cochrane, David (2000) *America Noir: Underground Writers and Filmmakers of the Postwar Era*, Washington DC: Smithsonian Institution Press

Cohen, Josh (1996) 'James Ellroy, Los Angeles and the spectacular crisis of masculinity', *Women: A Cultural Review*, 7:1, pp. 1–15

Cookson, Catherine (1969) *Kate Hannigan*, London: Corgi

Cordy, Michael (2005) *The Messiah Code*, London: Corgi

Cornwell, Bernard (2004) *Sharpe's Escape*, London: HarperCollins

Cowley, Robert (2001) 'Introduction' in Robert Cowley, ed., *What if?* London: Pan, pp. xi–xiv

Cox, Simon (2006) *The Dan Brown Companion*, Edinburgh: Mainstream

Creasy, Matthew (2007) 'Manuscripts and misquotations: *Ulysses* and genetic criticism', *Joyce Studies Annual*, New York: Fordham University Press, pp. 44–6

Cruz, Anne J. (2005) '*Don Quixote*, the picaresque, and the "rise" of the modern novel' in John P. Gabriele, ed., *1605–2005: Don Quixote across the Centuries*, Madrid: Iberoamericana, pp. 15–28

Danytė, Milda (2007) 'National past/personal past: recent examples of the historical novel', *Literatūra*, 49:5, pp. 34–41

Darwin, Charles (1996) *The Origin of Species*, Oxford: Oxford University Press

Day, Aidan (1998) *Angela Carter: The Rational Glass*, Manchester: Manchester University Press

De Certeau, Michel (1992), *The Writing of History*, New York: Columbia University Press

De Groot, Jerome (2008) *Consuming History*, London: Routledge

De Vigny, Alfred (1829) *Cinq mars*, project Gutenberg e-text at www.scribd.com/doc/2400618/cinq-mars-volume-1-by-vigny-alfred-de-1797–1863

Derrida, Jacques (1967) 'Structure, sign, and play in the discourse of the human sciences', in Alan Bass, trans., *Writing and Difference*, London: Routledge, pp. 278–94

Dickens, Charles (1842) *Barnaby Rudge*, New York: Colyer

Dickens, Charles (1860) *A Tale of Two Cities*, London: Chapman & Hall

Dixon, Jay (1999) *The Romance Fiction of Mills and Boon*, London: UCL Press

Doan, Laura, and Waters, Sarah (2000) 'Making up lost time: contemporary lesbian writing and the invention of history' in D. Alderson and L. Anderson, eds, *Territories of Desire in Queer Culture: Refiguring the Contemporary Boundaries*, Manchester: Manchester University Press, pp. 12–28

Doyle, Roddy, (2000) *A Star Called Henry*, London: Vintage

Eagleton, Terry (1997) *The Illusions of Postmodernism*, Oxford: Blackwell

Eco, Umberto (1983) *The Name of the Rose*, trans. William Weaver, London: Picador

Eliot, George (1871) *Middlemarch: A Study of Provincial Life*, Edinburgh: Blackwood

Eliot, George (1977) *Felix Holt, the Radical*, London: Penguin

Faulks, Sebastian (1994) *Birdsong*, London: Vintage

Ferguson, Niall (2000) 'Introduction' in Niall Ferguson, ed., *Virtual History: Alternatives and Counterfactuals*, London: Basic, pp. 1–91

Flaubert, Gustave (1886) *Salammbô*, trans. J. S. Chartres, London: Vizetelly

Fleishman, Avrom (1971) *The English Historical Novel*, Baltimore MD: Johns Hopkins University Press

Fletcher, Lisa (2008) *Historical Romance Fiction: Heterosexuality and Perfomativity*, London: Ashgate

Fowles, John (1996) *The French Lieutenant's Woman*, London: Vintage

Fuchs, Barbara (2004) *Romance*, London and New York: Routledge

Ganim, John (2005) *Medievalism and Colonialism*, Basingstoke: Palgrave Macmillan

García Márquez, Gabriel (1978) *One Hundred Years of Solitude*, trans. G. Rabassa, London: Picador

Genette, Gerard (1997) *Paratexts: Thresholds of Interpretation*, Cambridge: Cambridge University Press

Gladfelder, Hal (1993) 'Seeing back: Alessandro Manzoni between fiction and history', *Modern Language Notes*, 108, pp. 59–86

Godwin, William (1797) 'Of history and romance', www.english.upenn.edu/~mgamer/Etexts/godwin.history.html (accessed 14 August 2008)

Goodman, Irene (2005) 'Why Anne Boleyn is the poster girl of historical fiction', *Solander: The Magazine of the Historical Novel Society*, 9:2, p. 15

Green, Anne (2004) 'History and its representation in Flaubert's work' in Timothy Unwin, ed., *The Cambridge Companion to Flaubert*, Cambridge: Cambridge University Press, pp. 85–105

Guanzhong, Luo, attr. (2004) *Three Kingdoms*, trans. Moss Roberts, Berkeley and Los Angeles: University of California Press

Guardian, The (staff and agencies) (2006), 'Brown wins Da Vinci case', 7 April, http://books.guardian.co.uk/danbrown/story/0,1749361,00.html (accessed 21 November 2008)

Gulland, Sandra (1995) *The Many Lives and Secret Sorrows of Joséphine B.*, London: Headline

Gullon, Ricardo (1971) 'Gabriel García Márquez and the lost art of storytelling', *Diacritics*, 1:1, pp. 27–32

Gurnah, Abdulrazak (2007), 'Themes and structures in *Midnight's Children*' in A. Gurnah, ed., *The Cambridge Companion to Salman Rushdie*, Cambridge: Cambridge University Press

Hackett, Francis (1939) *Queen Anne Boleyn*, London: Nicholson & Watson

Harris, Robert (1987) *Selling Hitler*, London: Penguin

Harris, Robert (1992) *Fatherland*, London: Arrow

Harris, Robert (2000) *Archangel*, London: Cresset

Hartley, J. and Turvey, S. (2001) *Reading Groups*, Oxford: Oxford University Press

Harvey Wood, Harriet (2006) *Sir Walter Scott*, London: Northcote House

Hayden, John O., ed. (1970) *Scott: The Critical Heritage*, London: Routledge

Henty, G. A. (1889) *With Lee in Virginia: A Story of the American Civil War*, New York: Hurst

Henty, G. A. (2004) *The Young Carthaginian*, Whitefish MT: Kessinger

Heyer, Georgette (1991) *Regency Buck*, London: Heinemann

Hogg, James (1824) *The Private Memoirs and Confessions of a Justified Sinner: Written by Himself*, London: Longman

Hollinghurst, Alan (2004) *The Line of Beauty*, London: Picador

Hopkins, Chris (2006) *English Fiction in the 1930s*, London: Continuum

Howells, Coral Ann (1991) *Jean Rhys*, London: Harvester Wheatsheaf

Hughes, Helen (1993) *The Historical Romance*, London and New York: Routledge

Humphrey, Richard (1993) *Waverley*, Cambridge: Cambridge University Press

Humphreys, C. C. (2002) *The French Executioner*, London: Orion

Hunt, Tristram (2004) 'Pasting over the past', *Guardian*, 7 April, www.guardian.co.uk/education/2004/apr/07/highereducation.news (accessed 21 November 2008)

Hutcheon, Linda (1988) *A Poetics of Postmodernism*, London and New York: Routledge

Hutcheon, Linda (1989) *The Politics of Postmodernism*, London and New York: Routledge

Iggers, Georg G. and Powell, James M., eds (1990) *Leopold von Ranke and the Shaping of the Historical Discipline*, Syracuse NY: Syracuse University Press

Ives, Eric (2004) *The Life and Death of Anne Boleyn*, Oxford: Blackwell

Jameson, Fredric (1996) 'Postmodernism and consumer society' in J. Belton, ed., *Movies and Mass Culture*, London: Athlone, pp. 185–202

Jenkins, Keith (2003) *Rethinking History*, London and New York: Routledge

Jibrail_rising (2006) '#22 enemies' at http://community.livejournal.com/historslash100/2706.html (accessed 4 October 2008)

Johnson, S. L. (2005) *Historical Fiction: A Guide to the Genre*, Westport CT: Libraries Unlimited

Keen, Suzanne (2006) 'The historical turn in British fiction' in James F. English, ed., *A Concise Companion to Contemporary British Fiction*, Oxford: Blackwell, pp. 167–87

King, Florence (1990) 'A yuppie in King Charles's court', *New York Times*, 15 April, at http://query.nytimes.com/gst/fullpage.html?res = 9C0CE0DC1E3AF936A25757C0A966958260& sec = & spon = & pagewanted = 1 (accessed 7 January 2009)

Knight, Peter (2000) *Conspiracy Culture*, London and New York: Routledge

Kunzru, Hari (2002) *The Impressionist*, London: Penguin

Kunzru, Hari (2006) e-mail to author, 19 November

Kunzru, Hari (2007) *My Revolutions*, London: Penguin

Kunzru, Hari, and Litt, Toby (2004) 'When Hari met Toby', http://books.guardian.co.uk/departments/generalfiction/story/0,1131770,00.html (accessed 14 November 2008)

Kustritz, Anne (2003) 'Slashing the romance narrative', *Journal of American Popular Culture*, 26:3, pp. 371–84

Lafayette, Marie-Madeleine de (1994) *The Princess of Clèves*, New York: Norton

Lane, Jane (2001) *Sow the Tempest*, London: Stratus

Lavery, Brian (2003) *Jack Aubrey Commands*, London: Conway Maritime

Lawson, Mark (2006) *Enough is Enough, or, the Emergency Government*, London: Picador

Leisy, Ernest E. (1950) *The American Historical Novel*, Norman OK: University of Oklahoma Press

Lethbridge, Olive, and John de Stourton (1912) *The King's Master*, London:

Levine, Philippa (1986) *The Amateur and the Professional: Antiquaries, Historians and Archaeologists in Victorian England, 1838–1886*, Cambridge: Cambridge University Press

Light, Alison (1989) '*Young Bess*: historical novels and growing up', *Feminist Review*, 33, pp. 57–71

Lofts, Norah (1963) *The Concubine*, London: Hutchinson

Lukács, Georg (1962) *The Historical Novel*, trans. Hannah and Stanley Mitchell, London: Merlin

Lyotard, Jean-François (1984) *The Postmodern Condition*, trans. Geoff Bennington and Brian Massumi, Manchester: Manchester University Press

MacAlman, Iain (1999) *Oxford Companion to the Romantic Age*, Oxford: Oxford University Press

MacCallum-Stewart, Esther (2006) 'The cause of nowadays and the end of history: First World War historical fiction', *Working Papers on the Web*, 9, http://extra.shu.ac.uk/wpw/historicising

MacDonald Fraser, George (2004) 'Rafael Sabatini (1875–1950)', *Oxford Dictionary of National Biography*, Oxford: Oxford University Press (www.oxforddnb.com/view/article/37926, accessed 1 September 2008)

MacDonald, G. and MacDonald, A., eds (2003) *Jane Austen on Screen*, Cambridge: Cambridge University Press

Manzoni, Alessandro (1984) *On the Historical Novel*, trans. Sandra Bermann, Lincoln NE: University of Nebraska Press

Manzoni, Alessandro (1997) *The Betrothed*, ed. David Forgacs and Matthew Reynolds, London: Dent

Marcus, Laura (2003) 'Detective and literary fiction' in M. Priestman, ed., *The Cambridge Companion to Crime Fiction*, Cambridge: Cambridge University Press, pp. 245–69

Maxwell, Richard (2008) 'The historical novel' in Richard Maxwell and Katie Trump-ener, eds, *The Cambridge Companion to Fiction in the Romantic Period*, Cam-bridge: Cambridge University Press, pp. 65–88

McAleer, Joseph (1999) *Passion's Fortune: The Story of Mills & Boon*, Oxford: Oxford University Press

McCarthy, Cormac (1990) *Blood Meridian or The Evening Redness in the West*, London: Picador

McCracken, Scott (1998) *Pulp*, Manchester: Manchester University Press

McEwan, Ian (2002) *Atonement*, London: Vintage

McEwan, Ian (2006) 'An inspiration, yes', *Guardian*, 27 November, http://books.guardian.co.uk/comment/story/0,1957845,00.html (accessed 21 November 2008)

McGann, Jerome J. (1991) *The Textual Condition*, Princeton NJ: Princeton University Press

McGarry, Daniel D. and Harriman White, Sarah (1973) *World Historical Fiction Guide*, Metuchen NJ: Scarecrow

McHale, Brian (1992) *Constructing Postmodernism*, London: Routledge

McKeon, Michael (2000) 'Watt's *Rise of the Novel* within the tradition of the rise of the novel', *Eighteenth-Century Fiction*, 12:2–2, pp. 253–76

Mills and Boon (2008) www.millsandboon.co.uk/books/historical.htm

Mink, Louis O (1970) 'History and fiction as modes of comprehension', *New Literary History*, 1, pp. 541–58.

Mitchell, Kaye (2006) 'Alan Hollinghurst and homosexual identity' in Rod Mengham and Philip Tew, eds, *British Fiction Today*, London: Continuum, pp. 40–53

Mitchell, Kaye (2009) '"That library of uncatalogued pleasure": queerness, desire and the archive in contemporary gay fiction', forthcoming

Montefiore, Janet (1996) *Men and Women Writers of the 1930s: The Dangerous Flood of History*, London: Routledge

Moretti, Franco, ed. (2007) *The Novel*, Vol. I, *History, Geography, and Culture*, Princeton NJ: Princeton University Press

Morrison, Toni (2006) *Beloved*, New York: Knopf

Mosley, Walter (2001) *Devil in a Blue Dress*, London: Serpent's Tail

Munslow, Alun (1997) *Deconstructing History*, London: Routledge

Nield, Jonathan (1902) *Guide to the Best Historical Novels and Tales*, available as a Project Gutenberg e-book, www.gutenberg.org/etext/1359 (accessed 15 May 2008)

Nikolajeva, Maria (1996) *Children's Literature Comes of Age: Toward a New Aesthetic*, New York: Garland

O'Gorman, Ellen (1999) 'Detective fiction and historical narrative', *Greece and Rome*, 46:1, 19–26

Pamuk, Orhan (2001) *My Name is Red/Benim Adim Kirmizi*, trans. Erda? M. Göknar, London: Faber

Partner, Nancy F. (1986) 'Making up lost time: writing on the writing of history', *Speculum* 61, 90–117

Peace, David (2006) *The Damned Utd*, London: Faber

Peters, Ellis (1988) *The Hermit of Eyton Forest*, London: Macdonald

Pittock, Murray, ed. (2007) *The Reception of Sir Walter Scott in Europe*, London: Continuum

Plaidy, Jean (2006) *Murder Most Foul*, London: Arrow

Pullman, Philip (1985) *The Ruby in the Smoke*, Oxford: Oxford University Press

Pushkin, Alexander (1962) *The Queen of Spades and other Stories*, trans. Rosemary Edmonds, Harmondsworth: Penguin

Radway, Janice A. (1987) *Reading the Romance: Women, Patriarchy, and Popular Literature*, London and New York: Verso

Ranke, Leopold von (1824) *History of the Latin and Teutonic Nations from 1494–1514*, http://germanhistorydocs.ghidc.org/sub_document.cfm?document_id = 358

Reade, Charles (1861) *The Cloister and the Hearth*, www.gutenberg.org/files/1366/1366.txt

Rhys, Jean (2000) *Wide Sargasso Sea*, London: Penguin

Roberts, Adam (2005) *Science Fiction*, London: Routledge

Robinson, Emma (1854) *Westminster Abbey*, London: Mortimer

Roth, Philip (2005) *The Plot against America*, London: Vintage

Rushdie, Salman (1991) *Imaginary Homelands*, London: Granta

Russell, Corinna (2005), 'The novel' in Nicholas Roe, ed., *Romanticism*, Oxford: Oxford University Press, pp. 368–90

Sage, Lorna.(1996) *Angela Carter*, London: Northcote House

Said, Edward W. (1977) *Orientalism*, London: Penguin

Said, Edward W. (1993) *Culture and Imperialism*, London: Chatto and Windus

Sanders, Andrew (1978) *The Victorian Historical Novel, 1840–1880*, London: Macmilllan

Sanders, Julie (2005) *Appropriation and Adaptation*, London: Routledge

Sansom, C. J. (2007) *Dissolution*, London: Pan Books

Scott, Sir Walter (1816) *The Antiquarian*, Edinburgh: Ballantyne

Scott, Sir Walter (1985) *Waverley*, ed. Andrew Hook, Harmondsworth: Penguin

Sewell, Keith C. (2005) *Herbert Butterfield and the Interpretation of History*, Basingstoke: Palgrave

Shaw, Harry E. (1983) *The Forms of Historical Fiction*, Ithaca NY: Cornell University Press

Shiller, Dana (1997) 'The redemptive past in the neo-Victorian novel' in *Studies in the Novel*, 29:4, pp. 538–60

Slee, Peter (1986) *Learning and a Liberal Education: A Study of Modern History in the Universities of Oxford, Cambridge and Manchester*, Manchester: Manchester University Press

Slotkin, Richard (2005) 'Fiction for the purposes of history', *Rethinking History*, 9:2–3, pp. 221–36

Spivak, Gayatri Chakravorty (1988) 'Can the subaltern speak?' in Cary Nelson and Lawrence Grossberg, eds, *Marxism and the Interpretation of Culture*, Urbana IL: University of Illinois Press, pp. 271–313

Squires, Claire (2007) *Marketing Literature*, Basingstoke: Palgrave

Sternlicht, Sandord (1999) *C. S. Forester and the Hornblower Saga*, Syracuse NY: Syracuse University Press

Stevenson, Jane (2001) *Astraea*, London: Cape

Stone, Leonard (2006) 'Minarets and plastic bags: the social and global relations of Orhan Pamuk', *Turkish Studies*, 7:2, pp. 191–201

Sutcliff, Rosemary (1954) *The Eagle of the Ninth*, Oxford: Oxford University Press

Tew, Philip (2007) *The Contemporary British Novel*, London: Continuum

Thompson, Willie (2004) *Postmodernism and History*, Basingstoke: Palgrave

Thurston, Carol (1987) *The Romance Revolution: Erotic Novels for Women and the Quest for a New Sexual Identity*, Urbana IL: University of Illinois Press

Todd, Richard (1996) *Consuming Fictions: The Booker Prize and Fiction in Britain Today*, London: Bloomsbury

Todorov, Tzvetan (1977) *The Poetics of Prose*, Ithaca NY: Cornell University Press

Tolstoy, Leo (2007) *War and Peace*, trans. Andrew Bromfield, London: Harper Perennial

Touchstone, Timothy (1820) *A Letter to the Author of Waverley*, London: Hatchard

Tremain, Rose (1989) *Restoration*, London: Hamish Hamilton

Tremain, Rose (2000) *Music and Silence*, London: Vintage

Tremain, Rose (n.d), 'Author statement', www.contemporarywriters.com/authors/?p = auth97#criticalperspective

Turtledove, Harry (2003) *Ruled Britannia*, London: Penguin

wa Thiong'o, Ngugi (1994) 'The language of African literature' in Patrick Williams and Laura Chrisman, eds, *Colonial Discourse and Post-colonial Theory: A Reader*, New York: Columbia University Press

Wachtel, Andrew (2002) 'History and autobiography in Tolstoy' in Donna Tussing Orwin, ed., *The Cambridge Companion to Tolstoy*, Cambridge: Cambridge University Press, pp. 176–90

Wagner, Tamara S. (2002) 'Mrs Hubback's *The Younger Sister*: the Victorian Austen and the phenomenon of the Austen sequel', *Victorian Web*, www.usp.nus. edu.sg/victorian/previctorian/austen/tsw7.html (accessed 6 October 2008)

Wallace, Diane (2005), *The Women's Historical Novel*, Basingstoke: Palgrave Macmillan

Walpole, Horace (1765) *The Castle of Otranto*, London: Lowndes

Walter, Natasha (1999) 'The seductions of the past', *Independent*, 30 August, at http://findarticles.com/p/articles/mi_qn4158/is_19990830/ai_n14247704

Warnicke, Retha (1989) *The Rise and Fall of Anne Boleyn*, Cambridge: Cambridge University Press

Waters, Sarah (2002) *Tipping the Velvet*, London: Virago

Waters, Sarah (2003) *Fingersmith*, London: Virago

Waters, Sarah (2006) e-mail to author, 31 October

Waugh, Patricia (1984) *Metafiction: The Theory and Practice of Self-conscious Fiction*, London: Routledge

Waugh, Patricia (1989) *Feminine Fictions: Revisiting the Postmodern*, London: Routledge

Weir, Alison (2003) 'The allure of Anne', *History Today*, 53:5, pp. 94–5

Wells, H. G. (1895) *The Time Machine: An Invention*, London: Heinemann

Wells, Lynn (2006) 'The ethical otherworld: Ian McEwan's fiction' in Rod Mengham and Philip Tew, eds, *British Fiction Today*, London: Continuum, pp. 117–27

White, Hayden (1978) *Tropics of Discourse: Essays in Cultural Criticism*, Baltimore MD: Johns Hopkins University Press

White, Hayden (2005) 'Historical fiction, fictional history, and historical reality', *Rethinking History*, 9:2–3, 147–57

Whiting, B. J. (1951) 'Historical novels, 1949–1950', *Speculum*, 26:2, pp. 337–67

Williamson, Edwin (1987) 'Magical realism and the theme of incest in *One Hundred Years of Solitude*' in B. McGuire and R. Cardwell, eds, *Gabriel García Márquez: New Readings*, Cambridge: Cambridge University Press, pp. 45–65

Winterson, Jeannette (1987) *The Passion*, London: Penguin

Wood, Michael (1987) 'Review of *One Hundred Years of Solitude*' in G. R. McMurray, ed., *Critical Essays on Gabriel García Márquez*, Boston MA: Hall, pp. 36–40

Woolf, Virginia (1928) *Orlando: A Biography*, New York: Harcourt Brace

Woolf, Virginia (2000) 'Modern fiction' in Michael McKeon, ed., *Theory of the Novel*, Baltimore MD: Johns Hopkins University Press, pp. 739–44

Yeats, W. B. (1990) *The Poems*, ed. Daniel Albright, London: Dent

Index